BIG ED WALSH

ALSO BY JACK SMILES

*"Ee-Yah": The Life and Times of Hughie Jennings,
Baseball Hall of Famer* (McFarland, 2005)

BIG ED WALSH

The Life and Times of a Spitballing Hall of Famer

Jack Smiles

McFarland & Company, Inc., Publishers
Jefferson, North Carolina, and London

LIBRARY OF CONGRESS CATALOGUING-IN-PUBLICATION DATA

Smiles, Jack, 1947–
　Big Ed Walsh : the life and times of a spitballing
Hall of Famer / Jack Smiles.
　　　p.　　cm.
　Includes bibliographical references and index.

　　ISBN-13: 978-0-7864-3278-3
　　(softcover : 50# alkaline paper) ∞

　1. Walsh, Ed, 1881–1959.　2. Baseball players — United States —
Biography.　3. Chicago White Sox (Baseball team) — History.
I. Title.
GV865.W343S65　2008
796.357092–dc22　　　　　　　　　　　　　　　　　2007043096
[B]

British Library cataloguing data are available

©2008 Jack Smiles. All rights reserved

*No part of this book may be reproduced or transmitted in any form
or by any means, electronic or mechanical, including photocopying
or recording, or by any information storage and retrieval system,
without permission in writing from the publisher.*

On the cover: Ed Walsh, 1911 (Library of Congress)

Manufactured in the United States of America

*McFarland & Company, Inc., Publishers
　Box 611, Jefferson, North Carolina 28640
　　www.mcfarlandpub.com*

To the memory of the anthracite
coal miners of Northeastern Pennsylvania,
including my ancestors Thomas and Robert Smiles.
Though they died long before I was born,
they are my heroes.

Acknowledgments

This book would have been an impossible task without the help of Fred Buccheri, Marty Straub, John Carney, and Bob Petro. Fred was my man in Meriden, Connecticut, where Big Ed lived all of his adult life. Fred tracked down information about Big Ed's days in Meriden, especially before and after his major league career.

Marty, John and Bob researched virtually every one of Ed's pitching appearances from 1906 to 1911. Fred, Marty and John all worked for love, not money, and Bob worked as an unpaid intern from Luzerne County Community College in Nanticoke, Pennsylvania.

Also, thanks to Michael Bielawa from Bridgeport, Connecticut. Michael found important information about Big Ed's season as a manager in Bridgeport.

Special thanks to my cousin and proofreader, Phil "Dude" White.

Above all, thanks to my wife, Diane, and daughter, Sadie, who have always given me their unconditional support and encouragement.

Table of Contents

Acknowledgments — vii
Preface — 1

1. Big Ed: Coal Miner — 3
2. Big Ed: Rookie — 15
3. The Spitter — 29
4. Ze Meestaire Walsh — 43
5. The Hitless Wonders — 50
6. Big Ed: World Champion — 69
7. South of the Border — 81
8. Sox Are Tamed by the Tigers — 87
9. Big Ed: Ironman — 100
10. The Holdout — 113
11. Big Ed Opens Comiskey Park — 127
12. Big Ed Owns the Cubs — 137
13. What's the Matter with Big Ed? — 151
14. Arm Trouble — 181
15. Big Ed: Manager — 187

16. Big Ed Doesn't Like the Jeers   194
17. Little Ed and Big Bob   200
18. Big Ed: Old-Timer   207

Notes   215
Bibliography   221
Index   223

Preface

This is a biography of Big Ed Walsh, not a book of poetry, but there are eight poems in it, all of them written during the deadball era and published in newspapers of the day. I decided to include the poems because each advances the story of Ed's career and life. A lot of sportswriters wrote poetry about the players and teams during Ed Walsh's career, but Big Ed seems to have the record for inspiring rhyme, perhaps because his drive, his determination, and his self-confidence were inspirational.

I know his story was inspirational to me. As a descendant of men just like Ed Walsh, men who may have worked in the very same mines where Big Ed worked, and as a writer and baseball fan, I was compelled to research and write about Big Ed.

This is my second deadball era biography for McFarland. The first was on Hughie Jennings. Hughie and Big Ed had identical backgrounds. They were born just five miles apart in Northeastern Pennsylvania hard coal country, the sons of Irish immigrants. Hughie and Big Ed both left school about age 12 to work as breaker boys in the local mines. Both men used baseball to escape from the mines and both wound up in the Hall of Fame.

But their stories are vastly different, too. Hughie went to college, became a successful lawyer and rather wealthy man, but died in his early 50s. Big Ed never prepared himself for life after baseball. He lived until he was 78 and in the end had to rely on the charity of friends.

A note on Big Ed's middle name: His Hall of Fame plaque has his middle name as "Augustine." But that is disputed in his hometown area in Pennsylvania where it is always said to be "Augustin."

It was certainly not Armstrong, as was sometimes written. That was a nickname given to hime by *Chicago Tribune* writer Charles Dryden. And it was not Arthur, which was his older son's middle name. His son's first name was Ed.

1

Big Ed: Coal Miner

One day in the summer of 1901, 20-year-old Ed Walsh cranked his auger with the practiced skill of an experienced coal miner, and his drill whirled into the breast of coal some 500 feet below the city of Wilkes-Barre, Pennsylvania. When the hole was drilled the length of the bit, he pulled it out and filled it with black powder. He placed a squib — a small parchment tube filled with fine black powder and sealed at the ends with wax — over the hole. Yelling the warning "fire in the hole," he lit a fuse attached to the squib and scrambled 15 feet down the narrow tunnel away from the breast and around a corner into the gangway, the heavily timbered highway of the mine where the mine car tracks ran.

After the blast Ed and his butties, as the miners called their laborers, looked over the huge chunks of ore the blast had blown from the breast. Judging the ore would be enough to fill his day's quota of cars, Ed worked to prop up the roof over where he had advanced the breast that day, while his butties loaded the ore into cars and cleaned up the breast to get ready for the next day's work.

Wilkes-Barre — the hub city of the Wyoming Valley, a Susquehanna River valley in Northeastern Pennsylvania — was originally settled by 200 explorers for the Susquehanna Company of Connecticut in 1762. They built log homes and planted wheat, then went back to Connecticut for the winter. They returned in the spring with their families, but were routed by the Delaware Indians who killed 30 settlers and drove the rest back to Connecticut. In 1768 the land was purchased from the Indians and in 1769 the settlers from Connecticut resettled the area, establishing five townships, including Wilkes-Barre — named in honor of John Wilkes and Colonel Isaac Barre, members of the British Parliament who sympathized with the colonists during the Revolution — and Plains. Armed men loyal to Pennsylvania twice tried, and failed, to evict the residents of Wilkes-Barre in what came to be known as the Pennamite Wars. After the American Revolution, the conflict was resolved so that the Connecticut settlers retained title to their lands but transferred their allegiance to Pennsylvania.

The early settlers found outcroppings of exposed coal along the Susquehanna River as early as 1768. Little could they have known these outcroppings were the tip of an iceberg of 16 billion tons of anthracite, or hard coal, three-quarters of the known worldwide deposits. Some sources say the first industrial use of the coal was in a forge to make firearms in Carlisle, Pennsylvania. Another source claims it was first used to make nails in 1788. In any case it is known that in 1808 Jesse Fell, an early Wilkes-Barre judge, successfully burned anthracite coal on an open air grate in his tavern, thus proving it could be used as a fuel for heating and for steam engines. This discovery, which helped launch the Industrial Revolution, also fueled a stunning population and economic boom in Wilkes-Barre. Scores of mines were established in and around Wilkes-Barre and thousands of English, Welsh and Irish immigrants poured into the city to work them. By 1900, the anthracite fields around Wilkes-Barre were producing 50,000,000 tons of hard coal a year. In 1810 the population of Wilkes-Barre Township and Borough combined was around 1200. By the turn of the century Wilkes-Barre was the 75th largest city in the country with 51,721 residents counted in the 1900 census.

The success of the coal industry brought a steady stream of entrepreneurs to Wilkes-Barre. J. C. Atkins built the Wilkes-Barre Lace Manufacturing Co., Fred Kirby opened his first five-and-dime store, and Charles Stegmaier began brewing beer and by 1916 was turning out over 200,000 barrels a year. Silk and garment mills became major employers for miners' wives and daughters with companies such as the Empire Silk Mill importing silk from Japan. Richard Jones, a mill worker, founded Vulcan Iron works in 1849, which grew to 1,600 employees, producing locomotives and iron products.[1]

The anthracite that caused all this economic action was more expensive than common bituminous coal, but it was in great demand because it could be burned hotter, cleaner and longer without emitting soot. The Lackawanna Railroad, which served the Wilkes-Barre area, was dubbed "The Road of Anthracite" and advertised widely that travelers on the line could make railway journeys without getting their clothing blackened by

1. Big Ed: Coal Miner

Big Ed left school at age 12 or 13 in the 1890s to work as a breaker boy, like the ones pictured in the mines around Wilkes-Barre.

soot. The advertisements featured a white-clad woman named Phoebe Snow and poems containing lines like, "My gown stays white / From morn till night / Upon the road of Anthracite."

Riding on an anthracite-fueled train may have been a glamorous bit of fun for the rich in 1900, but for the men who mined it, anthracite was a killer. The earliest year with comprehensive accident statistics is 1900. According to a Bureau of Mines report, 363 collieries in the anthracite region employed 143,826 employees in 1900, one-fourth of them boys under 16. Accidents in anthracite mines in Northeastern Pennsylvania that year killed 411, injured 1,057, made 230 widows and left 525 children fatherless. In 1909 Ed's brother David would become one of those statistics.

In the late 1890s, John Mitchell, the legendary organizer of the United Mine Workers, successfully organized bituminous coal miners, achieving higher wages and better working conditions. In the early 1900s, Mitchell turned his attention to the anthracite coal mines in Northeastern Pennsylvania. In May of 1902 Mitchell led the anthracite miners into a strike. Since anthracite was the main fuel for heating homes, running factories, and operating trains and steamships in the Northeast, where most of the country's population lived, the strikers were in a strong position. When the strike continued into October, and with the winter months approaching, President Theodore Roosevelt became the first president to personally intervene in a labor dispute. Roosevelt met with representatives of the United Mine Workers and coal operators in the White House on October 3, 1902. But the coal operators refused to deal with the United Mine Workers until Roosevelt threatened to send military forces to take over and operate the anthracite mines.[2]

That ended the strike. Both sides agreed to settle based on the recommendations of a commission appointed by the president. The miners won a 10 percent increase in pay and a shorter work week, but the commission didn't recommend union recognition or address child labor and the hazardous working conditions. Still, for the first time the federal government acted to settle, rather than break, a strike.

None of this affected Ed Walsh. By the time the strike ended he had found another line of work — baseball. Edward Augustin Walsh was born in Plains, a Wilkes-Barre border town, on May 14, 1881. He was one of 13 children, three girls and 10 boys. All the boys worked in the mines or in related jobs. Ed, as did most Irish boys of the time, left school at 12 or 13, in 1893 or 94, to work as a breaker boy in the mines, picking out slate and other waste from the coal as it poured down chutes with a deafening, dusty roar. Ed's parents were Catholics. The church was a big part of the family's life, as was singing, as Ed would explain years later in a magazine story. "When my father came home from work at night black with coal dust he enjoyed himself by singing. My mother was in the church choir, so I grew up in a musical-minded family. As the kids got older they all sang. It was one singing family and one happy family, too.

"We sang all the old Irish songs like 'Danny Boy' and when we all sang together it was enough to bring tears to your eyes. I sang tenor along with the other boys, except Johnny. He had a high-pitched voice, almost like a girl's. Pop used to kid him about it."[3]

As Ed was a big strong boy capable of sturdy work, he progressed in the mines going from breaker boy to door tender, to mule driver, to laborer and finally to certified miner in 1900 when he was 19 and fully grown at 6 foot 1 and 190 pounds. He earned his miner's certificate the usual way. After two years' experience as a laborer he went before the mine examining board and answered 12 questions in the English language pertaining to mining. Once certified, he signed a contract with a mine operator to work breasts at a certain price per car. Miners like Ed supplied their own

1. Big Ed: Coal Miner

Here's how the breaker boys worked to separate shale and other waste from coal. As a big strong worker, Big Ed was quickly promoted and didn't have to do this for long.

tools and powder and paid the laborers. A miner's day's work was done when he cut enough coal to fill the cars assigned him by the mine boss. Many days that meant Ed got out of work early enough to play baseball. By the turn of the century Ed had developed a local reputation as a baseball player that caught the attention of Fordham University in New York City. Though he had attended parochial school only to age 12, Ed enrolled at Fordham. He lasted two days. The only known reference to his Fordham experience came from Ed himself, in an interview with the *Sporting News* in 1957, when he was 77. "I was about 18 when I entered Fordham. I was there two days. Then I quit and went back home to Plains. In New York I lived in a rooming house with a wild bunch of students and grown men. I didn't like them. I was used to the quiet folks back home."[4]

Once back in Plains the Miner-Hilliard Company of Miner's Mills — a small border town between Plains and Wilkes-Barre — hired him as a miner and to play for the company's team. Baseball wasn't just a popular form of recreation for the miners, it was also seen as a salvation, a way out of a life of drudgery in the anthracite mines. Hughie Jennings had paved this way out, becoming an idol to many of the young miners. Jennings, 10 years Walsh's elder, had come from Pittston, just a couple of miles from where Walsh was born and reared. Like Walsh, Jennings had left school at age 11 or 12 to work as a breaker boy. Like Walsh, Jennings moved up the miner job ladder, but unlike Walsh, Jennings left the mines in his late teens to start his baseball career. Jennings became an international celebrity as a player for the Baltimore Orioles in the 1890s where he teamed with John McGraw and Wee Willie Keeler to form one of baseball's first modern dynasties. He later served as the manager of the Detroit Tigers and Ty Cobb. His famous coaching box cry of "Ee-yah" was imitated by many young boys in the anthracite fields.

Ed was given some liberty from work in the mines by the Miner-Hilliard Company because of his baseball talent, but, even so, he didn't see himself as a Hugh Jennings. In a magazine story years later, he said, "When I left the breakers I passed from grade to grade until I became a miner. All my friends worked in the mines and while I knew it was hard and cheerless enough, it was the only world I knew. When I became a full-fledged miner, I never thought about any other occupation, for I didn't suppose there was any other occupation I was fitted for. I could mine coal as well as the rest and it was the only type of work I had ever done and felt I could do."[5]

A right-handed batter and thrower, when he did play baseball, for Miner-Hilliard or the Plains town team, he played some third base, but mostly outfield. In later years Ed told conflicting stories about how much ball he played as a kid and what positions he played. In one story he said he was an outfielder, and in another he said he played third base. In one he claimed baseball wasn't a consuming passion for him as it was for his peers. In another he said it was his only recreation.

In a 1912 *Washington Post* story he said, "Oh yes, a little ball game now and then, but not very much of that. I never played ball as much as you would imagine, nor did I seem to take the same interest in the games as did my little aspiring and perspiring pals.

"But somehow I did become quite adept at walloping the ball and straining 'em from the dirt around third base, in spite of myself, although I guess at that time I was a better coal heaver than a ball player."[6]

In 1913 he recalled his early baseball playing differently in *Baseball Magazine*. "My only recreation was baseball, and I played it whenever I could. Generally I used to pitch, but when I couldn't get in the box I played in the outfield."[7]

The late Martin Corcoran—who grew up with Walsh in Plains and played football, baseball and handball with Ed—recalled in a letter to the Baseball Hall of Fame how Ed became a pitcher. "Walsh was an outfielder," Corcoran wrote. "He had the finest throwing arm I had ever seen. He liked to give throwing exhibitions to the plate and all the other bases. His

1. Big Ed: Coal Miner

throws to the plate were perfect strikes. Blazing rifle-like throws without a bounce into the glove. He would have made the majors as an outfielder."

Corcoran was the third baseman and manager of the Plains team. During a game against Miner's Mills the Plains pitcher was injured and couldn't continue. Another version of the story has it that Plains' opponent was a local all-star team. In either case, according to Corcoran, the infielders had a meeting at the mound and Corcoran signaled for Ed to come in from centerfield and pitch.

"He objected saying he had never pitched a game and didn't like the idea, but after some talk I persuaded him that all we needed him to do was throw pitches over the plate as hard as he could. He finally agreed." Corcoran claims Ed, throwing nothing but straight fastballs, struck out 18 batters in 6⅓ innings. One batter popped out.[8]

Corcoran's letter didn't say when he brought Ed in to pitch for the first time but it had to have been sometime before the coal strike in May of 1902. This has to be the case because on May 2 Ed was signed for the first time as a professional player to pitch for the Wilkes-Barre entry in the Pennsylvania State League (PSL). The team was owned by Ernest Landgraf. Wilkes-Barre's catcher was Frank Burke, who would go on to play 40 games in the major leagues with the Giants and the Boston Beaneaters in 1906 and 07.

Other players in the league were George "Hooks" Wiltse, who would win 139 games between 1904 and 1915 with the Giants and Dodgers, and Ed Rainey, who later became president of the baseball division of Spalding and Brothers. Wiltse and Rainey formed a battery for the Scranton team in the PSL. The league was nicknamed the Poverty Stricken League and it lived up to the name. It lasted only from May 3 to May 24 before it disbanded. Ed pitched the opener on May 3 and lost to Williamsport 7–6. He walked seven, hit a batter and threw a wild pitch. He lost to Williamsport again on May 12, 9–8. On May 17 he beat Scranton 12–1 for his only win. While Ed was technically a professional with Wilkes-Barre and had a contract for $45 a month to prove it, practically he wasn't. When the league folded he was owed three weeks' salary which he never recouped. His record was 1–2 with 20 strikeouts in 36 innings. Landgraf tried to find another team for Ed. He took him to Reading to try to sell him, but Reading didn't have enough money. While he was there Walsh had fun throwing a 75 cent baseball. "I could do more tricks with those balls than with the spitball I learned later."[9]

Back in Wilkes-Barre, with the strike still on, Ed went back to playing amateur ball for Corcoran. In July, Burke, his catcher at Wilkes-Barre, recruited him to play in a July 4 game in Downingtown. This single game would start the unambitious coal-cracker down the path from obscurity to celebrity and from Wilkes-Barre to Cooperstown, New York.

Downingtown, 23 miles west of Philadelphia and 120 miles south of Wilkes-Barre, was founded as a mill town along Brandywine Creek in the early 1700s when the area was on the edge of the unsettled western frontier. Thomas Moore erected a water corn mill in 1716 and Roger Hunt established a grist mill in 1739, thus the town became known as Milltown. What's left of the Hunt mill survives in Downingtown to this day and is on the National Register of Historic Places. In 1761, John Downing opened a tavern on the east side of the creek. During the American Revolution the town was a supply depot for Colonial troops, and was called Downing's Town, which evolved into Downingtown.

By the late 1800s Downingtown was a borough of 4500 and a railroad and manufacturing center whose town baseball team was embroiled in a heated and one-sided rivalry with its much bigger neighbor, West Chester, the county seat of Chester County, with a population of almost 10,000. The West Chester area was originally known as Turk's Head, after the inn of the same name located in what is now the center of the borough. To the citizens of Chester County the July 4th game between the rival towns was bigger than a Harvard-Yale football game. Onto that big stage strode Ed Walsh.

It's established that Ed pitched for Wilkes-Barre earlier that season, yet in a *Washington Post* story years later he claimed he was not a pitcher and had wound up pitching for Downingtown only because of an injury to their pitcher. He also claimed that he won the game because of a rabbit. "Though never an active pitcher before, I had always hoped to be, so I mounted the mound full of hope and best wishes. West Chester was the opposing team and it looked like a tough game, as Downingtown had not beaten them in 15 years, so they had forgotten how, while the other fellows had the habit and habits are hard to break. Well, I was in there trying to break this one and was doing fairly well, as we had them beat by a run in the eighth inning. The crowd was wild. Not a win in 15 years and now a one-run lead with three outs to go. The last of the ninth came with only three outs to go, it still seemed like an impossible number, I guess the crowd was thinking for they became strangely quiet and crossed their fingers.

"I'll never forget that game as long as I live. I remember it as vividly as I do the one yesterday. I can see the West Chester short stop coming up and he can hit. He knows it and is not nervous. I was the nervous one now. I fed him a fast one in close and bang! He is squatting on first the result of a safe hit."

After the hit two errors loaded the bases with no outs. Walsh continues the narrative: "My heart was sinking. I faced the next man in a dizzy and dazed manner. It seemed like fighting against the inevitable. Hadn't they won every game for 15 years. What right had I, pitching in my first game, before my first real crowd. What right had I to stop them?

"I hopelessly grip the ball and am about to start the wind up of my arm — and the game no doubt — when from the far corner of the field I hear shouts; they are spreading in volume and now the whole park is in an uproar. I look and racing frantically across the field was a rabbit. He had been dislodged from his home in the high grass in far right field by the immense crowd that infringed the diamond. Round and round the shouting field he goes until after many tiresome and fruitless efforts to get away the frightened and exhausted rabbit drops in the pitcher's box. A good luck sign? The thought flashed through my mind. I thought of the left hind foot and the spectacular and theatrical way the whole thing happened. I carried the fear-stricken rabbit to the bench, feeling a sense of confidence come over me. Our nerves were relieved of tension and the Westchester attack was flustered. Then I struck out the next three men. I am not superstitious but I believed then and I still believe now that I was mighty lucky. If that is not luck why there is no such thing. If it wasn't for that rabbit I probably would not be here today. That victory was the beginning of my success. The next day I received my first offer to play professional baseball."[10]

Back home the next night, Ed was sleeping when he was awakened to get a telegram from a Cornelius J. Danaher, a lawyer who owned the New Haven and Meriden clubs in the Connecticut League. Danaher had learned about Ed the same way as the Downingtown team had. Frank Burke, who had been a catcher for Meriden as well as Wilkes-Barre, recommended Walsh to Danaher after the July 4 game. Burke told Danaher he doubted Ed would go to Connecticut, given that Ed was a lifelong coal miner who had never been farther away from home than Downingtown. Danaher, hoping to prove Burke wrong, wrote in the telegram an offer of $125 a month. In those days $100 was considered top minor league pay.[11]

By July 10 Ed Walsh, who a week earlier had been resigned to a life underground cutting coal and who had never left Pennsylvania, was a professional baseball pitcher for Meriden in the Connecticut State League. In two years he would be a major leaguer.

Except for an occasional Scottish mine boss, Ed hardly knew anyone who wasn't Irish and he had never even been away from home for more than two days when he left Plains in July of 1902 for Meriden, an ethnically-diverse city of 24,000 in south central Connecticut where he didn't know a soul. Clean and prosperous, Meriden was known as "Silver City" as it was the world headquarters of The International Silver Company, a major producer of silver products.

The Meriden area was first settled as the Gilbert farm in 1661. In the 1700s the area was a rural sector of the town of Wallingford and a way station for travelers between Connecticut Colony in the north and New Haven Colony in the south. Belcher Tavern was one of its well-known stops. By 1724 there were 35 families living in the area. In 1727 they raised a meeting house for religious services and by 1728 the parish was known by the name Meriden. In 1806 the Meriden parish was recognized as a town. The railroad arrived in 1839. In 1867 Meriden was incorporated as a city.

In the 1800s many small manufacturers sprang up. Belts, hoops, pewter, guns, cutlery, nails, buttons, lamps, ivory combs, tinware, organs, and coffee grinders were among the products of Meriden. In 1898 International Silver was incorporated in New Jersey after gobbling up 12 small silver companies including the Meriden Britannia Company and Wilcox Silver Plate, also in Meriden. Worth $20 million at its incorporation, Insilco, as the company came to be known, was centered in Meriden.

If Ed felt lonely or out of place in Meriden, three things likely helped him overcome his homesickness. One was baseball. The city and the surrounding towns were serious about their baseball and the Connecticut League was a highly regarded minor league. None other than Connie Mack had gotten his start in Meriden. A second thing that helped Ed adjust in his new home was the outdoors. Meriden is framed on three sides by geological features called traprock ridges, prominent rust-colored cliffs of erosion-resistant igneous rock commonly called traprock. From West Peak, elevation of 1,024 feet, one of the finest views in Connecticut can be seen. The area atop the ridges and in the rural area around Meriden offered small game hunting, Walsh's favorite pastime, almost as good as that in Pennsylvania.

The third and most important thing Walsh found in Meriden was Rosemary Carney, an ice cream vendor at Hanover Park where the Meriden baseball team, also known as Silver City, played. Ed met her within days of his arrival in Meriden. "That year I met and fell in love with Rosemary. After I met her, I suddenly liked ice cream. I used to eat enough to sink a ship and all the time I'd talk to Rosemary. Sometimes, and this is no fib, I ate two or three quarts of ice cream a day. Rosemary was a beautiful girl and tall, too, at five foot, seven. We married in the spring of 1904 just before I went to spring training with the White Sox for the first time."[12]

Ed's first appearance for Meriden in 1902 was a start on July 9 in Bridgeport. He pitched a six-hitter with 10 strikeouts and won 2–0. Walsh would recall years later that he threw nothing but a fastball that day. The newspaper account of the game differed a little.

> A husky youngster who hails from Wilkesbarre [sic], Pennsylvania and stands 6 feet, two inches in his stockings twirled for the Meriden team at Bridgeport yesterday afternoon and had no trouble in making the Park City contingent look like change for a bad nickel. He went through a few mysterious motions and soon had the Orators hypnotized. He had them so completely under his control that he had them batting at everything. High, low and wide ones they all looked alike to them. Someone told the Orators he was throwing curves and they believed it. They never opened their eyes to see if it was true or not. Mr. Walsh was inconsiderate enough to take advantage of their dozy condition and threw the speediest kind of straight balls. If they went whizzing by an Orators's head he struck at them frantically. If they tickled his toes, he swung the bat just the same. If they went two feet off the plate the striking Orator hit just as wildly at it.
>
> Mr. Walsh used a curve ball once in a great while but found it unnecessary. The frightened Orators went up to the plate prepared to hit anything he pitched and so he simply put on steam and sent them straight ones. He came from somewhere around Quakertown where they breed baseball players about as the Stratford Meadows turn out mosquitoes.

Four days later, Bridgeport, which was tied for first place with New Haven while Meriden was in last, beat Ed 9–6. Wildness hurt him. In the third and fifth innings combined, when Bridgeport scored seven times, he walked six, hit a batter and threw two wild pitches As a batter Ed was 4 for 4 with a long double which was called "one of the longest hits in the Bridgeport grounds this season."[13]

That loss was one of only five for Ed that season. He also played outfield. As a pitcher he won nine in a row from August 4 to August 28 to finish with a 15–5 record. In 182 innings he struck out 98, walked 48 and gave up 125 hits.

Ed went back to Plains after the season, but missing Rosemary, he went back to Connecticut after the new year. He started the 1903 season with Meriden. By July he already had done a season's worth of work for the last place Silver City squad. He was 11–10 with 126 k's, and 46 walks in 182 innings when Walter Burnham, the owner of Newark in the International League, bought him for $1,000, a figure that Danaher, the Meriden owner, could not refuse. Burnham signed Ed to a $1,800 contract. Ed was just as effective in the IL as he had been at Meriden. In his first start for Newark he beat Worcester 2–1, and in his second start he shut out Baltimore. Soon he usurped Bruin Magee as fastest pitcher in the Eastern League. He completed all 14 of his starts including two double headers.

Against Hartford he pitched a double header. Both were shutouts. He gave up five hits and struck out 19 in 18 innings. In an exhibition game against the A's he struck out 11 including Topsy Hartsel twice and Socks Seybold, the 1902 American League home run king, three times. By the end of the season he was being called the "Ironman" McGinnity of the Eastern League.[14] He was also being called, as he would be for the rest of his life, "Big Ed." He finished 1903 in Newark with a 9–5 record with 77 strikeouts and 28 walks in 117 innings, and major league teams came calling.

Newark was considered a camping ground for the Athletics in those days and it was expected that Big Ed would go to Philadelphia. After he pitched a game against Buffalo, Bison manager George Stallings, who later managed the 1914 Miracle Braves, recommended him to Charles Somers of Cleveland. In the end, though, it was Charles Comiskey of the White Sox who drafted him for the $750 draft price and signed him to a major league contract. Years later Big Ed said Comiskey gave him a "slight raise" above the $1,800 his Newark contract called for.

2

Big Ed: Rookie

Big Ed Walsh, former coal miner, was three months shy of his 23rd birthday when he donned Major League togs for the first time on March 6, 1904. Oddly, they were blue and he pulled them on in a train car in Fort Worth, Texas. Manager Jim "Nixey" Callahan of the White Sox had brought two sets of uniforms along on the spring training trip. One set was white, normal White Sox wear, and the other blue. The players were divided into two teams, the Whites and the Blues. Big Ed had arrived in Chicago on March 2 to catch the train to Texas with the team. The train left on the 4th. For two days he stayed with Larry Hoffman, a player with the Chicago Spalding indoor team who had been Big Ed's teammate at Meriden. The *Chicago Examiner* got a good look at Big Ed and he made an impression: "Six feet and over in his stocking feet. Every ounce looks like good whalebone and muscle. 23-years old, with the rosy healthy cheeks of a country boy, the clear eye of the mountaineers and the loose easy action of a man of great power.

"Such is Edward A. Walsh, the likely looking youngster from the Newark, N.J. team of the Eastern League. Walsh was born in the rugged Pennsylvania mountains and grew tall and straight and vigorous as the pines of the hills where he rambled as a boy.

"Commy, who knows a ball player when he sees one, thinks very well of Walsh. Indeed he hopes to have discovered a phenom and if past records and present indications are a criterion he will be a tower of strength to the pitching staff of the White Sox."[1] Big Ed would become that tower of strength, but not for over two years. In 1904 Callahan considered him a big lug with speed but no control who was a butcher fielding bunts.

Fort Worth was a stop on the way to the Sox' 1904 training camp, 120 miles farther south, in Marlin Springs, Texas. They hit Fort Worth at 7:10 in the morning. After a workout, nine players were designated Blues and, with catcher Billy Sullivan as their manager, were left in Fort Worth to play a game against the Fort Worth team of the Texas League, while Callahan and the Whites went on to Dallas to play there. They were to meet up in Marlin Springs the next day. Big Ed was initially penciled in for center field by Sullivan, but before the game he was asked to warm up and pitch. His appearance was described this way in the *Chicago Tribune*: "Ed Walsh, the Newark lad, tall, stocky and pink-cheeked pitched the first three innings and let Forth Worth down with two hits and a run."

He struck out two and hit a batter. He played the rest of the game at second base handling seven chances and booting two for errors. As a batter he hit a triple and scored a run. Attendance was 2000.[2] The account called Big Ed "a Newark lad" because he had pitched there in 1903. Comiskey drafted him for $750 after the season. But as late as March 11, manager Walter Burnham of Newark filed a formal protest claiming that Big Ed was exempt from the draft because he signed a contract with Newark for 1904. The *Wilkes-Barre Record* sided with Burnham. "Burnham justly contends Walsh is his property," but the National Commission rubber-stamped the deal for Comiskey.

Big Ed must have thought this Major League baseball business was pretty decent once he got to Marlin Springs where he found this: "A well appointed hotel in a modern town of 5,000 people, baseball grounds located a mile from quarters and mineral baths well suited to the eradication of soreness and lameness."[3] No wonder it was considered the best spring training facility in the country. The weather was ideal, as well. "A temperature which would drive Chicagoans to negligee shirts, a perfectly cloudless sky, and sun hot enough to burn one's face red in an hour's time."[4]

The day they arrived they practiced after lunch for two hours. Big Ed was so eager to pitch that Callahan had to caution him against "shooting" the ball too fast so early in the season. The next day was the first full day of practice and the Sox had two sessions from 10 A.M. to noon working on bunting and fielding and an afternoon session of hit and run and bunting. Big Ed, it was said, looked a little overweight. "But he's a horse for work and should take off flesh quickly."[5]

Two days later something happened that was noted only in passing, but it was something that would eventually transform Big Ed's life. Pitcher Elmer Stricklett, whom Comiskey had brought from the Pacific Coast

League, cut lose with his spitball for the first time as a White Sox. Stricklett was a right hander and it was said he could make the spitter move like a left hander's dry curveball. Though Big Ed learned the spitter from Stricklett that spring in '04, there is no evidence that Walsh threw it to live batters for over a year. On March 13 in 1905 the White Sox were in New Orleans. The regulars and the Pelicans went over to the nearby town of Thibodaux to play a game for the fans there. Big Ed was one of eight players left behind. The eight held a practice. The *Tribune* account of that practice was the first time that Big Ed was associated with the spitball in print. "Walsh developed a 'spit ball' which he says will fool the best of them and put Chesbro in the dark this season. The Sox certainly had trouble hitting him."[6] But in March of 1904, Big Ed wasn't fooling anybody with his fastball and traditional curve. On the 10th the Whites and Blues played a game in Marlin billed as "The Championship of Texas." Businesses closed in Marlin and admission was charged, but only 300 paid to see it. Big Ed, in his first game-condition pitching against Major League batters, was unmercifully bombed by the Whites. In one inning he gave up two singles, a double, two triples, a home run, and seven runs. He also walked a batter and hit a batter. He threw the ball hard, but without any movement or change of pace, it went out hard too.

One night the team was invited to a dance at the Arlington, a club in Marlin, where the players were the hit of the night. When it was over, the organizer approached manager Jimmy Callahan and told him it was appropriate for guests to help defray the cost of the dance and asked him for "ten bits."

"You'll have to translate that for me," Callahan said. Told it was Texan for $1.25, he paid up. When the incident reached the hotel manager he told the dance organizer to return the cash with an apology for taking Callahan for an ordinary citizen instead of the leader of a major league club. When this got back to the boys "it cost the manager several times ten bits to stop the ribbing they gave him."[7]

A few days later the Blues went over to Dallas and Big Ed had his best outing of the spring to that point in front of Comiskey, who had arrived there a day earlier. Pitching against the Dallas State League team, he gave up a walk, two triples and two runs in the first but Dallas didn't touch him after that. Over the next four innings he struck out eight, including the side in the second. It was encouraging, but it was against minor leaguers whom he blew away with straight heat. Dallas scored two off Nick Altrock in the bottom of the ninth and won 6–5, touching off a celebration. The Dallas players came up to the grandstand and the fans threw money at them. Back in Marlin for another Blues versus Whites exhibition game, Big Ed pitched the last three innings for the Whites. His mound opponent was Stricklett. Big Ed gave up a run throwing almost nothing but fastballs; Stricklett pitched shutout ball throwing almost nothing put spitballs.

On March 20 the Sox broke camp in Marlin to play themselves north. The weather had been so good they were sorry to leave. The regulars went with Callahan to New Orleans to play the Pelicans, while Comiskey took the second team to Galveston. The *Tribune* made this note of Big Ed as camp broke: "Of the new slabmen Ed Walsh has attracted the most attention, not so much for his pitching as for his batting. He has a good eye, steps into the ball and hits it hard all the time. He has the same action in every way as 'Tip' O'Neill used to have and may become his double."[8] O'Neill, a pitcher turned outfielder from Canada, had led the American Association in batting average, hits, doubles, triples, home runs and RBI with St. Louis in 1887. In Galveston, Big Ed pitched four innings for the Blues against Texas Christian University. He struck out four and gave up one hit. The Sox won 3–0. On March 23 it was reported in the *Chicago Tribune* that the Milwaukee Brewers would get four players, two of them pitchers, from the Sox on April 10. It was speculated based on the way the team was split up that Big Ed would be one of the four.

On the 25th the teams reunited in New Orleans and Big Ed pitched three scoreless innings against the Pelicans in an 18–4 win in a full squad game. The next day he pitched for the Pelicans against the Sox for three innings. This was his second live game against Major League hitters and he gave up five hits, two fewer than Altrock and Frank Owen, who gave up seven each in their three-inning stints. "None of the three was breaking his arm, however, to strikeout his teammates," the *Tribune* noted.

As the regular season approached, Comiskey and the Chicago writers expected the team to do much better than their 60–77, seventh place finish in '03. It was thought that moving Lee Tannehill from short to third and inserting George Davis at short would make a big difference. Davis had been a player-manager with the Giants from 1895–1901 and had led the National League in RBI in 1897. He was considered the second-best shortstop in the National League to Honus Wagner. In 1902 he jumped to Chicago in the upstart American League that was not honoring the N.L.'s reserve clause, which bound a player to his original team. He was the Sox' regular shortstop in 1902, but in 1903 Davis jumped back to the Giants, where McGraw was willing to make him the highest paid player in baseball. But Davis played just four games for the Giants in 1903 before a court ordered him to play with the White Sox or not at all. Davis sat out the rest of 1903 before going back to Chicago for '04. The Sox also bought first baseman Jiggs Donahue from the Browns and elevated Billy Sullivan to regular catcher. Sullivan had jumped to the White Sox from the Boston National League franchise in 1901. A suspect hitter, he was a superb backstop who would have a profound impact on young Ed Walsh.

Another key for improvement was to get Fielder Jones back to play center. Jones had hit .287 in '03, but had yet to report. Jones — an astute businessman with interests in oil, lumber and orchards — was considering retiring to go into business full time and had threatened to leave baseball before. Eventually he signed and met the team in Chicago.[9]

As the spring wore on there was a lot of speculation about Stricklett. One report had Stricklett going to Milwaukee in the American Association. Late in March the *Tribune* published this report: "Manager Frank of New Orleans announced that Comiskey has loaned him Stricklett for the season. This is not true, as Stricklett was left in New Orleans to help out the Pelicans for one week and will rejoin the Sox in Memphis on Sunday."[10]

As things turned out Stricklett did make the Sox' opening day roster, but he pitched in only one game and was sent to Milwaukee in June. He resurfaced with Brooklyn in 1905. Stricklett's association with Walsh and the Sox was short, but his influence on Big Ed during those few weeks of spring training in 1904 changed Big Ed's life and the fortunes of the White Sox, but the change wouldn't begin for another two years. As things would develop in 1904 Big Ed would be the sixth starter as a rookie behind Frank Owen, Nick Altrock, Doc White, Frank Smith and Roy Patterson.

The Sox stopped in Mobile where Big Ed struck out six locals in three innings of work. He also had a hit and scored two runs. The next stop was Montgomery on March 28, where Big Ed was hospitalized with a severe cold. The next day they went back to Mobile where Altrock pitched a complete game in a 3–1 win. Cy Young and Buck Freeman, a Wilkes-Barre resident, played for Montgomery. Young and Freeman were with Boston and arrived a day early for an exhibition game between Boston and Montgomery.

By March 31, Big Ed was out of the hospital and back on the mound in Birmingham. He was hit hard by the locals, giving up eight hits and four runs in five innings. In Memphis on April 2 Altrock pitched a complete game in a 6–2 win. The next day Tom Dougherty pitched a complete game in a 5–2 win. On the 3rd in Springfield, Big Ed threw his first complete game in a 13–2 win over the local squad. The Sox got 20 hits off three pitchers. The next day, for the first time since they left Chicago for Texas, the Sox missed a day due to weather. An all day rain stopped just long enough for them to jog a mile. Meanwhile, it was reported that Frank Isbell, the regular first baseman in '03, would join the team in Kansas City the next day. Also pitcher Roy Patterson of St. Croix, a former boy wonder, joined the team. And veteran pitcher Frank "Nig" Smith was signed and was expected to report to Chicago in time for the opener. He had won 18 in 31 appearances with Birmingham in 1903. The signing of the two pitchers did not bode well for Big Ed's chances of sticking with the Sox once the final regular season roster was announced.

After two days in Kansas City, where the Sox were rained out and worked out at the Missouri Athletic Club, the team split up with half going to Omaha for two games and half to Des Moines. But Big Ed went home. His mother was on her deathbed. Big Ed had buried his father and a brother over the winter. While he was gone the Sox played a game in a snowstorm in Omaha and beat the locals 7–4 with Owen pitching.

In Des Moines Isbell made his first appearance and had three hits as the split squad lost 7–6. Altrock and Dougherty pitched the next day in Des Moines in an 8–3 win. The Sox arrived in Chicago on the 12th. On the 13th they worked out at the Thirty-Ninth Street ballpark. Callahan told reporters that Big Ed's mother was extremely ill and that he would not return to the team for an indefinite period. "He will be back soon and will make a fine pitcher if he has the nerve. He's a big fellow, weighs 220 in condition and surely cut out to be a ball player."[11] Despite the praise, when asked to name his pitching staff Callahan mentioned Ed last after Owen, Altrock, Smith, Patsy Flaherty, Patterson, and Stricklett.

Big Ed's mother recovered, at least temporarily, and he went back to Chicago arriving on the 17th, expecting to be assigned to Milwaukee. To the surprise of the scribes, who had predicted Big Ed would be sent to Milwaukee, Comiskey and Callahan put him on the Sox' opening day roster. But three weeks into the season Big Ed had not pitched and fans were wondering why he was being carried. It was often joked that he was a relative of Commy's. "There was more than one person," Big Ed said, "who asked Comiskey why he kept that big stiff on the payroll, referring to me. Some of these remarks I overheard and some were told to me. They weren't pleasant to listen to, but a wise player merely grits his teeth and makes use of such remarks as a spur to drive him on."

Critics weren't the only thing spurring Big Ed on. "When I went to Chicago I had only my arm and my determination to make good. But I had a spur which most ballplayers do not have. The shadow of the coal mines was on me and I used to say to myself, 'It's make good or go back to the mines.' Then, too, I had recently gotten married and that made it all the harder for me to face defeat."[12]

As he waited to be called into his first major league game, Big Ed didn't sit around and pout. He paid attention.

> No one ever watched baseball closer than I did. When a good pitcher for a visiting team was working I never lost a chance to crawl as close behind the catcher as possible to see what he was doing, to study how he pitched to certain batters and how he used his curves. I think I spent nearly all of one season trying to get a balk motion that was not a balk, and finally I succeeded. I had sense enough not to ask many questions, but to keep my eyes and ears open and try to learn all I could. In those days the White Sox had a lot of smart pitchers, men who did things, and who used their heads all the time. Every time I saw one of them pull off something I made a sneak over toward the clubhouse and tried it myself, to see whether or not I could do it.

A very young-looking Big Ed, probably in his second year (Library of Congress).

> I don't think anyone ever worked harder than I to succeed. All my life I have been fond of children. Every big league player is a hero to kids. So every morning I used to get into the ballpark with a crowd of kids and pitch to them hour after hour. It was great sport for them and it did me good too.[13]

Big Ed's debut finally came on May 7. Altrock started the last of a three-game series against the Browns in Chicago and was hit early and often. After the Browns scored four runs on seven hits through three innings, Callahan called on rookie pitcher "Eddie" Walsh, as he was called in a game account, to put out the fire in his first major league appearance. Walsh did just that, pitching shutout ball for five innings. Meanwhile, the Sox scored six runs and Big Ed took a 6–4 lead into the ninth. "That ninth was a wonder," said the

Chicago Tribune account of the game. Big Ed easily retired the first two Browns he faced and seemed to have the game in hand. But then Wallace and Hill singled to right field. When Big Ed got two quick strikes on Tom Jones, once again he looked poised to close out his first win. "Eddie must have given Tom a straight one, for he whacked it swiftly along the left field foul line, with Holmes in full cry after it. Two runs would have scored anyway on the hit, but fortune was with St. Louis for the moment. The ball squeezed itself under the left field bleachers, and Jones scored, too, with the run that looked like a sure winner."

Despite the description of the ball going under the fence, it was ruled a home run. Big Ed got the next out, but he and the Sox entered the bottom of the ninth down 7–6. Davis grounded out to start the Sox' ninth. Donohue and Dundon singled to right. Donohue took a chance going to third and slid in just under the tag with Dundon taking second on the throw. Sullivan hit one into the left center gap scoring both runners and winning it for the Sox and Big Ed 8–7.[14]

Callahan didn't call on Big Ed again for 12 days, when he gave him his first start on May 18 in Washington. Throwing nothing but a fastball and curve he was nearly perfect. He pitched a 2-hit shutout facing only 28 batters, one over the minimum, as the Sox won 5–0. In the third Stahl doubled, but was doubled off on a fly to left as Holmes made a running catch and threw to second. In the fifth Cassidy doubled but was caught trying to steal third to end the inning. Big Ed retired the next 11 batters and with two outs in the ninth had faced the minimum, when Jacobsen reached on a error by Davis. Big Ed struck out three and, of course, had no walks.

Statistically it was a stunning performance, but the Senators were an easy mark. They were the worst team in the A.L. and would finish 1904 38–133 in last place 55½ games behind the pennant winners, the Boston Americans. Callahan must have sensed that pitching against a weak team would help Walsh's confidence. Four of Big Ed's eight starts in 1904 would come against the Senators.

Big Ed faced good teams, too. Five days after his first start, he started in Boston against the eventual A.L. pennant winners and lost 6–2. He gave up eight hits, two of them triples, one in a two-run first, and one in the two-run seventh. He struck out five and walked three. Batting in the eighth Big Ed hit a home run which was described this way in the *Tribune*: "Walsh opened the eighth with a slashing wallop to right center, which gave him a home run." It was one of only 14 hit by the Sox all season. Fielder Jones led the team with three.

Back home on June 3 Callahan gave Big Ed a start against the Senators, whom he had owned in his first start two weeks earlier. The results were far different this time. He fell behind every batter and was pulled in the fourth having given up four runs, four walks and three hits. Altrock finished the game and was the winner as the Sox pounded out 17 hits and won 13–7. Big Ed was 2-for-2 with a double.

Two days later Callahan, on what would be his last day as manager, sent Big Ed out to start again against the Senators. He pitched well enough, scattering eight hits and striking out seven, but lost 2–0 to Jack Townsend, who somehow kept the Sox off the board despite giving up 10 hits, one a single by Big Ed. One of the Senators' runs scored on a Big Ed wild pitch which went into the grandstand.

The next day Callahan, who was the regular second baseman, resigned as manager. Fielder Jones, who was the regular center fielder, replaced him in what was described as an entirely amicable arrangement among Comiskey, Callahan and Jones. Second base was a new position for Callahan, who had been an outfielder, and he said he felt he could learn the position faster and strengthen the team if he wasn't the manager. There was more to it than that. Callahan was a heavy drinker and carouser who was lax on discipline, which Comiskey didn't countenance.

Fielder Allison Jones was born August 13, 1871, in Shinglehouse, Pennsylvania, a timber town in the northwestern part of the state. His parents were Benjamin Franklin Jones and Laura Ellen Parmenter Jones, a *Mayflower* Pilgrim descendant. After a good season at Springfield, Massachusetts, in 1895, he was drafted by Brooklyn of the National League, where he played from 1896 to 1900 and helped win two National League pennants. As George Davis had, Jones jumped to the A.L because the new league was not honoring the reserve clause. Clark Griffith, who jumped from the Chicago N.L. franchise to partner briefly with Comiskey with the White Sox, raided N.L. teams. Jones was one of his spoils. Jones signed with the White Sox in 1901. He hit .311 as the Sox won the inaugural A.L. pennant. After his deal with the Sox expired, and without the reserve clause in his contract, Jones, as Davis had, signed a three-year deal to play for the Giants starting in 1904. He expected to be free to move to New York, but after the 1903 season the A.L. agreed to honor the reserve clause and Jones was stuck in Chicago.

Comiskey elevated Jones to manager to keep him from trying to leave Chicago or quit baseball, as well as to remove Callahan from the job. Jones proved to be an innovative manager of the Hanlon-McGraw school who coached his batters to get on base, bunt and run, a formula that worked in 1906 when the Sox were last in team batting, but third in runs scored.

Two weeks passed before Jones used Big Ed. On June 19 in Chicago against Boston he brought him in to relieve White in the first inning. White lasted seven batters. He gave up five hits and a walk and four runs. Big Ed came in with two runners on and struck out two to end the inning. Over two hours and 11 innings later, Walsh finished the game, a 13–10 loser. He shut out the Americans for 5⅔ innings but gave up nine runs and 10 hits over the last five. He walked two batters, hit one and struck out five.

On July 4 in Chicago the Sox were swept in a double header by Detroit. Despite the pair of losses the Sox were in pretty good shape. When they left for St. Louis on July 6 to start a month-long Eastern swing, they were in third place with a 39–28 record, 3½ games behind first place Boston and 1½ behind second place New York. During the second game at St. Louis, a 1–0 shutout win by Altrock, Big Ed received a wire from Wilkes-Barre. His mother was dead. He left for home immediately. After the funeral he caught up with the Sox in Philadelphia on the 15th. On July 19 he was brought in to mop up the ninth in a 12–1 win over the Senators in D.C., his first appearance in over a month. The next day he was given a start. The *Tribune* story speculated as to why Big Ed wasn't being used much. "Big Ed Walsh was sent in to perform for the White Sox, and acquitted himself well. He has not had much chance this season, for Chicago has a surplus of twirling material, and consequently his feat today is the more meritorious." That feat was pitching a 1-run, six-hit game without walking a batter and striking out five as the Sox won 5–1.

On July 24 in New York he got a start against the Highlanders and spitballer Jack Chesbro. Though Big Ed got behind most batters, gave up 12 hits and walked two, he emerged a 5–4 winner, accounting for two runs as a batter. In the fifth he hit an RBI triple to right center and scored on a single by Jones. Of his pitching with runners on base the *Tribune* wrote: "By putting it over at these critical moments and making them hit the ball he gave the other eight members of the team a chance to help do something, with the result that New York could not get leather to safe territory when most needed."

On July 28, with a day off in the midst of a series in Boston, the Sox went over to Lynn, Massachusetts, to play an exhibition with the locals. Big Ed pitched the first seven innings. Lynn got 10 hits off him, but he gave up just two runs in a 5–2 Sox win. The *Tribune* was not impressed: "Walsh, who started the game, was wild and the Lynn team hit him hard."

Back home on August 3 Big Ed started against Washington for the

2. Big Ed: Rookie

fourth time in his seven starts. He shut down the Senators through six, but they bunched three hits together in the seventh for two runs, and the Sox went into the bottom of the ninth down 2-0. A single by Donohue and a double by Tannehill made it 2-1. An infield single moved Tannehill to third. Isbell batted for Walsh and hit to second. The Senators went for two, but Isbell beat the throw to first and Tannehill scored the tying run. Smith pitched a scoreless 10th inning and the Sox won it in the bottom. With the bases loaded and one out, Donohue hit back to the pitcher who threw home looking for a 1-2-3 double play, but Senators catcher Kittridge's throw to first hit Donohue in the back and the winning run scored. The win was the fifth straight for the Sox and their 12th in 14 games. With a 56-35 record they were in second place just one-half game behind Boston and they were the talk of the American League. On the same date the year before they had been 39-46 and in seventh place 14½ games out.

On August 7 Big Ed played the ringer role. He was sent to Kenosha, Wisconsin, to pitch for Kenosha against Racine in the first of a best-of-three series that was billed as the semiprofessional championship of Wisconsin. A crowd of over 5,000 saw Big Ed strike out 13 in five innings, but the Kenosha catcher, last name Donavan, couldn't handle it. "Donavan was unable to hold him and Walsh was forced to let down after a few innings," said a newspaper story. Big Ed hit two batters, walked three, gave up 10 hits, most of them, presumably, after letting up for the catcher's sake, and lost 9-6. Kenosha made five errors, which according to a game account were crucial in Racine's six-run sixth. It was alleged that $10,000 was bet on the game.

Back with the Sox, who were in a pennant race, Big Ed didn't pitch again for over a month. It was likely that Jones didn't trust him in crucial games and, as tight as the race was, every game was crucial in August and most of September. On August 4, the day after Big Ed beat the Senators, the Sox won again and moved into first place one-half game ahead of Boston and one and one-half ahead of the New York Highlanders. On August 5 the Philadelphia A's, who were only five and one-half out, came to Chicago for a four-game series. The A's Plank beat Owen in the opener 4-3. The Sox won the second game 8-1 with Altrock beating Chief Bender 8-1. The third game was on a Sunday and the Sox needed it to stay in first place. The officially announced crowd of 27,000 was the largest in the history of South Side Park, but it was estimated that over 30,000 crammed themselves into the park. Many of them, according to the *Tribune* account, "were among the hoodlum element." Neither the White Sox officials nor the police were prepared for the onslaught of fans. "Some semblance of order was maintained until the latter half of the game, when the hoodlums, in an ugly mood at defeat, began to encroach on the playing field from all directions, until the sight surpassed anything anyone had ever seen at a prairie lot contest."

The thing that most caused the hoodlums' ugly mood was Rube Waddell. The A's hayseed pitcher struck out 11 and had a shutout going into the ninth. The A's won 5–2. During the Sox' ninth inning rally the fans ran at A's catcher Schreck to try to stop him from catching a foul pop a few feet behind home plate. For the fourth game, game one starters Owen and Plank pitched again and the A's made it three of four with a 6–5 win. At the end of the day the Sox were in third place by percentage points with the A's only three and one-half behind them.

The Sox stayed within at least one and one-half games of the top for next 20 days, as the Sox, Boston and New York traded the lead. On August 10 the Sox beat the Highlanders 5–1, and knocked out Chesbro, breaking his string of 30 straight complete games. Chesbro caused a sensation in 1904, winning 41 games throwing the spitball.

Comiskey showed his appreciation for his team's showing in the pennant race by buying each player a $30 suit of clothes. They were measured for their suits on August 17, promptly went out and lost seven of 10 and fell to fourth place, though only three out of first. On the 18th the Sox were no-hit by Boston's Lee Tannehill, who retired the last 25 Sox batters after hitting one and walking one in the first inning. Big Ed pitched the last six innings. He struck out the first two batters he faced, four overall, and didn't give up a run until Boston got two in the ninth. He also caught two line drives with his bare hand. "It seems as if either must have smashed his pitching hand, but Walsh did not even look to see if his fingers were intact. This led the bleachers to inquire if the hand was made of chilled steel."[15]

His hand may have been made of steel, but Jones didn't let him use it again for another month. Big Ed could only watch as the Sox fell to five games out in early September, even though they passed the A's to regain third. A spate of doubleheaders in early September, seven in two weeks, gave Jones no choice but to give Big Ed a start. On September 17 he started the second game of a double-header in St. Louis. He hadn't pitched since August 17 and it showed. He walked six, threw a wild pitch and lost 6–5 in 11 innings. The Sox also lost the first game and they dropped to six games out. But the Sox didn't fade any further in September and on the 29th Big Ed helped them get within three games of Boston and New York, who were tied for first, by beating Washington in relief. Big Ed got in after

In 1904 as a rookie Big Ed was the Sox's sixth starter. He got in only 18 games (Library of Congress).

starting pitcher Altrock and manager Jones were tossed from the game in the fourth for arguing a close play at second base. The Sox were losing 3–0 at the time, but while his teammates scored four runs over the last five innings, Big Ed pitched no-hit ball and faced the minimum 15 batters. One batter reached on a walk but was erased on a double play. He struck out three.

The next day, September 30, the Sox beat Chesbro and the Highlanders. Boston lost, too, and the Sox trimmed the lead to two games. The next day, October 1, "Jack Chesbro came back, spit ball and all, and got ample revenge on the White Stockings." Big Ed made his last appearance of 1904 in that game, pitching the final three innings in a 7–2 loss. He didn't give up a hit or run and struck out the side in the eighth. It was Big Ed's 18th appearance of the season. It was Chesbro's 38th win. The Sox never got any closer after that loss and they finished 89–65, six games behind the pennant-winning Boston Americans who beat the Highlanders by one and one-half games. Even so, the 89 wins and third place finish were dramatic improvements over the 60 wins and seventh place finish in 1903. The rise was fueled by the pitching. Owen won 21, Altrock, 19 and Smith and White, 16 each. At one point White pitched 41⅓ consecutive scoreless innings.

Walsh finished his rookie season 6–3. He started eight games and completed six, with one shutout. He was used in relief in 10 games and finished all 10, a league leading statistic. His ERA was 2.60. He walked 32 and struck out 57 in 110 innings. As a batter he was 9 for 41, .220, and hit one of the team's 14 home runs.

3

The Spitter

By any name — mystery vapor float, cuspidor ball, salivated slant, eel ball, or moist shoot — the pitch that Ed Walsh helped make famous was co-invented by George Hildebrand and Frank Corridon at Providence in 1902. Hildebrand was an American League umpire from 1912 to 1934 who got an 11-game cup of coffee as an outfielder with Brooklyn in 1902. Before he went up to Brooklyn he was a teammate of Corridon's at Providence. In a letter he wrote in 1920 Hildebrand said he saw Corridon throw a drop pitch after wetting the tips of his fingers. In an attempt to one-up Corridon, Hildebrand "slobbered all over the ball. I held the ball the same as Corridon, only wetting it a great deal more. The ball I threw broke a good deal more than Corridon's."

Later in the letter Hildebrand recounts that after he was released by Brooklyn he went back home to California and finished the season with Sacramento in the Pacific Coast League where he taught the pitch to Elmer Stricklett. It was Stricklett who introduced it to Jack Chesbro of the New York Highlanders that fall when Chesbro came to Sacramento barnstorming with an all-star team.[1] And it was Stricklett who introduced the pitch to Ed Walsh at the White Sox training camp in Texas in 1904. The Hildebrand-Corridon story was also told in the May 1913 issue of *Baseball Magazine* in an article titled "A Question Which Has Caused a Great Deal of Discussion and Never Before Been Correctly Answered" by P. A. Meany. Though Corridon and Stricklett were important spitball pioneers who are linked to Chesbro and Walsh, they had very limited success in the big leagues themselves. Corridon's career record was 70–67 and Stricklett's was 35–51.

In 1919, Fred Mitchell, then manager of the Cubs, claimed that Chic Fraser, Mitchell's teammate with the Phillies in 1903, was the first pitcher to throw a spitball in a regulation major league game. In a newspaper interview Mitchell said Fraser had been monkeying with the spitball at least a year before Stricklett, but never used it much because he couldn't control it. "Chief Zimmer was catching for the Phillies late in a game they had in hand when Mitchell, as a practical joke, told Fraser to throw a spitter. Zimmer called for a fastball and Fraser threw the spitter. The batter missed it by two feet and so did the astonished Zimmer. The batter wound up on second."[2]

While the George Hildebrand story may explain how the spitball was introduced into modern baseball, it seems logical to assume pitchers probably stumbled on the effect of throwing a wet baseball long before 1902. After all, wetting the fingers is a common way to aid grip in everything from turning the pages of a book to swinging an ax. And, after all, as long as there have been baseball games played in rain, there have been wet baseballs.

In their book *The Pitcher*, John Thorn and John Holway suggest that Bobby Matthews first used the spitter in the minor leagues in 1868, throwing underhanded. Cap Anson, in a 1919 newspaper article, backed the claims about Matthews. "Many of the old pitchers wet the ball and nothing was thought of it. Matthews rubbed the ball white on one side and then would moisten it with his fingers. The ball would curve and other times drop. Reports of the game in newspaper clippings which I now have will bear me out."[3]

Whatever its origin, in 1903 the spitball was a novelty pitch little talked about and thrown, infrequently and ineffectually, by no more than a half dozen American League pitchers. That changed in 1904 when Chesbro threw a coming out party for the spitter. Throwing a spitter almost exclusively, he won an all-time record 41 games, starting 51 and completing 48. He worked 454 innings with a 1.82 ERA. Most significantly, throwing a pitch previously believed to be uncontrollable, he walked only 88 batters, an average of fewer than two per nine innings. Because of Chesbro's success in 1904, the spitball was the talk of the major league training camps in the spring of 1905. From the Giants camp came word that all their pitchers were working on spitters. "According to Manager McGraw the spitball will be a conspicuous feature of Giants pitchers this year. Everyone of them has been experimenting with the particular bender and each claims to have it under perfect control. Mathewson is going to use it in the repertoire of his curves, as will Taylor and Elliot. All three used it in practice yesterday and had the catchers hopping around."[4]

3. The Spitter

Comiskey even referenced the pitch when talking about Koury, a Russian general in the Russo-Japanese War which was being waged at the time. "All he has done so far is build a breastworks and then start running for home. He tires his soldiers out building defenses and they haven't anything left to defend them. How would it look if I kept my players up all night before a game practicing spitballs? They would be all in when they met the enemy wouldn't they?"[5]

In the White Sox camp there was more talk about 20-year-old rookie Louis Fiene and his spitter than there was of Big Ed. Fiene, who had been with Cedar Rapids in 1904, claimed to have mastered full control of the pitch over the winter. While it's considered gospel that Big Ed learned the spitter from Stricklett a year earlier in the spring of '04, just how that happened isn't so clear. Over the years Big Ed told conflicting stories about his relationship with Stricklett and just how he learned the spitball from him. Sometimes he said Stricklett didn't teach him the pitch with hands on demonstrations, but rather that he picked up the pitch by watching Stricklett work out. "I first took lessons from Elmer Stricklett, lessons he gave me without knowing it. I was in Marlin Springs with the White Sox. One day Comiskey got him out to see what he could do and I heard Elmer tell him he had something good. That was enough for me, I certainly hadn't. I stood there rubber necking and saw the spitball. I watched him and tried to solve his delivery. I saw how Elmer did it and tried it myself. From the first the spitball appealed to me."[6]

But Billy Sullivan, who caught Big Ed throughout both their careers, remembered things differently. Almost 50 years later Sullivan told *Baseball Digest* that the spitball did not appeal to Big Ed initially. "Our manager Fielder Jones told Walsh his one

One way or another, Ed learned the spitball from this man, Elmer Stricklett, in 1904, but he didn't use it for two years. Stricklett was released by the Sox in 1904 and resurfaced with Brooklyn.

chance to stay with the club was to learn the spitter. Practically ordered him to learn it. Walsh was depressed, thought it would ruin his arm, but he worked on it."[7]

Some newspaper accounts said that Big Ed and Stricklett were roommates that spring. Big Ed never confirmed that, but in an interview in 1915 said that he and Stricklett hung out together and that Stricklett did teach him the pitch with hands on lessons. "When I first reported to the White Sox they were training in Marlin Springs, Texas. Stricklett was in camp. He confided to Comiskey that he had something in the way of a new fooler. Commy advised me to watch Stricklett and observe the mysterious slant. Stricklett and I had been chumming and I attended his workout. He showed me how it was done and I started to master it."[8]

By the 1950s Big Ed's version of the story had evolved to where it had been Stricklett's idea for Walsh to learn the spitter. Toward the end of his life he recounted a conversation he had with Stricklett this way:

"Why don't you throw the spitball?" Stricklett asked.

"Spitball, what's a spitball?" I asked.

"He showed me what he meant and threw the spitball and I saw something. It broke two ways, down and out."[9]

Big Ed also contradicted himself in describing just when he used the spitter in an American League game for the first time. He always insisted that he worked on the pitch for two years before he threw it in an A.L. game. "I worked on it all that first spring after I learned it in Marlin Springs. Then for two years after, every minute that I was not actually at work in a game I was out behind the grandstand working on that spitter. It's difficult to throw a wet ball with accuracy at first, but you can learn it like anything else."[10]

Yet here he is quoted in 1914 saying he used it in his rookie season: "I reduced the spitter to a fair point of effectiveness while training at Marlin, but not until 1904 did I use it in a major league game. I used it for the first time in desperation. It was a case of wetting the ball or getting walloped. It was against Cleveland and the Naps were hammering me to all angles of the garden. Sullivan goaded me into taking a chance with the spitter and with its help, I succeeded in restoring calm."[11]

Either "1904" is a typo in the passage, or time fooled with Big Ed's memory. Since 1904 was his rookie season and since by all accounts he picked up the pitch that spring from Stricklett, he could hardly have practiced it for two years before using it against Cleveland that same year. A check of box scores of the Cleveland-Chicago games in 1904 shows that Big Ed did not pitch against Cleveland either as a starter or in relief.

3. The Spitter

He appeared in only 18 games in '04, starting just eight. Accounts of those games make no mention of his throwing the spitball. Was he a year off in his memory of the first time he threw the spitball in a major league game, or was he two years off? If it was against Cleveland, it may have been on May 9 in 1905 in his first start of the season. From an account of that game: "Walsh is another of these twirlers who have been warming the bench for several weeks chewing slippery elm bark or something else to aid them in accumulating the wherewithal to toss the 'eel ball' over the plate."[12]

As an avid outdoorsman Big Ed was familiar with slippery elm bark, but whether he started to chew it as nervous habit akin to chewing tobacco, or as a purposeful method for inducing saliva for the spitball isn't clear. And while the "eel ball" was one of the many nicknames for the spitball, it isn't clear that Walsh threw the pitch in that May 9, 1905, start. Again, though the spitball was all the rage in the spring of '05 because of Chesbro's sensational '04 season, and while pitchers all over the A.L. practiced it and threatened to use it, few did use it in 1905. Harry Howell of the Browns was one pitcher who did throw the spitter in '05. Though he was 15–22 with the hapless Browns, he did have a 1.98 ERA, down from 3.53 in 1903, and led the league in complete games. On opening day he shut out the White Sox with a two-hitter and 10 strikeouts.

But when did Big Ed first throw the spitter? That May 9, 1905, start loosely fits his memory of the game in which he first threw the spitball. It was against Cleveland and it was a game in which he was hit early and then settled down. But it wasn't like he was hammered in that game and then became unhittable. He gave up a run in the first inning on a single, sacrifice and a double. He gave up four hits and a run the rest of the way and won 3–2.

A game on April 22 in 1906 fits better because it is two years after he learned the pitch. Again he started against Cleveland. Again he started poorly, walking the lead-off batter and giving up two runs in the first and then settled down. He pitched four scoreless innings, then gave up a run in the sixth and three in the seventh. He was relieved by Altrock, who won it in 12, 7–6. It is likely — given his insistence that he worked on the pitch for two seasons and part of another before he tried it in a major league game — that the April 22, 1906, start against Cleveland in Chicago was the start of Ed Walsh's career as King of the Spitball.

Just how did Big Ed throw the pitch? In 1914 he described his mechanics this way:

I think that many pitchers smear the ball with an unnecessary amount of spit. I just moisten my two fingers and rub them on the ball until it is damp. Then I reach down and pick up some dirt and rub the dirt on the wet spot until it is thoroughly black. Finally I rub my fingers on my trousers. Then I am ready to throw the spitball. Many people have the idea you can only throw one kind of twister with it; as a matter of fact you can make a spitball follow any curve. The physics back of the spitball is the reverse twist. I'd grip the ball with my fingers close together and my thumb underneath. I let the ball slip from underneath my wet finger tips. By wetting the fingers held on top of the ball and keeping your thumb perfectly dry you make the ball spin over forward, that is to say it spins away from your fingers and toward your thumb. The result is a perfectly astounding pitch downward. It goes straight for the batters head, then swerves out and takes a sudden dive downward. Depending on my grip, I could break the pitch four ways. To a right hander I could break the ball down and away, straight down and in, and up. To get the rise I threw underhand, but the other pitches were thrown with the same motion as my fastball. After you learn to control it is an assassinator of batting averages.[13]

Here's a similar description from a 1910 newspaper account:[1] "Walsh uses a piece of slippery elm bark in his mouth to keep up the stock of moisture needed through a nine-inning contest. He moistens a spot an inch square on the ball between the seams. His thumb clutches the ball length wise on the opposite seam and with a mighty overhand delivery the big fellow hurls the ball straight toward the pan. Sometimes it will jump two feet downward or outward."[14]

Big Ed always talked freely about the spitter. He never tried to hide his technique. "People think the spitball is some mysterious secret, some black art that the ordinary man cannot learn. I believe there is nothing to such reports. There are just two things necessary to make a spitball pitcher, speed and practice. Any one in the world is at liberty to watch me. I have never made the slightest effort to conceal anything. The various positions that my hand assumes in manipulation of the spitball have all been photographed and are public property. I have taken a good deal of pains to try to teach the art of the spitter to other big league players and when I coached at Yale I told them all I knew about it."[15]

Learning to throw the spitball may not have been a "mysterious secret," as Big Ed said, but why it broke as it did was mysterious. There were various theories. John Ward described it this way in *Baseball Magazine*, "The spitter is thrown just the same as you'd throw a dry ball. There's no twist to it. A straight ball or a curve is necessarily thrown with a twist that makes it revolve rapidly and maintains the ball's center of gravity. That's why straight and curve balls can be thrown with absolute accuracy. But the spitter, having no particular center of gravity, wobbles and careens first to one side and then the other in the most irregular manner. That's why it is so hard for the batters to hit it."

Clarke Griffith, who managed Chesbro with the Highlanders when Chesbro won 41 in 1904, put the spitball effect this way: "This principle in brief is that where one side of the ball is smoother than the other the ball can be released from the pitcher's hand in such a way as to completely alter its proper rotation as it shoots through the air. And the altering of this rotation is what gives the ball its peculiar break as it ducks across the plate."[16]

Here's another theory on why the spitball did what it did. "For a spitball after all, is only a special type of fastball. It is pitched with great speed with the first two fingers wet. The friction of these two fingers gives it a peculiar spiral motion and this motion coupled with the great speed causes it to break sharply."[17]

After his sensational 41–12 1904 season with the New York Highlanders, Chesbro proposed his own theory. "The thumb, and the thumb alone, directs the spitball. The saliva on the ball does not make it drop. In fact, the saliva does not affect the ball in any way. The ball must be moistened simply for the purpose of making it leave the fingers first and thumb last. Curves and fastballs leave the fingers last. By moistening the ball the fingers slip off first and the thumb last. The thumb does the trick on the spitball and does it well."[18]

Larry Cheney, one of the few National League pitchers to rely on the spitball, developed it late in his career. After leading the N.L. in wild pitches from 1912 to 1915 and in walks in '15 with 140, he was traded to Brooklyn where used the spitball in 1916 to go 18–12 with a 1.92 era and help the Dodgers win the pennant. "I never knew how to pitch until I came to Brooklyn," Cheney said after the 1916 season. "Until I perfected the spitter my whole idea was to throw the ball past the bats. I found out that the boys at the plate hit them back at you faster than you can throw them up, if you stick to that method of pitching. I wish I had the spitter working when I was with the Cubs and knew as much about pitching as I do now. I'd have hung up a record or two myself. A good husky fellow breaking in young with a good spitter ought to set any league on fire. I took it up pretty late. Still it's done a lot for me. I'm afraid I might not be in the big leagues today if I hadn't mastered it."[19]

Cheney said the spitball's motion was about friction. "The ball is twirled with two fingers gripped on one side and the thumb on the other.

The ball is made moist at the point it is touched by the fingers so it rolls off with just the slightest degree of friction causing the ball to take a whirling flight over a short distance until the friction overcomes the revolving motion, when the break occurs — the sharp zigzagging jump that has baffled some of the greatest curve-ball hitters. When pitched with an overhand motion the spitball shoots almost straight downward, and when the sidearm movement is brought into play with the thumb toward the body it breaks as fast as a curve does, downward and either outward or inward."

However thrown, given the success Chesbro had in 1904 and the success Big Ed would have in his breakout year of 1906, the popularity of the pitch exploded. By 1910 Cleveland was the only A.L. team without at least one full time spitball pitcher.

Though the spitball would not be outlawed in the major leagues until 1920, prominent baseball men spoke out against it almost as soon as Chesbro and Big Ed popularized it. Deacon McGuire, who played, managed and umpired for 28 years, was one of them. He was the Cleveland manager in 1910 when the Naps were the only team in the A.L. without a spitball pitcher.

"Some spitters are all right. I'm not saying anything against men like Walsh," McGuire said, "and some others who have mastered the spitball without it affecting them physically, but just the same I prefer recruits who depend on good old speed and curves and change of pace. When you have a few spitters on your pitching staff you are always running the risk of having your catchers put out of business."[20]

There were three main objections to the spitball. One: it hurt the game's popularity, because it was too hard to hit and fans liked batting and scoring. Two: it was unsanitary. Three: it slowed down games because pitchers had to pretend to wet the ball before every pitch, even when they weren't throwing a spitball, so batters wouldn't be tipped off to when it was coming.

From a 1915 newspaper story: "When two hurlers addicted to the spitball work against each other it has been proven that it requires considerably longer to play nine innings than when two men who depend entirely on curves and fastballs are opposed on the slab.

"It takes more time to moisten the ball for a spitter. Although a pitcher may deliver only one spitball in every dozen pitches he must be deliberate with every pitch otherwise the batsmen would detect the difference."[21]

Big Ed acknowledged the last point in an interview later in his life,

3. The Spitter

Big Ed appears to be working up some saliva in the photograph. He's probably sucking on a piece of slippery elm bark (George Grantham Bain Collection, Library of Congress).

but denied the pitch was unsanitary. "When I loaded up the spitter I kept the glove in front of my mouth. I didn't throw it on every pitch. I averaged two or three per batter. The other times I relied on the fastball which I threw with the same motion.

"As for the pitch being unsanitary that isn't true. You don't use a big gob of saliva. Most people have the impression the ball is soggy. It isn't. Two wet fingers are all that is necessary. I had such control that I could hit a tack on the wall with it."[22]

In a magazine interview in 1907 White Sox manager Fielder Jones came out against the spitball. Given that Jones and his Sox would not have won the A.L. pennant and World Series in 1906 without Big Ed and his spitball, Jones was an unlikely opponent of the pitch. Even so, here's what he said in the interview:

> I warned Comiskey against the evils of the "spit" ball two years ago. He laughed at me and said baseball was more prosperous than ever. That may be

all true, but I would be willing to wager that the crowds would be even larger if it were not for the "spit" ball. Comiskey was on the Rules Committee when I begged him to have a rule inserted prohibiting a pitcher from moistening the ball, but he thought that my fears were groundless.

In my opinion the "spit" ball is doing a great injury to the game. In the first place, it is not natural. In the second place, it is not cleanly. Lots of people do not like to go out to the park and watch a pitcher slobbering all over a ball. Thirdly, the use of the "spit" ball lengthens the games, as pitchers who depend upon the "spit" ball consume so much time applying the moisture. Another reason is that when a "spit" ball pitcher has good control of his "spitter" the opposing team can consider itself lucky if it gets a hit. The rooters like to see the ball hit or a fine piece of fielding.

Then again, with a "spit" ball man in the box, the fielders behind him are more liable to make errors in consequence of the slippery condition of the ball."

Bobby Wallace, the Browns shortstop, is often cited as evidence of this. Wallace was considered one of the most accurate throwers in the business, except when Howell pitched. He made a disproportionate number of his league leading 54 errors in 1907 in games Howell pitched.

Jones worried that spitball pitchers would take over the game. "By another year there may be twice as many and it would be no surprise to see all the pitchers within a few years using this delivery which injures the game. Now is the time to act. Let the league instruct its umpires to call every ball pitched in which the pitcher uses the saliva a ball and this delivery will be killed in short order."[23]

Another unlikely spitball opponent was Clarke Griffith, Chesbro's manager in 1904. As a pitcher with the Cubs in the 1890s, Griffith had used a trick pitch of his own — he scuffed the ball with his spikes — to win 20 or more for the Cubs for six straight seasons. In 1898 he led the N.L. in ERA. "I had a habit as far back as I can remember, of hitting the ball on the spikes of my shoe before I started to pitch. At first I think it was nothing more than a habit, just as some pitchers are always hitching up their belts or shifting their caps. But after a while I noticed that when I had scarred one side of a new ball with my spikes it would break a good deal better when it crossed the plate. Now the spitball pitcher accomplishes this end by wetting one side of the ball so that it slips away from under his fingers with the least possible friction. Why encourage the stranglehold which the pitcher has on batting? Batting is the most interesting part of the game. It ought to be encouraged."[24]

Big Ed defended the spitter in a 1912 interview. "With the beginning of the spring training," he said, "comes that six year-old discussion about how long the spit-ball will last. I have noticed of late that some of the critics have discovered that that particular delivery is on the decline and that in a short time, if there is no baseball legislation against it, the moist shoots will be thrown into the discard. Now, I might just as well take the bull by the horns at the start and say that the successful pitcher of the future, unless he has some other equally as effective delivery, will have to come to the spit-ball or fall behind."[25]

Addie Joss, who was something of a Big Ed nemesis, did not throw the spitball, but wanted it legal out of fairness, even while admitting it was almost impossible to hit. "It would hardly be fair to the men who depend on this form of delivery for their success. It took Ed Walsh a couple years to acquire the spitter and it would be a hardship to deprive him of it now that he has it down to a near science," he said in 1913.

In 1913 *Sporting Life* asked Chicago health commissioner Dr. George Young if the spitball was unsanitary. "I do not believe the spitting on the ball by the pitcher has any more effect upon the health of the player than spitting on the bait 'for luck' when fishing has to do with the size of the catch."

But Dr. Young did concede a point to a school principal who said the use of the spitball was "a disgusting and pernicious example to thousands of boys."

"Unquestionably, there is much to be said in your behalf [sic] when the question is viewed from the standpoint of esthetics," Young said.[26] A Dr. Martin Friedrich, a St. Louis health officer, disagreed. "The spitball is unsanitary," he said after watching Harry Howell pitch. "Consider for a moment the possibilities of the practice. Suppose he was a victim of tuberculosis — and base ball players are not immune, by any means — what would a man's feelings be with a batted ball covered with microbes coming at him like a shot out of a gun?"[27]

The first step toward the eventual banning was a ruling by National League president Harry Pulliam just before the 1905 season opened. "He instructed umpires to see that pitchers do not moisten the ball in an ostentatious and objectionable manner, for instance deliberately wetting the fingers in the manner of licking a postage stamp. A balk will be called on every pitcher doing so."[28]

Though an article leading up to the 1915 Major League meetings claimed the spitball would not be banned, its reprieve was only temporary. "It is not the intention of the rule makers to attempt to legislate the spitball out of baseball as it would prove too severe a handicap on some of the hurlers and even wreck some pitching staffs. Other freak pitches have been eliminated simply by enforcing one of the existing rules which forbids damaging or discoloring the ball.

"The emery ball and mud ball were ruled out under that section of the code. Prohibiting the emory ball put Russell Ford out of business." Ford, a Canadian, may have been as much to blame as any pitcher for the banning of the spitball and he didn't even throw it, though for years it was thought he did. In 1910 as a rookie with the Highlanders he was 26–6 with a 1.65 ERA. His key pitch was called the "slide ball." During spring training that year, some papers explained that it was actually a spitball with a new twist. "Ford worked at it until he has perfect control of the curve. In addition to the usual sharp break of the spitball Ford gives it an 'out' or 'in' twist at will."[29]

Ford kept the true source of the mystery pitch under wraps for a few years. Then the truth emerged: it was no spitter, but rather an emery ball, a ball he secretly scuffed with emery paper (similar to sandpaper). This practice was also outlawed in 1920.

Big Ed explained how Ford was outed. "Russell Ford was the first one to use the freak ball. He was putting floaters and funny twists over the plate that were hard to hit. Everyone was curious to know what he was doing with the ball and they might not have known to this day if he had taken care of his glove. One day one of the boys picked up his glove and saw the palm cut out. Underneath was a sheet of emery paper. That was the start and finish of the emery ball."[30]

After emery was outlawed, Jim Lavender of the Cubs, who was using emery, tried mud. He would wet the ball and touch it to the ground. He claimed a spot of mud on the ball would cause it to rise. He was stopped by umpires."[31]

The second shoe on the spitball's demise dropped at the American Association winter meetings in 1917. A story about the meeting cited Big Ed directly. "The American Association banned any foreign substance at their winter meeting in Chicago. There was agitation back in 1908 against it when Ed Walsh was knocking batters flat, but no action was taken. Since then have appeared the emery ball, the shine ball and the mud ball which act similar to the spitter. It was left to the umpire to determine if any foreign substances were being used. Fines shall be $25 each pitch. Under such conditions it would have cost Ed Walsh $2000 to pitch a game in 1908."[32]

New York Giants manager John McGraw came out publicly against the spitball in 1918. When McGraw talked baseball, baseball people listened. "My position as regards the spitball is well known. I have always been opposed to it. It is disgusting, unscientific and dangerous. Batting would be helped by a rule against the spitball, and the public wants batting. The chance of error making would be lessened, and the public wants cleanly fielded games. There would be less danger to batter and catcher with the freak deliveries out of the way, for not only are they hard to hit, but hard to catch."[33] A year later the spitter was banned. For all the talk about how unfair the spitball was to batters, after the pitch was banned, Big Ed claimed its effect was all in the batters' heads. "The spitball is nothing more than a curveball. It is not dangerous and it is not a handicap to batting. Much of the effect on a batter is psychological."[34]

Though Big Ed was out of baseball when the spitball was banned in 1919, he spoke out against the ban, and the live ball, for the rest of his life. Speaking before a crowd of 1,000 at an old timers banquet in Chicago in 1944, he railed against the "rabbit ball" and the modern pitcher. "Only one in 20 pitchers today can throw a real curve today. Put the spitball back in and let them get their curves with it. Or put a ban on this dangerous rabbit ball. Baseball is getting too home run crazy. You'd think that was the only thrill in the game."[35]

In an interview in 1957 he said:

> The lively ball being used today scares pitchers to death. It's made worry warts out of them and nobody can pitch good ball when he is fretting and fidgety. The ball they're throwing is like a golf ball. When it hits the fat part of the bat it soars like a tee shot. When the deadball of my day was tagged it went out like a seven iron.
>
> Baseball today is a hitters' game. The pitchers can't breathe out there on the mound. The umpires are itching to call a balk for any false move and the hitters are itching to smack a jack rabbit ball.
>
> When I pitched the home run was something special. Today it's an ordinary part of the game. They could move the fences back 75 feet in every park and there would still be a flock of home runs. Don't let anyone tell you the ball isn't juiced up. It sure is.
>
> The ball is too lively. Teams have no infields today, they have two outfields, because what was the infield now play back on the green. If they don't deaden the ball they should bring back the spitball as an alternative. Today's moundsmen need help and they need it bad. Pitching used to be 60 percent of the game — today it's about 30. The spitter would restore the balance between batting and pitching. Pitching duels would be more common and the home run would not be cheapened.
>
> Don't think I'm a cheat, but I know if I were pitching today I'd try and sneak a spitter in now and then in a tight spot. I'd never tell anybody I

threw the spitter, though, like Preacher Roe did a couple years ago. What good does that do. Throw it and keep your mouth shut.[36]

Of the 17 pitchers who were grandfathered to be allowed to use the spitball after the 1920 ban, Big Ed's favorites were Urban "Red" Faber because he was a White Sox and Stan Coveleski because he was a fellow coal cracker from the Northeastern Pennsylvania anthracite fields.

4

Ze Meestaire Walsh

Manager Jones had planned to use only Frank Smith and Big Ed in the first game of the spring against the Pelicans in New Orleans on March 13, 1905, but Big Ed blew up after two innings. After he hit a batter and forced in a run with a walk in the second, Jones brought in Lou Fiene. This was two days before the practice in which Big Ed was first associated with the spitball in print. At a practice the next day, which included an intra-squad game, pitchers were drilled on observing the balk rule which the American League umpires were to enforce to the letter in '05. That night Comiskey took McFarland, Donahue, Clarke, Patterson, Altrock, Dougherty, Morrison and Big Ed to Beaumont for a game and then for a week's stay in Galveston. Big Ed started a game in Galveston and had a rough first inning, giving up two runs with two walks and a wild pitch. He settled down and pitched the next three innings scoreless. He struck out six. There was no mention of spitball. Altrock pitched the rest of the game and Big Ed played shortstop. The next day in Galveston he played the whole game in center.

Back in Chicago the *Tribune* ran a profile of the players which revealed their marital status. That prompted a poem in a letter from a female fan which ran in the paper's "Diamond Chat" column on March 26.

> Ze Meestaire Walsh, he ees so g-r-r-r-r-an!
> Zer is no ozzair in zis lan'
> Viz hair so black, viz cheek so red.
> He ees SUPERB! But, he ees wed!
> I luffe' to vatch heem twirl zee ball,
> Zee leetle sphere, zat puzzles all

> Ze battairs, so zey cannot play.
> Ah! He has stole my heart away.
> An' now eet ees so full of fear.
> Ze world eet ees so dark — an' drear.
> I mus' forget heem, eef I can,
> For, alas, he ees a married man.

Big Ed may have been popular with the ladies, but he still had work to do to popularize himself with Jones. On April 1 he pitched against the University of Nebraska in Omaha and was hit hard in the sixth, giving up three singles and a home run in an 8–4 loss. He struck out four. He finished the game in right field and hit a double and a triple. On April 7 in Burlington, Iowa, he hit a two-run triple in the first inning while playing in center field and pitched the last four. On the day before the opener on April 14 in 1905 Jones was asked about the spitball. He worried about opponents using it, but made no mention of Big Ed. "I am going to see what the spitball does to us. Perhaps some may be able to hit it better than others. No, I don't think all the pitchers will be able to use the spitball, particularly in tight places, because they haven't mastered it yet, but many of them will master it and there are some of them who have it under control already. Those are the men who are going to play havoc with the batting."[1]

It didn't take long for the Sox to run into one of those. The Browns' Harry Howell threw an opening day two-hitter in Chicago, beating the Sox and Nig Smith 2–1. Howell struck out eight. The *Tribune* made note of the spitball. "There was Harry Howell and his perfectly tamed spitball who had the White Stockings at his mercy." The Sox line up for 1905 was substantially the same as it had been in 1904. The only meaningful additions were backup catcher Hub Hart and utility player George Rohe.

Big Ed didn't get his first start until the Sox' 19th game on May 9 in Cleveland. He won 3–2 to put the Sox over .500 at 10–9. He struck out three and didn't walk a batter. From the *Tribune*, "Six little hits were all Cleveland could gather off Walsh, and it was because manager Larry tore off two of the six at opportune moments that Cleveland scored at all. The remainder of the team was practically helpless before Walsh and his red sleeves."

Big Ed lasted only an inning and one-third in his second start at home against New York on May 15. In the first inning Dougherty singled and Wee Willie Keeler doubled. A ground out and a single made it 2–0. After an out in the second, a walk, passed ball and single produced another run and Jones ran in from center field and pulled Ed out. White came in and the Sox rallied to win for him 10–4. After that poor showing Jones held Big Ed back for nearly a month, until the Sox played Big Ed's favorite patsies, the Senators, on June 14 in Washington. He won the game 5–3. "The big miner"—as the *Washington Post* described him—hit a long home run. The *Post* said it was a "Navy Yard homer."

For the next 15 games Jones rotated White, Altrock and Owen. He even started Owen in both games of a double header on July 1 in St. Louis. "Yipsy," as they called him, pitched two complete games winning 3–2 and 2–0. He gave up only seven hits, four in the first game and three in the second. Jones had planned to use White in the second game, but Owen finished so strong that he asked Jones to let him start the second game.

The Sox left for Chicago immediately after the game, tied for first place with the Naps. Both teams were 37–21. In Chicago they played just one game, a makeup with Detroit which White won 1–0. They got back on the train and went over to Cleveland for a four-game set. They arrived in Cleveland tied for first with the Naps and left the same way as the teams split the four games. Altrock won the first and fourth games, while Smith and Owen lost the two middle games.

Big Ed didn't start again until his designated opponent, the Senators, came to Chicago on July 14. He dominated again, winning 2–0. He gave up seven hits, but didn't walk a batter and struck out three. Apparently he had his fastball working and the Senators had a problem with the umpire, as this bit of prose tells: "Walsh had the goods usually kept in a first class pitching store and delivered them in spite of the vigorous protests of the opposing strikers. Bases full, none out, and the whole tribe of Stahl inviting Walsh to a balloon ride while blue curls of evaporating profanity arose from portions of the stands. But Walsh didn't soar. Instead he shot the ball over so fast that only Sullivan could see it."[2]

With that win the Sox were 43–26 and one game behind the first place Naps. Two days later Jones couldn't resist a chance to throw Big Ed at the Senators again before they got out of town. This time it didn't work. He was wild and lost 7–4. It was his first loss of the season. He was 3–1, with one no decision and two mop up relief jobs. He had appeared in only seven of Chicago's 71 games. On August 5 he made his third consecutive start against the Senators, this time in Washington. It was a disaster. He was knocked out after five innings and lost 9–1. By this time the A's, winners of six of seven, were in first place, ahead of the Sox by two games, who were one-half game ahead of the Naps. On August 22 the Sox were three and one-half games behind and with five consecutive home double headers coming up in as many days. The first two of the twin bills were against the A's and both were split. Next Boston came in for three double headers on the 25th, 26th, and 27th. The Sox won all six games. Big Ed pitched the second game on the 26th and won 4–3 to the surprise of the *Tribune*. "A man could have offered 25 to 1 without finding any sane takers for Ed Walsh hooked up with Jesse Tannehill in the second scrap, for that sou'-paw has had the Sox faded all season." Big Ed was sharp in the middle innings when he retired nine straight. He struck out eight and didn't walk a batter. He also had a hit and scored a run. When the Sox won the double header the next day, they moved into first place by a game. But the stay on top was short lived. The A's won 11 of 12 from August 26 to September 9 to overtake the Sox by four and one-half games. After Big Ed beat Cleveland 6–1 at Cleveland on September 1, the Sox lost five straight from September 2 to September 5, a single game at Cleveland and a pair of double headers in Detroit. In the first game of the second double header loss to Detroit, Altrock took a 5–2 lead into the ninth, but the Tigers scored four to win 6–5. Before the game it was announced that Jones was suspended indefinitely for calling umpire O'Loughlin a crook the day before. In the second game Big Ed lost 3–2. In the fifth inning Cicotte opened by rolling one to Donohue back of first but Big Ed didn't cover the bag. Cicotte later scored when the Tigers pulled off a double steal with two outs. Oddly, for a player considered a good fielder, Big Ed had a mental block about covering first as a rookie. After failing to get to the bag cost him a run in the loss to Detroit, he did it again in the first inning of his next start on September 9 in Chicago against Cleveland and again it cost him a run. In the third inning he nearly did it again. This time he got to first base late and, after catching the toss from Donahue, had to slide into the bag to avoid a collision. He survived his errors this time and beat Addie Joss 5–2.

The win by Big Ed was the fourth straight for the Sox, who won 15 of 18 between September 6 and September 26 to get within one-half game of the A's. Big Ed won three of the 15 games — the 5–2 win over Joss on the 9th, a 9–6 win at Cleveland on the 20th and a 3–1 win over Boston in the second game of a double header on the 26th. In the 9–6 win over Cleveland he gave up 13 hits in 7⅔ innings and was losing 6–1 in the eighth, when the Sox scored eight. Cleveland made seven errors and the Sox got six hits, including a double by Big Ed. Altrock pitched the ninth and the Sox won 9–6. In the 3–1 win at Boston Big Ed pitched a four-hitter. He walked four and struck out six. He had a base hit but was thrown out trying to stretch it into a double. At the end of the day the A's were 85–52. The Sox, having played three more games, were in second place by one-half game with an 86–54 record.

That was as close as the Sox would get though they hung on, at least mathematically, until October 6, two days before the end of the regular season. The A's backed into the pennant, clinching it when the Sox lost to St. Louis. The Sox still had four games to play and the A's had two, but even if the Sox won out and the A's lost all four the A's would win the pennant with a .617 winning percentage to .614 for the Sox.

As it happened the Sox finished 92–60 with six ties which were nongames. The A's were 92-56-4. The White Sox had no choice but to accept the results, as that's how things were done then. Tie games were not replayed. Comiskey accepted that, but he was livid about what the National Commission did two days earlier on October 4, while the Sox were still mathematically alive. The commission announced details and dates for a World Series between the A's and the National League champion New York Giants.

"If we should win the pennant," Comiskey said, "and I have by no means given up hoping we will, I shall decline to have anything to do with the proposed New York series, but instead will go ahead with the post-season games with the Chicago Nationals.

"Who said I had given up winning the pennant? Was I quoted in today's or yesterday's papers as saying anything of the kind? I consider it a most discourteous thing for the commission to go ahead, while the race was still on, with a close, important finish in progress and announce details of the series on the assumption that the White Sox were beaten. I did not solicit these interviews remember, but when I was asked what I thought I expressed my convictions.

"Why has the commission taken this deliberate slap at me. Is it to affect the spirit of my players? My club has been making a grand fight and it was deserving of better treatment."[3]

On the last day of the season in Boston on October 9, in a preview of things to come, Big Ed pitched both games of a double header. In the first game he relieved Doc White, who asked out with a bad arm after pitching to only two batters. Ed came in cold, threw five warm up pitches and went to work. In first he gave up two singles and walked three as Boston scored five. But Big Ed shut out Boston the rest of the way and the Sox won 10–5. He struck out four. He started and completed the second game and won 3–1. He gave up just five hits and four walks and struck out five. He had a hit in each game. It was dark by the time Sullivan caught Freeman's pop foul to end the second game and the Sox' 1905 regular season.

There was still the city series to be played, but despite Big Ed's strong outing in Boston on the last day, he made only one appearance, as a pinch hitter, in the Cubs' series, won by the Cubs 4–1. Players from both teams split $10,802

Why didn't Jones and Comiskey use Big Ed more in 1905? Typically in that era pitchers pitched. But Big Ed started only 13 games in '05, fewer than any fifth starter in the league. He finished '05 8–3, with a 2.17 ERA, 29 walks, and 71 strikeouts in 136 innings. The ERA sounds credible, but it was the highest on the staff. Manager Fielder Jones may have thought that Big Ed just wasn't good enough to start over the Sox' big four — Frank Owen (21–13, 2.10), Nick Altrock (23–12, 1.88), Frank Smith (19–13, 2.13) and Georgetown University trained dentist Guy "Doc" White (17–13, 1.76) — especially as the Sox were in a pennant race all season. The big four started 136 of the Sox 152 games in 1905. Big Ed never complained publicly about the inactivity, but he did talk to his wife, who talked about 1904 and 1905 in a newspaper article after the 1906 World Series. "He used to say, 'I wish I could get more chances. I'm sure I could win.' He was pretty blue in those days, and yet always maintained confidence in his ability."[4]

The first time Big Ed said anything publicly about his first two seasons with the White Sox was in a magazine story in 1913. "The first of my

Billy Sullivan was very important in Ed's development, having been given the job of finishing Big Ed's pitching education. He helped him tame the spitball (Library of Congress).

experience in baseball was not over-pleasant. Things did not go very well with me, and for more than two years I was on the ragged edge of nowhere. I worried a good deal about my condition, or rather lack of it. It was my disposition to worry — a bad habit, but hard to break. I was glad enough, when the season was over, to take my gun and go off into the woods and forget for a time that there was any such thing as baseball."[5]

Despite appearances, Jones and Comiskey weren't keeping Big Ed around just as a spot starter. They had plans for him. Jones realized that he might have a budding Chesbro on his hands, so he went to Comiskey and asked for more time for Big Ed to master the spitball. Jones gave catcher Billy Sullivan the job of finishing Big Ed's pitching education. Sullivan said they were hard lessons. "He had me hopping around as he tried to master the spit and gain control. Walsh fairly soaked the ball with moisture, but eventually got better results with just a little."[6]

After Big Ed had a breakout year in 1906, the fans justifiably wondered why Jones and Comiskey held him back for two years. They knew nothing of the hours Walsh had spent in obscurity learning to pitch and throw the spitter with Sullivan watching and coaching him.

"Whatever success I have had in baseball is due to hard study and hard work," Big Ed said. "I had sense enough to keep my eyes and ears open when I joined the White Sox. The team had a lot of smart pitchers, men who used their heads all the time. Every time I saw one of them pull off something I made a sneak over toward the clubhouse and tried it myself to see whether or not I could do it. I worked as hard in those days as any man worked in a mine or a mill. Comiskey and Jones both coached me, told me what to do and how to do it, but they could not make me a pitcher. A fellow has to do that for himself. When I began to use the spit ball I worked like a horse. I must have pitched two or three games a day trying to get control and make that ball go where I wanted it to go."[7]

In 1906 the ball would go where he wanted it to go.

5

The Hitless Wonders

Charles Albert Comiskey was born in Chicago on August 15, 1859. His father, John, was an alderman for 12 years in the old Seventh and Eighth wards. He and his six brothers and one sister went to Holy Family school. Charles spent more time playing baseball than on school work so his father apprenticed him to a plumber. Comiskey resisted and the fights between him and his father over baseball and plumbing led Comiskey to leave home at 17 and sign with an independent team in Milwaukee. The manager, Ted Sullivan — who would in later years work for Comiskey as a White Sox scout — agreed to pay his new pitcher $60 a month.

The next season Comiskey pitched for a team in Elgin, Illinois, and reportedly had an undefeated season. This was when the pitcher pitched from a box 45 feet from home plate and batters were able to call for a low or high ball. In 1878 he signed with Dubuque in the Northwestern League, another team managed by Sullivan. The team was owned by D.B. Henderson, who was later an Illinois congressman and speaker of the house. Comiskey played all positions except catcher. He was paid $50 a month and Sullivan got him a job in the off season as a sales representative for Sullivan's news agency. Comiskey stayed with Dubuque through 1881. In 1879 Comiskey played exclusively at first base and Dubuque won the league pennant. Future Hall of Famer Charley "Old Hoss" Radbourn was the number one starter.

As a first baseman Comiskey was a pioneer. He invented a new style and though he never led the league fielding statistics, he had a greater influence on first base play than even Hal Chase ever did. Before Comiskey, first basemen were guys like Dan Brouthers, Dave Orr and Roger Connor, big immobile targets who played near the bag. Comiskey played first base like another infielder. He played deep, moved around. He was ridiculed at first until it became apparent that he was getting to the bag in plenty of time, while covering twice the territory as any other first baseman in the American Association.[1]

In 1914 his first base style was recalled in *Baseball Magazine*: "Thirty years ago first base was the next station before the jumping off place for fading veterans or a trial spot for the undeveloped recruit. Most who played the position hugged the base. Comiskey with St. Louis Browns of A.A. took a stand well toward second base which enabled him to cut off many balls that otherwise would have gone into right field. He practiced with his pitchers each morning to teach them to cover the bag on such plays. Within a few years all first basemen were doing it."[2]

After an exhibition game against the Browns in 1882, Comiskey was offered a contract for $125 a month by owner Chris Von der Ahe of the American Association St. Louis Browns. Comiskey took over as player-manager of the Browns in '83 and from '85 to '88 won four consecutive American Association pennants for Von der Ahe, who called himself "Der poss president of der Prowns."

Comiskey was a career .250 hitter, but hit .368 in 1887 and was considered dangerous with runners on base. He led the Browns in steals each season. He stole 62 bases in 1887 and 77 in 1888. After the 1886 season a world championship series was arranged between the Browns and the N.L. champion Chicago. There was some bad blood between the teams because of what had happened during a post-season series the previous year. In that series only the receipts of the first four games went to the players. Because they had won three of the first four games the Browns claimed victory, even though the seventh game was declared a tie. To prevent any such shenanigans in the 1886 series, the entire gate receipts went into a pot, half of which would go to the players. During the sixth game, with the Browns leading the series 3–2, a special train waited on a siding to carry the players to Cincinnati for a seventh game if Chicago won. The sixth game went into extra innings. In the 10th, with the Browns' Curt Welch on third, Chicago catcher "King" Kelly called for a high inside pitch with the intention of making a snap throw to third to get Welch, but Kelly missed the pitch and Welch scored to end the series. The play became known as the "$10,000 passed ball," as that was the amount by which the winners' share was greater than the losers.' Comiskey kept a ball from that game inscribed with the score in gilded letters and numbers.

Comiskey jumped to the Players League in 1890 to manage the

Left: Comiskey was considered a pioneer of modern first base play, even without a glove. *Right:* This card depicts Charles Comiskey as a player-manager for St. Louis in the American Association about 1887 or 1888 (both photographs from Library of Congress).

Chicago team for $8,000. When the league folded, Comiskey went back to the Browns for 1891, where one of his players was Clarke Griffith. In '92 he signed to manage Cincinnati for three seasons at $7,500 per season.[3] In Cincinnati Comiskey met Ban Johnson, a writer for the *Cincinnati Commercial-Tribune*. The pair became fast friends. Together on November 20, 1892, at a meeting in Detroit of minor league teams from around the Midwest they helped organize a western league. A western league had existed in various forms since 1879, but the most recent version had gone bankrupt. Comiskey attended the meeting and recommended Ban Johnson for president. Comiskey had considerable clout and Johnson was voted in. While Johnson is largely given credit for founding the Western League which eventually became the American League, and fairly so, it might not have succeeded without Comiskey. *Baseball Magazine* said the league was Comiskey's idea, which he sold to Johnson during a hunting and fishing trip. The theory was that Comiskey wanted to be an owner and figured if he could help establish a league with his friend as its president, he'd get his franchise.

But he had to wait two years. Cincinnati owner John T. Brush, who would later own the Giants, would not let Comiskey out of his contract, which ran through '94. After the '94 season Comiskey bought the Sioux City team and moved it to St. Paul, Minnesota. He built a ballpark in St. Paul for $12,000 and then built a second one outside the city limits for $16,000 because he couldn't persuade St. Paul to allow Sunday ball. He played in 13 games with St. Paul, his last as a player.

In 1900, after five years in St. Paul, he moved the team to Chicago. In 1901, when Johnson declared his renamed American League a major league, Comiskey was in on the ground floor with his White Sox, a name he took from a team he had played against years earlier in St. Louis. The plan worked. By 1906 Comiskey was a rich man, having cleared $100,000 in 1905 alone, the equivalent of over $2,000,000 today. Johnson, who ran the league for 35 years, became a wealthy man too. So it seems incredible that two men who enjoyed such a mutually beneficial friendship could have a falling out over a back-up outfielder, but that's what happened in 1905.

In September of '05 a regular Sox outfielder "went on a spree," as the *Washington Post* put it, and Ducky Holmes took his place. Holmes was a notorious troublemaker, the exact type of player Johnson did not want in his league. After Holmes got tossed out of several games by umpires, Johnson ordered him suspended. Comiskey sided with Holmes. "Because a regular player was on a toot and the substitute could not keep his tongue down a long friendship broke down," wrote the *Washington Post*. The animus was so strong, it lasted into 1906, when Comiskey moved the White Sox offices out of the Fisher Building where Johnson had the American League main office.

Holmes became an owner in Lincoln, Nebraska, in 1906 and came back to Chicago for the winter baseball meeting in February. After the meeting Holmes stayed in town and met with Comiskey and the pair agreed to have the White Sox play in Lincoln on April 9 and 10, further irritating Johnson.[4] The American League schedule was released at the American League winter meeting. The Sox got 17 Sundays, 12 Saturdays and July 4 at home. The league addressed the issue of how to call batted balls which left the playing field. This is what they came up with: "When a batted ball passes outside the ground or into a stand, the umpire shall decide fair or foul according to where it disappears from the umpire's view.[5]

In early February when Big Ed returned his signed contract to

Comiskey, little notice was taken. Comiskey was more concerned about Frank "Nig" Smith and a pending deal to get George Stone from the St. Louis Browns. Smith and Stone, Comiskey thought, were the keys to catching the Philadelphia Athletics, who had won the 1905 pennant by two games over the White Sox.

Smith was holding out and threatening to jump to Harrisburg of the outlaw Tri-State League. Comiskey wrote to him asking for his terms. He had been 19–13 in 31 starts in '05, but, according to his telegraphed reply to Comiskey's letter on January 12, he wasn't holding out for more money as much as he was for more respect. He alleged that in '05 the team refused to play ball behind him, particularly Lee Tannehill.

"Had I no one to deal with but 'Commy' I would have no trouble. But I can't get along with some of the men on the team and I have given up trying. I hope Comiskey will appreciate my position and consent to dispose of my services to another team."

As this was a common complaint for the paranoid Smith, Comiskey ignored him and Smith eventually capitulated and signed. The *Post* agreed with Comiskey's assessment, writing, "His grievance is more fanciful than real. He blames defeat on others."[6]

In February a trade was rumored between the Sox and St. Louis Browns — Gus Dundon, Danny Green, George Rohe and $100 for outfielder George Stone, who had led the league in hits in '05. Since the Sox had batted .237 in '05, fifth in the 8-team league, getting Stone for the anemic Sox lineup would have been a coup for Comiskey, but it never happened. Browns manager Jimmy McAleer stopped in Chicago on February 12 and met with Comiskey, but a deal could not be worked out.

Comiskey did make some moves. To replace retired outfielders Ducky Holmes and Nixey Callahan, Comiskey drafted Bill O'Neill from Milwaukee, where O'Neill wound up after being released by Washington in '05. Pitcher Roy Patterson signed February 3, the same day as Big Ed. Catcher Eddie McFarland signed on the 9th. First baseman Jiggs Donahue, who had tied for the team high in hits with shortstop George Davis in '05, withheld his contract for three weeks before signing for a slight raise. While he waited he bowled with his four brothers on the best team in Springfield, Ohio.[7]

Comiskey drafted left handed pitcher Earl Kruger from Cedar Rapids and bought right hander Louis Fiene, who had been in camp with the Sox in '05, from Toledo of the American Association. Comiskey was high on the two prospects, especially Fiene, whom he valued over Big Ed. As things turned out Kruger never even made it north and Fiene would appear in

5. The Hitless Wonders

just six games. Doc White, who was 17–13 with a 1.76 ERA in 33 starts in '05, was given leave from spring training to coach the Navy baseball team at Annapolis. He didn't have to report until April 14. This was fortuitous for Big Ed, as he got more work in the spring than he might have. The White Sox left for spring training in New Orleans on March 9. The next day they stopped in Jackson, Mississippi. They worked out at the local park from 9:30 A.M. to 11, then ran the mile back to the hotel. This was repeated from 2 to 4:30 in the afternoon. The squad was split into two teams for games the next day. Big Ed pitched for the second team, nicknamed the Jacksons to honor the town. Comiskey had his houseboat put into the White River in Arkansas, a tributary of the Mississippi, from where he could mix business and pleasure, baseball and hunting and fishing.[8]

To avoid the Mardi Gras crush the Sox didn't push on to New Orleans until March 14. The plan was to practice for two days before playing two games against the locals, the New Orleans Pelicans, on March 17 and 18, but the plan was waylaid by weather worse than even the most wizened old timers could remember. Record cold, 32 degrees on the 15th, and steady rain cut the four scheduled practice sessions to one. They worked out on the afternoon of the 16th on soggy grounds in winter-like weather. To make matters worse, ballplayers had been banned from the Young Men's Gymnastic Club, considered one of the finest in the country. Ballplayers were banned because of bad behavior by the Philadelphia A's, who had been there a few days earlier. They were accused of abusing the hospitality of the club by "making roughhouse in the cafe, insulting members, abusing attendants, parading through parlor with spikes on, crowding members out of the pool."[9]

As there was nothing else to do, the White Sox found badges for the Fair Grounds in their boxes and went to the races. Everybody on the team won money on Guiding Star at 2-to-1 in the Crescent City Derby, but all lost on a subsequent race.

The first game against the Pelicans was canceled. On the 18th the field was finally ready. Big Ed pitched three innings and faced the minimum. One batter bunted for a hit but was caught stealing. He struck out three and had three easy ones hit back to him. The Sox played the Pelicans two more times on the 24th and 25th. Big Ed started on the 24th and, while what happened was only little noted at the time, the three innings pitched by Big Ed that day in New Orleans dramatically changed his life and career and the fortunes of the Chicago White Sox. From the *Chicago Tribune* account of the game: "Walsh made a hit with his spitball, a feature he perfected since coming here and now has under full control."

That passage marks just the second time Big Ed's name was associated with the spitter in print and that game was the first time he used it in competition with another team. He faced 10 in the three innings, with one hit allowed, no walks and one strikeout.[10] The next day he pitched the third through seventh innings in an 11–2 win over the Pelicans. It was the first time in three springs that a big league team took three from the local team. He walked one, struck out four and gave up one run. After the third game against the Pelicans, the Sox started north. They spent a week in Alabama and two days in Memphis, March 31 and April 1. From there the club split into two teams, one going to Louisville for April 7 and 8 games and the other to Nebraska for games against Ducky Holmes' Lincoln team as agreed. Comiskey followed the second team on the Mississippi in his boat, but not for long. On March 26 he was called back to Chicago by a court case. August Auerbach won a verdict of $10,000 from the White Sox for injuries when he was hit by a foul ball four years earlier. The suit said he was unconscious for two days and was "made a nervous wreck as a result of the blow." The jury gave him the full amount of the suit. Comiskey was unrepentant. "It is unprecedented in baseball history. Real fans will not stand for wire screens in front of them. It was so hard to sell box seats in the grandstand behind the wire netting that we had to take down part of it."[11]

The bad weather followed the Sox north. They played more chess and checkers than baseball. Some games were played, but that was about it. As the *Trib* put it: "Both Chicago teams chased all over the middle south for nearly four weeks in search of sunshine."

Big Ed pitched in most of the games and was practically unhittable. In three innings in a 3–2 win at Memphis after a week of idleness due to rain he struck out three without a walk and allowed one hit. In a 6–2 win at Nashville, played at Peabody College, Big Ed pitched the fourth, fifth and sixth and stuck out six and walked one. Nashville got one run on two misplayed bunts and a clean single. On April 7 in Louisville Big Ed got a rare day off in a 13–2 win. The next day he split a game in Louisville with Owen pitching the first four innings and Walsh the last five.

Three days later in Springfield, Ohio, Big Ed pitched four innings and batted twice with two hits and two runs, but so did everybody else as the Sox won 22–5 batting against Rob Eberly, a Chicago schoolboy, and Charles Stroup, a schoolteacher from Fayetteville. Springfield was the home of "Jiggs" Donahue. Charles Rowlus, a former mayor, presented him with a gold watch and an elegant umbrella. The last stop was Grand Rapids. On the 14th they played to a 0–0 nine-inning tie in damp, near-

5. The Hitless Wonders

freezing conditions. Owen and Altrock pitched a one-hitter. In the final exhibition game the next day at Grand Rapids, Big Ed pitched the last four in a 2–1 Sox win. He gave up a run and two hits and struck out two.

The team that would come to be known as the "Hitless Wonders" opened the 1906 season three days later, April 17, in Detroit. This was the opening day roster. Catchers: Billy Sullivan, Ed McFarland, Hub Hart; pitchers: Doc White, Frank Owen, Nick Altrock, Nig Smith, Roy Patterson, Lou Fiene, and Big Ed. Infielders: Jiggs Donahue, Gus Dundon, George Davis, Lee Tannehill, Frank Isbell, and George Rohe. Outfielders: Fielder Jones, Bill O'Neill, Frank Hemphill and Rube Vinson.

Hemphill played in only 13 games and Vinson in only 10. They were replaced by Ed Hahn and Patsy Dougherty, who were bought from the Highlanders on May 10 and June 6, respectively. Once Hahn came on board the regulars were Hahn, Jones, and a platoon of O'Neill and Dougherty in the outfield; Bill "Sully" Sullivan, catcher; Donahue, 1B; Davis, SS; Isbell, 2B; and Tannehill, 3B.

Owen started the opener for the Sox and beat the Tigers 5–3. Big Ed started the second game and lost 3–2 to the Tigers' Siever. Big Ed walked one, hit a batter and struck out two, but didn't throw the spitball. Though he gave up eight hits, he pitched well enough to win and he hit a triple off the center field scoreboard, but he hurt himself in the field. From the *Tribune* story: "Walsh himself was chiefly responsible for the defeat, as his brief balloon trip in the fourth inning accounted for the two runs scored and these added to a lucky one in the first proved to be enough. He pitched well, but his inability to handle bunts proved his undoing."

A telegram came to the Tigers' bench during the game informing of the death of Siever's father. It was kept from him until after the game. When he read it, he collapsed on the home bench and cried. The Tigers made it two of three by winning 3–1 the next day on a mighty home run by Sam Crawford over the wall and over the lumber yard beyond right field. Big Ed got his second start on April 22 at home versus Cleveland. This is the game in which he likely used the spitball for the first time in a regular season major league game. He lasted seven giving up six runs, nine hits and two walks and made a critical throwing error. Altrock relieved with the score 6–6 and won 7–6 in 12 innings. For the first of only seven times in 31 starts during the season, Big Ed did not finish what he started.

Though Big Ed did throw 5⅔ hitless innings with the spitball after the rough first inning, he didn't get another start for over a week. On May 1 he was matched with Siever again and Siever won 2–1 in 10 innings. Big Ed was now 1–2 with a no-decision in four starts. On May 6 in Chicago he took a no-hitter into the ninth in a 6–0 win against Cleveland and Addie Joss. He missed pitching a no-hitter by inches when Bemis grounded a single past Davis at short leading off the ninth. Big Ed had walked the second batter he faced in the first inning, then retired 23 consecutive batters before the Bemis hit. The last two batters in the ninth hit into force-outs and he faced only two batters over the minimum. He struck out five. In the second he retired the Naps on four pitches. And he did it all without throwing a single spitball. "Walsh used only speed and reduced the size of the ball in the visitors' eyes to the size of one of those nutmegs of his native state. Not once did he let loose the eel, usually his mainstay."[12] He had pitched games like this intermittently, but not consistently, over the past two seasons as he demonstrated in his next start, again versus Cleveland, on May 10. In just three innings, Big Ed was hammered for eight runs and eight hits in a 15–1 loss. He walked two without a strikeout. Smith finished the game. The loss was the Sox' sixth in eight games and it dropped them to seventh place in the eight-team American League with an 8–11 record. The A's led with 14 wins. It wasn't noted at the time, but Big Ed pulled a muscle in his side in that game. Apparently, Sox secretary Charley Fredricks didn't believe the injury was bad enough to let Walsh see a doctor, so when the team got to Philadelphia Big Ed borrowed $100 from Frank Isbell and went home to Meriden, Connecticut, to see his own doctor, who diagnosed a wrenched side and prescribed 10 days of rest. When Comiskey found out what had happened, he sent Big Ed a telegram and told him to take all the time he needed.[13]

With Big Ed gone, Jones rotated Owen, Altrock, Smith and Patterson as starters. Big Ed rejoined the team in New York City on May 22 and the next day Jones called on him to relieve Patterson, who gave up four runs and eight hits through the first four innings. Big Ed pitched the last five without allowing a run. He struck out three without a walk. Two days later, on May 25, Doc White, who had spent the spring coaching Navy, made his first start, bumping Big Ed further down the rotation. White started again on the 25th and 30th.

It took a double header to get Big Ed another start. On May 31 he pitched the first game of a double header at Detroit. He held the Tigers without a hit through three and had a 2–0 lead, but wound up losing 4–2. He gave up five hits, walked three and struck out three. The Sox also lost the second game and at the end of May were 14–18, in sixth place and 7½ games behind the first place A's. Back in Chicago on June 3 Big Ed lost yet again, 2–0, to Cleveland and Joss in Chicago. Walsh allowed six hits, struck out three and walked two. From the *Tribune*: "Eddie Walsh pitched almost as good a game, but his support was of the kind that is inimical to the public's health."

It was inimical to the health of Big Ed's record, too. He fell to 1–5. But help was on the way; Washington was coming to town. Big Ed started two of the three games against the Senators. He started on June 12 and with only a day's rest on the 14th. Leading 2–0 in the eighth in the first game, he gave up a walk, double and single and it was 2–1 with no outs and two runners on. Jones brought in Owen. He got out of the eighth, but gave up the tying run in the ninth. Owen was still in there when the Sox won with a run in the 12th. Big Ed's line was two hits, one run, four walks and four strikeouts. Nig Smith shut out Washington 2–0 the next day, then Big Ed, as he had done in the two previous seasons, started a second game of a Washington series on one day's rest. He pitched a five-hitter with five strikeouts and zero walks in a 2–0 win. Big Ed was evolving into an ironman. But before the evolution was complete, Big Ed went back to his role as fifth starter after Owen, Altrock, White, and Smith and didn't pitch again for six games over nine days. When he finally did start on June 23 at home against Detroit, he was mysteriously pulled after only three innings having allowed only two hits and no runs. Owen and Altrock finished up and the Sox won 3–2 in 12. Accounts of the game do not explain why Jones took Big Ed out though he did have a shaky third inning. "The end looked near in the third, when a double by Warner, a single by Eubanks, and a pass by Davy Jones filled the bases with only one out. But Tannehill made a stop of Lindsay's high bounder and caught Warner at the plate."[14]

The win was the sixth consecutive for the Sox and at the close of the day on June 23 they were in fourth place at 29–26, five games behind the Naps, who led the A's by a game. Another six days passed before Big Ed's next start and it was a disaster in Cleveland. Jones took him out in the second inning after five Naps batters produced four hits and a sacrifice. The Naps won 9–2.

So it was that when Big Ed took his next turn as starter on July 9 he was nothing more than an obscure sixth starter with a 2–5 record on a fourth place team. Seven weeks later he was 13–5 and being celebrated as the best pitcher on a first place team, if not the best in the American League. "From an unknown second rate pitcher, Walsh suddenly developed into one of the best pitchers in the country and perhaps the sensation of the year and for six weeks mowed down everything in sight."[15]

During this stretch of games from July 10 to August 27, the White Sox won 11 straight games in which Big Ed started. From August 2 to

August 23 they won 19 straight overall. During the team winning streak Big Ed started and finished seven games, five of which were shutouts. He allowed only two runs in seven games and pitched 55 consecutive scoreless innings, then a major league record. Walter Johnson broke the record in 1913 with 55⅔ scoreless innings, which stood until Don Drysdale pitched 58⅔ scoreless innings in 1968. On August 3, in Big Ed's first win during the Sox' 19-game winning streak, against Boston in Chicago, he took a no-hitter into the ninth for the second time that season. Boston's manager Eddie Collins inserted himself as a pinch hitter to open the ninth and Walsh struck him out. Then outfielder Jack Hayden broke up the no-hitter with what the *Boston Globe* described as a "dinky" hit. The bloop single landed just out of the reach of shortstop Davis and left fielder Hahn.[16] Hayden was forced out at second on a ground ball by Parent, and Big Ed tossed out "Chick" Stahl, ending the game. Big Ed and the Sox won 4–0. He walked three and stuck out five. Unlike the first time he took a no-hitter into the ninth, back on May 6 when he threw nothing but fastballs, this time he threw mostly spitballs.

"Walsh used the spit ball continually to baffle the Bostons. It deceived Walsh too, once in a while he could not get it over the plate. To start the first, second and fourth innings, Eddie let the first man up walk to first base. Of course none of these passes did any harm, as nobody could advance the deadheads."[17]

From that point on he used the spitball almost exclusively. He once said he threw it on nine of 10 pitches. On August 5 the first place A's came to Chicago seven and one-half games ahead of the Sox, who were in fourth place. When the A's left five days later the Sox were in third place, two and one-half out. Big Ed pitched the second game of the five game sweep, a three-hit shutout. He struck out four and walked two. Patterson shut out the A's 1–0 the next day. White won two of the five games and Owen one.

The Highlanders were the next victims. They came into town on the 10th and Big Ed beat Chesbro 2–1. Big Ed pitched a five-hitter with six strikeouts and a walk and scored the winning run in the eighth. He reached on an error by Yeager at second base with one out. Hahn bounced to the mound and Chesbro inexplicably threw to first for the out, allowing Big Ed to get to second. O'Neill singled just over a leaping Hal Chase at first base and Big Ed, "his neck flaming triumphantly," scored.[18] The next day White won easily 8–1 for the Sox 10th straight win. Going for the kill, Jones brought Big Ed back on just one day's rest on the 12th. It was a Sunday and 25,000 to 30,000 came out, the largest crowd ever to see a game

5. The Hitless Wonders

on the South Side. At 2 o'clock, an hour before the first pitch, the stands were filled and thousands poured onto the grounds lining the fringe of the field 10 to 20 deep, held back by 200 policemen. The gates were closed at 2:30 with thousands left outside lining 39th Street for three blocks in each direction.

Big Ed thrilled the crowd with a shutout the hard way. Through the first six innings he gave up nine hits and a walk, but "Sully" threw four runners out trying to steal and a fifth was wiped out by a double play. Big Ed retired the last nine batters in order as the Sox won 3–0. He also had a hit and scored a run. Meanwhile the A's lost for the third straight time in St. Louis. With that score already posted, chaos ensued in Chicago as the fans realized the Sox had ascended into first place. "The crowd, held on a leash for so long was ready for the finish, and when Tannehill, by a brilliant effort fielded Laporte's hot bounder and heaved the ball across to Donahue it broke all bounds and rushed across the field like one seething maelstrom of humanity. The chief object of each one seemed to be to pat Big Ed on the back, but Walsh and his fellows escaped.

"Then followed for 15 minutes one of the most exciting cushion battles ever seen, the field crowd fighting desperately with the crowd in the stands with cushions as missiles. Women in magnificent raiment, crouching behind barricades of chairs urged their escorts to fight with the crowd below and the air was black with cushions."[19]

It was the Sox' 11th consecutive win and 15th of 16, all at home. The streak ended the next game, not with a loss, but with a tie. Chesbro, pitching for a second consecutive day for New York, and Doc White both pitched shutout ball for 10 innings until a truce was called at 5 o'clock so the Highlanders could catch their train.

The Sox caught their train the next day for a trip to Boston for the start of a 14-game eastern swing. For over a week the only thing that changed was where the Sox played, not how. They won another eight straight between August 15 and 23 in Boston, New York and Washington. Big Ed started and completed three of the eight games with two shutouts and a 1-run game. On the 16th he stopped Boston 6–0 on five hits, striking out six and walking one. On the 18th in New York he beat the Highlanders 10–0 in the opener of a four-game series, but it wasn't quite as easy as the score sounds. The Sox had just a 1–0 lead into the ninth when they batted around and scored nine times. Big Ed had a double and a single in the ninth. Again he gave up just five hits. He struck out three, including Wee Willie Keeler. For Keeler it was only the second time he struck out all season, both times against Big Ed.

"As for big Walsh, the Chicago moundman, he was cool and crafty as to mentality and as to physical endowment had a low, swinging out curve command, that enabled him to make the ball describe hairline flights across the corners."[20]

The next day was Sunday and there was no game. On Monday White beat the Highlanders 4–1. After a rain out Tuesday, Big Ed pitched the first game of a double header on Wednesday and won 6–1. Conroy hit an inside-the-park home run in the sixth to prevent a third consecutive shutout by Walsh. Owen won the second game 11–6. The Sox took a train to Washington right after the second game and the next afternoon Patterson beat the Senators 4–1 for the Sox' 19th straight win. When the win streak started on July 27, the Sox were in fourth place, nine games out of first. When it ended the day after Patterson's 4–1 win in Washington on August 19, the Sox were in first place by five and one-half games.

After an off day, the Senators finally stopped the win streak, by beating the Sox in a double header on the 20th. The team's streak was ended, but Big Ed's continued the next day in Philadelphia when he blanked the A's 1–0 for his 11th straight win. The game was played in continual rain, until the grounds were so soaked that the right fielders were standing in ankle deep water. Umpire Connolly called it a game after six innings, during which Big Ed struck out nine and gave up just one hit, a single by Hartsell, which was the only ball hit out of the infield by the A's. When the game the next day was rained out, Jones came back with Big Ed the following day and the A's ended his streak. The teams were to play a double header, but were lucky to get in five innings. After five the A's led 4–3. Big Ed gave up five hits, walked a batter and plunked two in the five innings. In the top of the sixth the Sox got two runs and were ahead 5–4 when the rains came again. Umpire Hank O'Day waited a half hour and then called the game. The score reverted where it stood at the end of the fifth and the A's won, 4–3, ending Big Ed's winning streak.

"I don't know how it happened," Big Ed told the *Washington Post* after the game. "I guess they didn't break right. I would have bet 10 years of my life that I could have shutout the Nationals without a run in that last inning."

In his next start in Cleveland on September 1, Big Ed, having pitched three games in six days, was mortal. He gave up nine hits and six runs and had to be relieved by Nig Smith. The Naps won 7–0. Batting in the sixth inning, Cleveland pitcher Bill Bernhard hit a foul tip that hit catcher Billy Sullivan on the thumb. According to the *Trib* report the ball "smashed out all semblance of a thumb. The most skillful surgery was necessary to put

Sully's hand in such shape that he will ever be able to play again, without the slightest hope that he will get into the harness again this season. President Comiskey had the plucky backstop hurried into his automobile and taken to Mercy Hospital." A Dr. J.B. Murphy was called in to perform the surgery. The loss of the game was one thing as the Sox were still 70–47 and in first place by one and one-half games over the Highlanders and four and one-half over the third-place A's. The loss of Sully was more worrisome. Though the Sox carried a backup, Ed McFarland, Jones didn't like him. The *Tribune* called McFarland "recalcitrant." So Comiskey signed Hub Hart, whose only major league experience was 11 games with the Sox in 1905, and Jay Towne from Des Moines and took them to Cleveland the next day for a single game and then a Labor Day double header. The Sox won the single game Sunday, then lost both games on Labor Day. Meanwhile in New York on Labor Day the Highlanders swept a double header to go ahead of the Sox by percentage points. In the first game Highlanders shortstop Kid Elberfield assaulted umpire Silk O'Laughlin and had to be forcibly removed from the field by police. In the second game, Willie Keeler collided with A's shortstop Lave Cross trying to field a ground ball and two runs scored, tying the game at 3–3. O'Laughlin didn't call interference, and the A's argued so vehemently that O'Laughlin forfeited the game to New York.

Fearful that too much work might ruin Big Ed for the stretch drive, and that the untested catchers couldn't handle him, Jones gave Big Ed nine days off after the 7–0 loss on September 1, the day Sully was injured. While Big Ed rested the Sox went 5–4 and stayed in second place. On September 10, Big Ed started again and lost 2–1 to Detroit in Chicago despite striking out nine. In the ninth Davis bunted for a hit, but was called out at first by umpire Evans. Instantly a shower of bottles from the first base bleachers drove Evans into the outfield out of range. Order was restored long enough for Detroit to get two more outs and finish the game, but as soon as it ended the fans along first base rushed for the exits to look for Evans as the umpire ran to the third base side amid another shower of bottles. After waiting for the threatening crowd to calm, Evans and Secretary McRoy of the American League left the park under police escort. An angry mob confronted them at the park entrance but the police kept them away and Evans made his getaway on a street car.[21]

The Sox lost again the next day, September 11, and dropped two games behind the Highlanders. Unfortunately for the Highlanders their last 25 games were to be on the road while the Sox had 22 of their final 24 games at South Side Park. The Sox regained a tie for first place on the 14th with a double header sweep of the Browns in Chicago. Altrock won the first game 4–3 and Big Ed returned to the form he showed during his 11-game winning streak. He pitched a 3-hitter, struck out 12 and walked one. At the end of the day the Sox and the Highlanders were both 79–51. Roth caught both games and earned praise for handling Big Ed: "He showed his nerve and pluck by backstopping both games and handling Walsh's difficult delivery steadily and confidently."[22]

The double header wins were the first of six straight for the Sox, a streak that gave them a two-game lead over the Highlanders. Big Ed contributed one win, 5–4, over the A's in Chicago on the 17th in an 11-inning battle with Rube Waddell. Big Ed struck out 12 and Waddell struck out 11. In the second inning, with the bases loaded and no outs, Walsh fanned Oldring, Shreckengost and Waddell in succession. In the Sox' 11th, with darkness falling and the fans in a frenzy, Jones surprised everybody by sending McFarland up to pinch-hit with a runner on second. The *Tribune* wrote that McFarland "had been in the sulks all season," but he came through with a ground single up the middle to win the game.

The A's shortstop that day was a rookie appearing in his first game. An 18-year-old Columbia University junior, he was listed as "Sullivan" and in his first at-bat he singled off Big Ed. His real name was Eddie Collins, a future hall of famer. Years later Collins explained what happened. "On the Sunday following Labor Day in 1906, I met manager Connie Mack in the Fifth Avenue Hotel in New York City and signed a contract to play with the Athletics the next season. The interview was arranged by Billie Lush manager of the independent team at Rockville, Connecticut, where I had played for several weeks of my summer vacation. I didn't sign until Mack agreed not to trade, sell or farm me to a minor league team. As I had nothing to do until school opened I agreed to go to Philadelphia and practice for a week or two and then make the last western trip with the Athletics.

"The day I reported Mack called me 'Sullivan' in front of the reporters, because he did not want me to risk losing my spot as captain of the Columbia team. But I was found out and did lose captaincy, but was named coach. In my first at bat I made a safe hit. When I realized I had singled against the mighty spitballer, I experienced a strange thrill and never in my life have I run faster than I did on my way to first base."[23]

The Sox had a two-game lead after the Collins game, but blew it when the Highlanders came to town the next day for a four-game series. The Sox lost three of the four to drop one game back. They lost a double header the first day with Big Ed taking the loss 6–3 in the second game.

When Big Ed hit the Highlanders' catcher, Red Kleinow, in the head, the Highlanders shortstop, Kid Elberfeld, accused him of doing it on purpose and had to be restrained from going after Big Ed. White won the third game 7–1 and Jones came back with Big Ed on one day's rest hoping to retake the lead, but he lost 1–0 to Bill Hogg. Big Ed gave up a run in the first inning. He struck out seven and walked three. The good news was that despite the dire description of Sully's injuries in the newspaper, he was back in uniform during the Highlander series practicing with the team on the 18th. On the 22nd he entered a game for the first time as a pinch runner. On the 26th he was back behind the plate.

After the Highlanders series the Sox won three straight against visiting Boston. Big Ed saved the second game thanks to a spectacular play by Jones, who made an unassisted double play from center field. Big Ed relieved Altrock in the ninth with a runner on first and no outs and the Sox leading 3–2. After a sacrifice, Wilkes-Barre resident Buck Freeman hit a shot to deep left center that looked like a sure triple. From the *Tribune* account, "Jones did not give up the ship, but tore desperately across, edging back at the same time and with one final jump lunged sideways and speared the ball in midair. Chadbourne had rounded third and was half way home before he knew the ball had not gone to the fence. Fielder wheeled and started to wing the ball to second after coming to earth again, but when he saw where the runner was decided to complete the play himself. Galloping in with a yell which could be heard above the rooting, the manager finished at second base by breaking the running broad jump record, then joined Davis and Dundon in a war dance."

The next day, when Sully caught for the first time since mashing his thumb, Big Ed started and won 2–0 to put the Sox back in first place to stay. He struck out seven and the Sox regained first place as the Highlanders lost to Detroit. Three times Big Ed struck out the last man in an inning with runners on bases. He closed the game by fanning Freeman.

The sweep of Boston was the start of a run of nine wins in 10 games. The only loss in the string was by Big Ed in the second game of a double header in his last start of the season against Washington on September 30 in Chicago, but it didn't matter as the Sox had a two and one-half game lead with six games to play. They won the next two days in St. Louis on shutouts by Altrock and Owen. They wanted to clinch the next day by beating the Browns again, but were rained out. Instead they clinched on October 2 dressed in their street clothes, a mile from the ballpark, dancing in the rain. "Oblivious to everything but the figures that sprung out one by one on a bulletin board a little group of big bronzed men danced around the street in front of a newspaper office while rain fell over them in sheets. They were drenched but they didn't care. All they knew about was that over in Philadelphia it wasn't raining and there was a baseball game. So they splashed about in the mud and rain waiting."[24]

When the A's beat the Highlanders 3–0 in the second game of a double header, the Sox ran through the crowd yelling "pennant, pennant." When the crowd realized the crazy men were the Sox they joined in the jubilation. Back at the hotel the dancing continued. McFarland, White, Owen, Dundon and Walsh played ring around the rosey with Jones in the center. Similar scenes played out back in Chicago where fans rejoiced that the White Sox had joined the Cubs as pennant winners and that the World's Series would be an all–Chicago affair for the first and, as it would turn out, only time. Crowds gathered in front of the Tribune building and on street corners all over town. A roar went up throughout the elevated train when word spread that the "Hitless Wonders" were pennant winners, too.

How deserving were the Sox of their nickname? The team hit an A.L. low seven home runs. The Sox were also last in the A. L. in team average, .230; and hits, doubles, and triples. But that didn't mean they couldn't score runs. They led the league in walks and hit batsmen and were third in runs scored. Their best hitter, shortstop George Davis, batted only .277 but drew 80 walks.

Nobody called the Sox the pitchless or catchless wonders. They had the second lowest ERA, 2.13 to the Naps' 2.09, gave up the fewest runs in the league, 2.99 per game, and led the league with 32 shutouts, 10 of them by Walsh who won 17 games and was third in strikeouts with 171. Frank Owen won 22 games, Nick Altrock, 20; and Doc White, who led the league in ERA at 1.52, won 18. The Sox were also second to the Naps in fewest errors and team fielding percentage. So how did the Naps finish in third place five games behind the Sox when they led the league in runs scored, ERA and fielding? The Naps were 21–25 in one-run games while Chicago was 29–19 and the Sox won the season series from the Naps 12–10.

The Sox played out the string with four games at home. In their first game back home after clinching they played Cleveland on October 5. Poor weather kept attendance to 7,000 fans, who didn't mind that Jones started only three regulars and who cheered every glimpse of a regular player they could get. Cleveland pitcher Addie Joss pitched five perfect innings, but a home run by Jiggs Donahue, the seventh of the season by a Sox player, lifted the Sox to a 3–1 win. Louis Fiene was the winning pitcher in his first start, and only his fifth appearance, of the season. Jones rested Altrock

5. The Hitless Wonders

and Big Ed over the last four games. White pitched the next day, a 9–5 win over Cleveland, then Owen pitched in a loss to Cleveland, then Fiene again to close out the season on October 7 in a loss to Detroit.

The Sox had little time to enjoy their celebrity as A.L. champs. The World Series versus the crosstown Cubs started just two days later.

The Cubs had opened their season on April 12 winning in Cincinnati 7–2 with this line up and batting order: Jimmy Slagle, cf; Jimmy Sheckard, lf; Frank Schulte, rf; Frank Chance, 1b and manager; Harry Steinfeldt, 3b; Joe Tinker, ss; Johnny Evers, 2b; Johnny Kling, c. The batting order never changed all season. When subs played they batted in the same spots.

On May 7 the Cubs won their 10th straight game and broke into the lead for the first time behind New York. It lasted only a day. They dropped into second with a loss to Pittsburgh the next day. The Cubs regained the lead on May 12 and again it lasted only a day. On May 20 McGraw and the Giants came to town. The Giants won three straight and reclaimed first place. They won 6–4 on Monday and 8–2 on Tuesday, a game in which Kling was injured when a foul tip broke a wire in his mask. After a rain out the Giants won again on Decoration Day 6–5. The next day, May 25, the Giants lost in St. Louis, while the Cubs beat Boston to regain first place, where they stayed for the rest of the season. On May 25 the Cubs were 26–13. The rest of the season they went 90–23. From August 6 through September 1 they were 25–1. They closed the season with a 50–8 run.

The Cubs led the N.L. in team average, hits and runs scored with 704, an average 4.57 per game. Chance led the league in runs and stolen bases and was fourth in average. Sheckard was third in runs. Steinfeldt led in hits and was second in average and RBI.

Guy "Doc" White was a Georgetown University–trained dentist. He and Big Ed made a good one-two punch for the Sox in the 1906 and 1907 seasons. White led the A.L. in ERA in 1906 (Library of Congress).

They led in team ERA, 2.31, and runs allowed with 381, an average of 2.47 per game. Mordecai Brown, 1.04; Pfiester, 1.51; and Reulbach, 1.65 were first, second and third in ERA. Brown won 25, second in the league; Pfiester, 20; and Reulbach, 19. Three other pitchers won 12 or more games.

The Cubs won 116 games and lost just 36. Three ended in ties. Their winning percentage of .736 is an all-time record. They won the N.L. pennant by 20 games. The Sox won 23 fewer games than the Cubs and won the A.L. pennant by three games. The Cubs scored 704 runs and allowed 381. The Sox scored 137 fewer runs and gave up 79 more.

No wonder then that bookmakers were offering the Sox from 3-to-1 to 8-to-5, but were finding few takers, as bettors held out for even better odds.

6

Big Ed: World Champion

Comiskey and President Murphy of the Cubs, President Pulliam of the N.L. and Secretary McRoy of the A.L., and managers Jones and Chance met on Thursday, October 4, to work out details for the World's Series. They chose the following Tuesday, October 9, as the start date. A coin flip decided the site of the first game, the Cubs' West Side Grounds, with the site alternating each day after that through the sixth game. The National Commission reserved the right to choose a site for the seventh game if it came to that. Johnstone of the N.L. and Silk O'Loughlin of the A.L. were selected as umpires. It was suggested that four umpires be assigned to alternate every other game, but that idea was later abandoned. All games were to start at 2:30. Ticket prices were doubled over the regular season to $2 for box seats, $1.75 and $1 for the grandstand, and 50 cents for bleachers. Comiskey objected to the ticket price increase, but the National Commission claimed jurisdiction.

The players' share was to be 60 percent of the gross of the first four games, 75 percent to the winners, 25 to the losers. To combat scalpers, ticket purchasers were limited to six tickets. The city assigned 500 policemen for each game to keep order inside and outside the field and arrest speculators, as ticket scalpers were called. The advance lot of tickets for the first game at the West Side Grounds was sold out Friday, hours after they went on sale. On the South Side $12,000 worth of reserved seats for the second and fourth games were sold out. Murphy ordered construction at the West Side Grounds to increase box seats by 1,200 and erect 6,000 circus seats in center field to increase capacity to 26,000. "That would be more people than have yet seen a baseball game anywhere," said the *Tribune*.

Slagle, the Cubs' lead-off batter, was not expected to play. He hadn't played since August 31 when he was severely bruised in the chest in a collision at the plate with Cincinnati catcher Admiral Schlei. The *Tribune* reported that Slagle was also "suffering from intercostal neuralgia." Chance declared that Hofman, Slagle's sub, was the best fielding outfielder in the country. The Sox' only injured player was shortstop George Davis. He had a bad back but was expected to play. His doctor said his back pain was due to a cold and "electrical treatment" was applied.

Ban Johnson went on record against betting on the series: "All true lovers of baseball should discourage betting on the results of the series between the two Chicago clubs. Gambling in any form is a serious menace to the game and should not be tolerated."[1]

Betting was light, even at the board of trade, where gambling was a favorite pastime. It wasn't Johnson's plea, but rather the long odds — 3-to-1 to 8-to-5 in favor of the Cubs — that discouraged betting, but the *Tribune* guessed there was another reason. "There seems to be such a general feeling of satisfaction at the victory of both teams that there is a disposition on the part of fans to be more or less impartial and stand back and say let the best team win."[2]

There was interest in the series all over the country. In Cincinnati a trip for 400 Reds fans to Chicago by special train was organized by members of the Macon, Peerless and Owl athletic clubs. They were going to root for Cincinnati natives George Rohe and Nick Altrock, who was a member of Peerless, and for Dayton, Kentucky, native Lee Tannehill. A train from Memphis was organized by the city attorney and included members of the city council. In Washington, the home of "Georgetown" Harry "Doc" White, plans were made to have wire service play-by-play descriptions called through a megaphone from a window at the *Washington Post* building.

The managers made their prediction on the eve of the first game. Chance: "I believe we will win from the White Stockings, but we will have no excuses if we are beaten. We are not going to underrate the strength of Fielder Jones's team, mind you, for we know their speed in base running and fielding. But I am confident of the result. Last year we beat the Sox easily and we are much stronger than then, while they have not added as much strength to their lineup as we have it seems to me. We are not going to be afraid of their left handed pitchers for we have seen a few of them all summer and are well equipped with right handed batters."

Jones: "It will be a contest between two of the greatest teams we have ever had. We will make no excuses if beaten and on the other hand, I hope

6. Big Ed: World Champion

Mordecai Brown and Jimmy Slagle are in the games at their best. I think we will win and want the honor of beating the best Frank Chance has. One team must win and the other lose but there will be no dishonor in a defeat by either of Chicago's great clubs. Last year we went into the post-season series with pitchers in poor shape and just after losing out in a fearful battle with Philadelphia for the pennant. The effect of defeat on our team is greater than anything else. But this year we won and can face the world's series with the confidence of winners. We are not afraid of their batting strength. The Cleveland team leads the American League and we are last in batting, but we won the pennant because runs count."[3]

The day of game one, which was the 35th anniversary of the Great Fire of 1871, turned out to be one of the coldest days anyone could remember for a baseball game. Outside the park plainclothes police officers arrested eight speculators, as fans streamed in dressed for football in bearskin and other fur coats, fur blankets, buffalo robes and heavy blankets called steamer rugs which were used on shipboard deck chairs. Some fans wrapped newspapers or programs around their necks. Among the fans in the boxes were "The Father of American Football," sportswriter Walter Camp, and two-time U.S. Amateur Golf champion H. Chandler Egan. Before the game the Hamilton Club presented identical silver loving cups to Chance and Jones, while two cornetists played "Auld Lang Syne" and the fans sang. In the Sox players' box Doc White's sister held a teddy bear cub with white socks on its feet. In another box female Cubs fans dangled a two-foot long teddy bear cub on a string and made him dance — but he wouldn't have much to dance about.

Jones had White and Big Ed rested, but started Altrock, who, he reasoned, worked better in cold weather. White admittedly didn't like to pitch in the cold and spitballs didn't work well below freezing. And it was that cold. It snowed off and on throughout the game. Chance started Mordecai Brown. As expected, Slagle did not play, but neither did the Sox' shortstop Davis. Third baseman Tannehill moved to shortstop and George Rohe started at third, where he had started 54 games during the season.

Through the first four innings Brown retired 12 consecutive Sox, while Altrock retired 11 consecutive before giving up a single to Schulte with two outs in the fourth. The Sox finally broke through with a run in the fifth. Rohe led off with a line drive to left that went under the bleachers for a ground rule triple. Brown struck Donahue out. Dougherty hit a slow roller toward third. Brown fielded it and threw home, but Kling dropped it for an error and the Sox led 1–0. The Sox made it 2–0 in the sixth when Jones singled, went to second on a passed ball, and scored on a single by Isbell.

In their sixth the Cubs threatened to tie the game when they put runners on second and third with one out. Altrock threw a wild pitch into the dirt, letting a run in and putting a runner on third with one out. Then two fielding plays saved the day for Altrock and the Sox. First Tannehill went into short left field for an over-the-shoulder catch of a pop up. Then Rohe fielded a grounder at third and threw wide and low to first, but Donahue stretched full out and caught the throw holding the bag for the third out. The Sox went on to win 2–1. When the game ended with a fly ball to Jones in center, hundreds of fans rushed onto the field looking to carry Rohe and Altrock off the field. They were rescued by policemen who surrounded them and escorted them through the crowd.

The winter-like weather, including periods of snow flurries, kept the crowd down to 12,693. Another 1,500 "watched" the game at the First Regiment Armory, billed as the biggest playhouse in the West, where the *Chicago Tribune* had set up an electric board. "The great score board with its numbers and signals, its system for moving the players around the bases on the board, and recording every play the instant it happened worked beautifully."[4] Tickets were free.

The next day Jones started Doc White for game two at the South Side Grounds. Big Ed hadn't pitched since September 30, but with the weather much the same as the day before, near freezing with snow flurries, Jones feared the spitball wouldn't work. At 12,595 attendance was less than hoped for, but remarkable considering the weather. Baseball legend Cap Anson and friends Fred Pfeffer, Jimmy Ryan and John K. Tener, all of whom went with him on a baseball world tour in 1888 and 89, occupied a box. A concession under the grandstand sold out of hot sarsaparilla.

When Jones came to bat the first time, the game was stopped and he was given a complete silver service in a mahogany chest from the fans, who cheered wildly. That was about all they had to cheer about. White was ineffective and the Cubs evened the series with a 7–1 win behind Ed Reulbach's one-hitter. The White Sox run was the result of a wild pitch and an error. Their only hit of the game was Jiggs Donahue's single in the seventh inning. Cubs third baseman Steinfeldt — the "other" member of the Cubs' famed Tinker-to-Evers-to-Chance infield and a .327 hitter — went 3 for 3 and Tinker had two hits and scored three runs.

On Thursday for game three the temperature moderated enough for Jones to give the ball to Big Ed and for 13,667 fans to come out. He

6. Big Ed: World Champion

responded with a game reminiscent of the many in his 11-game win streak in August and September. He pitched a 2-hitter in a 3–0 Sox win that put the Sox up 2 games to 1. In the first inning Big Ed gave a single to Solly Hofman, who was caught stealing, and a double to Frank Schulte, but he allowed no hits and only two base runners the rest of the way. He walked Chance with two out in the fourth. Gessler, batting for Pfiester in

A young-looking Big Ed warming up early in his career, probably about 1906, the year the Hitless Wonders won the World's Series.

the ninth, reached on an error leading off. A passed ball and an out put him at third base, but Walsh struck out Sheckard and Schulte to end the game, giving him 12 strikeouts (a World's Series record that stood for 23 years until the A's Howard Ehmke struck out 13 Cubs in the first game of the 1929 series.) The 8⅓ no-hit innings was a record until 1947 when Yankee Floyd Bevan went 8⅔ yet lost to the Dodgers 3–2. Big Ed said he threw the spitball almost exclusively after the first inning, "The spit ball is a difficult thing to throw and on a chilly day such as yesterday it is particularly hard to control. I told myself before the game that I might have trouble in the opening inning. I wasn't warmed up sufficiently. However I should have finished that inning without allowing more than a hit. I had Hofman struck out, but umpire Johnstone missed the third one. I don't blame him though, he called it as he thought. The next one I threw was a straight ball and he made a pretty hit to center. I fanned Sheckard using nothing but the spitball then Schulte came along and put the double to right. That was another straight ball.

"After that I was determined to cut out the straight ones and thereafter I kept the old spit balls humming over every time. I think that by holding the powerful Cubs to two hits and shutting them out I have demonstrated that the spitball, when properly thrown, is one of the most effective modes of attack a pitcher can possess."[5]

Big Ed didn't take all the credit. "I depended a great deal on the judgment of Catcher Sullivan. His knowledge of the Cubs was much more far reaching than mine. I look at Sullivan as the greatest catcher in the world and to him I ascribe much of the success I have had this year."[6]

Big Ed's wife said Big Ed was confident before the game. "When he left the house he said he was going to win if he had to ruin his arm forever to do it. He looked so determined when he said that and shut his teeth together so hard that I am sure I was the first person in Chicago who knew how that ball game was going to end. I just knew and that's all there is to it. The possibility of losing never entered my head. I simply knew he couldn't lose. I wasn't even frightened when they made those two hits in the first inning. I saw him shake his head and close his mouth tight and I knew they would get no more hits."[7]

The Sox got their three runs in the sixth on a two-out bases-loaded triple by Rohe, his second triple in three World's Series games, one fewer than he would hit in his 868 career at-bats. Tannehill started the Sox' sixth with a single. Big Ed followed and Pfiester, trying to prevent a sacrifice bunt, worked him too closely and walked him. Hahn batted next and Pfiester hit him in the face. Hahn was bundled in sweaters and hustled to

6. Big Ed: World Champion

the hospital with a broken nose. O'Neill ran for him. Pfiester got Jones to pop to catcher Johnny Kling, who leaned into the crowd to make the play. Pfiester almost saw his way out of the inning when he struck out Isbell. But Rohe bounced the first pitch into the left field stands for a ground rule triple, knocking in the only three runs of the game.

Suddenly Rohe, who was an obscure sub just days earlier, was getting star treatment. Again it took a phalanx of policemen to get him and Big Ed safely off the field amid a crazed throng of thousands of their worshippers. Charles Dryden, a writer for the *Tribune*, had a comical take on Big Ed's pitching and Hahn's broken nose. "A popular subscription was started on the south side tonight to endow Mr. Walsh with a diamond studded cuspidor—deserved tribute to his potent salivary glands. Aside from the round in which he changed the general topography of Hahn's nose, the pitching of Pfiester was great. Hahn had been saving his nose for an emergency play and the call came to him in the hour of need."[8] That night Sox fan Charles Martin, alderman of the Fifth Ward, the stockyard section, was arrested for disorderly conduct after a fight over baseball in a local bar.

Back at South Side Park the next day for game four, 18,385 saw the Cubs even the series at two games, with each team having won twice on the opponent's grounds. Mordecai Brown pitched no-hit ball for the first 5$\frac{2}{3}$ innings, allowed two hits overall, and out dueled Altrock 1–0. Evers drove in Tinker with a clutch two-out hit in the seventh inning for the only run.

At the West Side for game five the next day, October 13, Ed Haan, a Cubs fan from the board of trade, walked two live bear cubs around the bases before the start of the game. "They walked a little and pulled a little, but jumped the bags in clever fashion."[9] Daniel Shea—the business manager for George M. Cohan, a famous actor, singer, dancer, playwright, director and producer of the day and writer of "Give My Regards to Broadway"—presented Chance and Jones with watch fobs bearing gold pendants studded with 14 diamonds. The inscriptions read: "From George M. Cohan, a lover of baseball."[10] The first fans stood at the box office at 6:30 A.M. and by 8:30 a line formed. Ticket sales were cut off at 1:40 when it was judged that no more fans could fit in. But after an inspection the box office was reopened and standing room was sold at $1.50 per square foot until 23,257, the biggest crowd of the series, were jammed in. It was estimated there were that many more fans left outside, many of them reportedly willing to pay $5 to $10 for a ticket.

Before game four, Big Ed said he would be ready to pitch game five. "My arm never felt better. I could have kept throwing until 6 o'clock so good did it feel. I gave it a good hot water bath immediately after the third game and then it was given a hard alcohol rub. The result was I went to bed and slept fine. I'll be ready for work tomorrow."[11]

Jones was a believer. He came back with Big Ed on one day's rest for game five and he wound up the winner despite six errors by the Sox. The real story of the game was the Sox batting. After having scored just six runs on 11 hits in the first four games combined, they knocked both Ruelbach and Pfiester out with 12 hits, four of them doubles by Isbell, and won 8–6. Even Hahn, playing with a plaster cast on his nose, had a hit and scored two runs. Big Ed went six innings, struck out five and gave up just one earned run as the Sox went up 3 games to 2. Doc White relieved Big Ed in the seventh and pitched three scoreless innings.

On Sunday, October 14, for game six, fans, some with picnic baskets, lined up at the ticket windows as early as eight in the morning. Tickets went on sale at noon. At 12:45 ticket sales were stopped. A.L. secretary Fredricks said there weren't enough police to control more fans inside and that 5,000 more tickets could have been sold had there been more police. As it was the official crowd was listed at 19,249. At least that many waited outside on 39th Street and in a vacant lot on Wentworth Avenue listening for shouted updates from fans inside in the top rows.

In game six the Sox' unprecedented hitting continued. They made 14 hits and clinched the series with an 8–3 win, in the only game won by

A panoramic photograph of the 1906 World's Series. Walsh gave up one earned run in six innings, getting the win despite six White Sox errors that led to 5 additional runs (Library of Congress).

6. Big Ed: World Champion

a home team. The Sox knocked Brown out in the second inning and by the end of the frame led 7–1. Staked to the lead, Doc White pitched a complete game giving up seven hits. It was the first time all season the Sox scored as many as eight runs in consecutive games.

With two outs in the ninth Schulte hit a ground ball to first base. Donahue beat Schulte to first base and as soon as his foot touched down on the bag for the final out crazed fans swarmed over the field racing to be the first to pat some White Sox on the back. The outfielders made a mad dash for the exits beneath the stands as soon as the ball was hit, but fans from the infield seats were already on the field waiting for them. The fans surrounded their heroes, shaking their hands, stealing their caps, pounding on their backs and jostling their hair.

Spotting Cubs president Charles Murphy in the stands, the fans surrounded him and wouldn't let him leave until he spoke. "The White Sox played better ball than us and deserved to win," he said. "I am for Chicago and will say Chicago has the two best ball teams in the world. If I had to lose I would rather lose to Comiskey's club than any other club in the world."

A woman in the box where the White Sox wives were seated handed him a White Sox banner and he dutifully waved it to boisterous cheers, applause and shouts of, "That's right."

Somewhere in that throng of players and fans on the field was a White Sox pitcher who was as important a part of winning the World's Series as any of the Sox. Edward Augustine Walsh, just four years removed from the coal mines around Wilkes-Barre, had pitched and won both the third and fifth games, starting the fifth one on just one day's rest.

Johnny Evers was impressed. "Ed Walsh is the greatest pitcher I have ever faced, and I hope that I do not have to face more like him. Altrock was a mighty good man, but Walsh was better."[12]

Hours after the game 2,000 White Sox fans made the rounds of the homes of White Sox players who lived near the grounds, chanting "What's de matter wid de White Sox? Dey're all right. Who's all right? De White Sox." They stopped at Doc White's house, but he wasn't home. They headed for the manager's home. On the way along Cottage Grove Avenue they spotted George Davis in a restaurant. They pulled him from his seat and carried him on their shoulders to Jones' home where the manager was entertaining White and his wife. They yelled for a speech and Jones came out and said, "Boys, it goes deep with me to see the demonstrations our friends are making. Every man on the White Stockings team is as proud of Chicago as you are of them and I want to say it has been the individual work and hearty cooperation of every man that has landed the championship for us. That's the big title — the world's championship." Jones pulled out a piece of paper and waved it. "Look at this, a certified check for $15,000 handed me by president Comiskey at the close of the game. That's one sample of appreciation. That money is to be divided equally among the club. I thank you and all the other friends whose hearty support has been as vital as good ball playing."

The joyous crowd then marched down 36th Street to the Hotel Hayden to call on Rohe. After some commotion he stuck his head out the window of his second floor rooms and unfurled a six-foot long white stocking. The crowd went wild. They set a bonfire that blocked traffic on Cottage Avenue until firemen put it out. On Milwaukee Avenue two Sox fans and two Cubs fans who had made a strange bet attracted 1,000 fans to see the pay off. The losers, in bare feet, had to pull a buggy with the winners in it down the avenue. White stockings were hung from the buggy and the route was lit with Roman candles. The buggy fell into a cable car slot and the Sox fans, Patrick Ryan and Benjamin Jacobs, were thrown onto the street and severely injured.

Earlier in the evening at the Pomeranian Room of the Auditorium Annex, Comiskey made the presentation of the $15,000 check that Jones later waved at the fans. The $15,000 was added to the $25,000 winners' share from the players receipts from the first four games for a total of $40,000 to be split by the Sox. Each of the 21 Sox players got just under $2,000.[13] For many, including Big Ed, that doubled their salaries.

By winning in six the White Sox spared the National Commission from having to make a decision about the site for a seventh game. Had the Cubs forced a seventh game, things might have been interesting. Even in 1906 money talked and the commission had offers to host a seventh game from Fresno, California, for $25,000 and New Orleans for $15,000.

The parties and receptions went on for days, but Big Ed didn't stay in town. At the reception the night of the last game, the Sox fans begged him to stay in Chicago for a week, but he was in a hurry to get home with his wife and one-year old son, Ed. Before he left he was presented with seven suits of clothes, three overcoats and a dozen hats and pairs of shoes from his admirers. Big Ed caught a train with a Boston contingent which had been in Chicago for the World's Series. During the long ride from Chicago to New England the Boston fans had the time of their lives making Big Ed go over the games and the plays in the games he pitched. At every depot he was introduced as the man who beat the Cubs. Once the news spread, scores jammed into Big Ed's car to get a glimpse of the great man and hear a World's Series story.

6. Big Ed: World Champion

The Walshes arrived in Meriden at 3:18 P.M. on October 16. A crowd of 2,000 and a brass band met them at the station. The delegation was led by Mayor Thomas Reilly. At a reception a few days later sponsored by the Young Men's T.B.A. Society, Big Ed was presented with an inscribed gold watch. A stuffed bear cub wearing white socks sat on the dais next to the reception chairman. After the Meridan reception Big Ed, in response to a flood of telegrams, went to his old hometown, Plains, Pennsylvania, where he was known, not as "Big Ed" or "The Big Moose" as the national sportswriters called him, but rather as "Duck."

> The return of Ed Walsh was celebrated with a rip-roaring demonstration. It seemed as if every man, woman and child in the township was on the street to rejoice over his success and welcome him to his native home. All along the line of march, bands played, drums beat, horns tooted and people yelled and cheered. The scene was enlivened by the burning of colored fire sky rockets, Roman candles and other fireworks at every house on the route of the parade. Walsh arrived at Scranton from Meriden in the evening and was met by part of the reception committee. The party reached the station in Plains at eight o'clock when the demonstration began. "Duck," accompanied by his brother John, entered the first carriage. Then came carriages of clergy, the speakers, the reception committee, newspapermen, the school board, board of commissioners, baseball players, township officers and prominent citizens. The C.T.A.U. [Catholic Total Abstinence Union] band and the Irish-American drum corps of Wilkes-Barre headed the line. Company T of the C.T.A.U. regiment made a splendid appearance. They were headed by the Thistle Band of Plains. The parade proceeded to Sacred Heart Hall where a reception was held.
>
> P. J. Magnan reviewed Duck's work as a ball player, beginning with the time he began with the gritty little fellows known as the Black Diamond team of Plains. Martin Corcoran sang a solo. John P. Gibbons read original verses written for the occasion. Robert Condron sang a solo and was obliged to sing two encores. The last address was by Atty. T. M. Coniff. He congratulated the people on the great local pride they demonstrated and thanked "Duck" for the advertising the town received thanks to his pitching.[14]

In Wilkes-Barre a game to benefit two local hospitals was arranged for Mitchell Day, October 29, a coal country holiday named for legendary labor leader John Mitchell. Big Ed pitched for a team of locals, which he hand-picked, against a team called the All Professionals. In the morning over 2,500 union workers marched in a parade in Wilkes-Barre, along with several bands. That was considered a low turnout and the weather was blamed. It was World's Series weather — winter-like with a cold wind off the river.

"The game to be played at Driving Park between the All-Professionals and a team organized by Duck Walsh promises to be one of the great baseball events ever witnessed in this city. The All-Professionals will be captained by Buck Freeman and will comprise Brown, O'Hara, Burke, the two McCabes, Steamer, Flanagan, Kelly and others.

"Duck Walsh's club will be composed of the best talent in the upper end of Luzerne County and Lackawanna County. Cranston, Mullen, Golden, Hugh Jennings, Tom McAndrew of Scranton and Mike and John O'Neill of Minooka. W.J. Clymer, manager of Columbus, will umpire."

A committee representing the hospital arranged for 5,000 tickets to be made available and they were for sale at all the colliery offices and with various mine foremen and union officials. The weather, described as "a pneumonia-laden atmosphere," kept the crowd down to 2,000. Walsh received a tremendous prolonged ovation when he walked to the mound in the first inning. Jennings and the O'Neills were no-shows and Walsh lasted only two innings. In the second he tried to field a hit by Freeman with his pitching hand and split his hand between the third and little fingers. The professionals won 6–3.[15]

Back in Chicago the all–Chicago World's Series healed the relationship between Comiskey and Ban Johnson. In December Comiskey threw a banquet at the Auditorium Annex for his fellow club owners and he invited Ban Johnson. "The peace dove was present and did not have to be dragged in by the neck. Comiskey said in his speech that he and Johnson would never have any differences in the future. They signed a protocol yesterday after the siege of war covering two years."[16]

7

South of the Border

The celebration of the Sox' 1906 World's Series triumph lasted through the winter. On March 6, 1907, several hundred fans gathered at the Illinois Central station in Chicago to see the White Sox off on their spring training trip to Mexico City, a first for a major league team. The train, known as the Cuban Special, was dubbed the White Sox Special with four extra sleepers added. The two huge locomotives were decorated with American and Mexican flags and the cars with White Sox banners. Ted Sullivan, whom Comiskey had sent to Mexico as an advance agent, gave pointers and advice about Mexico to the players. George Rohe had several cameras. Some of the married players brought their wives and a total of 14 children. The oldest, George Rohe's son, was only six. Big Ed brought his wife and their sons, Edward Arthur, 2, and Robert, two months.

Fans sent four cases of champagne, and other kinds of wet goods arrived in cases and barrels, but Comiskey drew the line after the wine was on board. "The fans forgot this was a training trip and mistook it for a fishing trip," Comiskey said.[1]

When the train stopped in Kankakee, Champaign, Centralia, and Mattoon, Illinois, hundreds of fans gathered at the stations to see the champions. The train picked up pitching recruit Lawrence Cheney in Centralia and Altrock in Memphis. The train fell behind schedule. Hot engines waited at every relay and the train was cut into two sections, but it still got to San Antonio three hours late. The "bush league" locomotives of the Southern Pacific were blamed. In San Antonio players in the section of the train which did not have the dining car stormed a local restaurant thinking they had only a short time to eat, but it was later learned there would be a 24-hour delay. The players did some sight-seeing. Big Ed went to the Alamo and said, "Gee, I never knew that song was such a chestnut."

The next morning the players threw balls around in the rail yard as the sleepers were connected to the Sunset Limited, an 8 A.M. train to the border town, Eagle Pass. But before the train could pull away Frank Owen was arrested by San Antonio police for having a concealed weapon. He was showing his gun to players when a cop saw him. He spent several hours in custody before being released on the promise that he would return on March 20 for a hearing. From Eagle Pass the Sox finally made it into Mexico at Porfiro Dias, only to be delayed again. Halfway across the international bridge, Mexican custom officials stopped the train, dragged out every third trunk and searched it. The officials had no knowledge of baseball and didn't know what to make of the bats, balls and uniforms.

By the time they got going again the Sox had already missed one game in Mexico City and were in danger of missing a second, as they still had 1,000 miles to go. On the way the Sox ate six meals on the train prepared and served by a Chinese kitchen crew. Each meal contained quail. The train, due at noon, was stuck in San Juan del Rio. After some trouble a wire was sent and a special engine was sent to bring the team to Mexico City ahead of the regular run. They arrived at 2 P.M. The players changed into their uniforms in the train and went right to the field just in time for the advertised game. Big Ed did stop in the station just long enough to exchange an American 20 dollar bill for Mexican money and was given a wad of bills so large he couldn't get it in his pocket.

Two days late they finally played a game in Mexico City on March 10. Only 1,000 fans showed up, partly because no one knew if the Sox would arrive in time to play. Among the fans was Raman Carroll, the vice-president of Mexico, who sat in a box with Comiskey. There was a high sky, higher than any they had played under before, and the result was a lot of errors on fly balls. There were errors on ground balls, too. The players were exhausted by the train trip and many of them were hungry. The Sox hardly showed the Mexicans an example of championship baseball. The Blues, captained by Jones, beat Altrock's Whites 8–2. Big Ed pitched three scoreless innings for the Whites, had a hit in his only at-bat and scored a run.[2]

After the game the Sox went to the St. Francis Hotel, where accommodations had been made for only 24 and there were 56 in the party. Accommodations were made at other hotels. Two days later on March 12, the Sox beat the Records, the defending champions of the Mexican League

7. South of the Border

and their ace pitcher, Juarez, 12–2. The Sox made 13 hits off the Mexican ace, but the fans never wavered in their support for him. His popularity was said to be the same as the most popular matadors. White, Altrock and Big Ed each pitched three innings. Big Ed struck out three. The Records had two Americans on their team, Tobin from Cornell University, and Bell from the University of Nebraska.

On the 13th the Sox were supposed to play an all-star team, but only five players showed up, so it became a split squad game. Bucky Freeman — not the player from Wilkes-Barre, but a pitcher from Evansville, Indiana, by the same name — pitched five innings against the Mexican-Sox combination team. As the White Sox were the world champions, the Mexican fans expected perfection out of them and the Sox were far from it. Their errors were greeted by whistles from the fans. Mexican fans whistled rather than booed. The Mexicans considered whistling an insult. Whistling was for dogs, not men.

The next day, March 14, the Sox played their last game against Mexican players and beat a Mexican All-Star team 15–4. A dust storm hit as the players and fans made their way to the field and visibility was near zero for a time. The Sox hit the Mexican pitcher, a man named Caras, hard and the fans yelled, "Otro pitcher and agua pitcher," meaning "take the pitcher out, water the pitcher." Big Ed pitched two scoreless innings with a strikeout and two weak balls hit back to him. A Mexican player, known as the Mexican Miller Huggins, was said to be the smallest player in baseball. He was said to be half as tall as Walsh and he stood next to Big Ed to prove it.

While in Mexico Comiskey was publicly diplomatic about the conditions. He said he was planning for a return trip to Mexico in '08 using a steamer from New Orleans to Vera Cruz and then to Central America and the Yucatan. Privately Comiskey and the Sox couldn't wait to get out of Mexico and had no desire to go back. While on one hand the climate, with its warm rainless days and cool nights, seemed perfect for baseball in March, on the other hand it was too dry. Not only was there no rain in March, the locals said it hadn't rained since December. The slightest wind raised dust in the air. A lot of sprinkling was done on the field, despite the value of water, but to little effect. Most of the players developed cold-like symptoms, including severe sore throats and laryngitis. The sickness was blamed on alkali dust and the altitude. Mexico City is at 7400 feet. Most of the Sox were flatlanders and were easily overexerted in the thin air.

Eating properly was a problem, too. The Sox stayed at two high class hotels yet complained of hunger and "longed for one good meal of stockyard beef." The Sox ate more than most Mexicans. "The waiters view with alarm each invasion of the dining room by the Sox — who rapidly acquired enough native lingo to make their appetites known."

Crowds averaged only 1,000 in a city of 350,000. Bullfighting and pelota, a game described as a cross between handball and soccer, were popular with the masses. Baseball was in its infancy in Mexico then and was considered a game for Americans living in Mexico and upper class Mexicans. Tickets were $3 Mexican, about $1.50 American, at a time when a game could be seen in the states for 25 cents. Communication was a problem, too. The federal government owned the railroads and telegraph lines and they were notoriously inefficient. The only reliable means of communication was a telegraph owned by a private company from London.

About the only good thing about training in Mexico was that the players stayed out of trouble. The temptations of the big city were less because of the language barrier and the fear of crime. The players tended to stay on beaten paths. But the trip did have at least one scary incident. One night the whole hotel was awakened by a woman's screams on the first floor. Some of the Sox went to her room where she said a burglar had jumped out a window. Isbell was armed with a bat and Owen had his gun.

The Sox played their last game in Mexico on the 17th. The Blues won 9–8. Big Ed did not play. They left for the U.S. that night at 7:40. The "Sox Quartet"— tenors Big Ed, Altrock and White and bassist Donahue — entertained during the monotonous trip. Once the team got back to the states, the squad was split. The regulars went to New Orleans, the other squad went to San Antonio under the direction of Comiskey. Owen went with the San Antonio squad to keep his court date. In July Comiskey's son, J.L., the team's financial officer, announced that the Sox would not go back to Mexico. "Members of the team were thoroughly disgusted at the climate, their surroundings and everything connected with the trip," said Comiskey junior.[3]

On the 23rd Big Ed pitched against the New Orleans Pelicans and lost 1–0 to a pitcher named Guese, who pitched a three-hitter and struck out six. Big Ed pitched six innings and struck out five. He hit a double that shook the fence board in left field. He pitched against the Pelicans two days later, hit another double and lost again, 4–3. All four Pelicans runs came in the third inning. Before the game a fire caused by a gasoline engine that powered a well at the park burned 50 feet of the center field fence, a telegraph pole, two beer signs and one cigar sign.

In Vicksburg, Mississippi, Hahn was given a gold-handled umbrella from his fans there who remembered him when he played there in 1904. In Jackson on the Wednesday before Easter, entertainment was as much of a draw as the Sox. The Dockstraders black-face minstrels performed on Wednesday, as did Big Ed, whom handbills referred to as "the greatest spittoonist in the world." He gave up four hits and a run in four innings, but struck out seven. In the ninth he struck out the side in order. As a batter he had two hits, including a home run which was lost in the weeds in left center. Thursday was a day off and the Sox were invited by the Dockstraders to a wild west style show they were traveling with. The hit of the show was a Mr. C. Kilpatrick, billed as a one-legged cyclist and skatist. He rode around on a unicycle while shooting clay pigeons.

On the 28th the Sox were stunned to hear that Boston Americans outfielder Chick Stahl killed himself at home in Indiana. Stahl was a well-liked and, as far as anyone knew, a happy-go-lucky type. "Stahl was a fine fellow," Comiskey said. "I do not believe that baseball caused him to end his career so suddenly. Stahl was in baseball too many years to worry seriously over anything pertaining to the game. I think it must have been trouble of some other sort that prompted the deed."

Stahl had played 10 seasons, all in Boston with both the Nationals and Americans. In 1906 he led the league in games played, 155, and outfield assists. In August of 1906 he was named manager, replacing Jimmy Collins. He managed the last 40 games. Stahl had been in Jackson with Boston just before the White Sox. It was in Jackson that he resigned as manager. He told friends that the job was too big for him, went home and killed himself three weeks before his 34th birthday. Five years earlier Stahl had been shot on a street in Fort Wayne by Lulu Ortman, a woman "he refused to marry."[4]

In Kentucky on Good Friday, March 29, the Sox beat the Colonels 5–3, belting out seven hits with 15 new bats. The bats came wrapped in paper sausages, that bore the photos of Nap Lajoie and Honus Wagner. Big Ed did not play. On Saturday he did. He pitched the last four innings. The Sox trailed 2–1 in the eighth when they scored two to win 3–2. Big Ed reached on an error, followed by Hahn, who bunted for a hit. Jones bunted back to the mound, but Big Ed beat the throw to third. He scored on a hit by Dougherty.[5]

Early the next morning the Sox caught a train to Indianapolis where on April 2 Big Ed had his best outing of the spring. The spitter was unhittable and he struck out 11 in seven innings. He was just as impressive as a batter as he went 3 for 3 and scored half the Sox' six runs. Big Ed said that the spitter hadn't been working as well in the southern climes. "It made the ball wingy and the leathers soaked up the juice faster than he could rub it on."[6]

From Indianapolis the Sox went to Terre Haute and then Cincinnati, where they were feted at a banquet arranged by the Reds' president Hermann on April 6. About 200 of the city's most prominent residents gathered in the Sinton Hotel. That same day Comiskey finally heard from George Davis, who hadn't been heard from since November. He was in New York and planned to met the Sox in Chicago. With Davis on board, the Sox had their team intact from 1906 and were seen as favorites in 1907. Even Fielder Jones, who in the past never made predictions, said he expected the Sox to repeat in the American League. "He figures he has the best pitching staff in the country, that he is long on catchers and veterans in the infield and outfield. The manager fears New York the most and Cleveland next."[7]

Jones told the *Chicago Tribune* if Smith emulated Big Ed, the Sox would be tough to beat. "Smith was becoming a strong pitcher before he stopped using the spit ball," Jones said. "Then he was less successful. I have been pointing out to him how Walsh came to the front once he acquired mastery of the spit ball and now Smith is working hard and conscientiously to get control of the delivery he discarded. I believe he will be as successful as Walsh. If he does have success and we are not shot to pieces by hard luck, they will have to beat the Sox to win the 1907 pennant."[8]

The roster was set at 22. Three players from '06,—Jaye Towne, a backup catcher, and utility players Gus Dundon and Tip O'Neill—were sent to Milwaukee. Their places were filled by Mike Welday, an outfielder from Des Moines, and Lee Quillen, a third baseman from Lincoln. The Sox opened defense of their American League Championship in St. Louis on April 11.

Fielder Jones managed the White Sox and was the full-time center fielder from 1904 to 1908. He was patient with Big Ed (Library of Congress).

8

Sox Are Tamed by the Tigers

Just before the 1907 season began the Sox, and Big Ed, were given some added incentive. Comiskey offered the players a $15,000 bonus and a trip to Ireland if they won the A.L. flag. Meanwhile, Highlanders manager Clarke Griffith predicted Ed Walsh would flop. Griffith believed a spitball pitcher could not have two good seasons in a row.[1]

Jones selected Altrock for opening day in St. Louis. Altrock gave up only one run, but the Sox were shut out by Harry Howell. On the 13th Jones started Big Ed and he was a winner, 6–4, as much with his bat as with his arm. He hit a two-run homer into the bleachers in left in the fifth and doubled and scored in the eighth. He struck out five but gave up 10 hits. "The Browns would slam the spit ball no matter how much the big chap painted it."[2] Back in Chicago on April 19 Walsh beat the Browns again 1–0, tied the record for total chances by a pitcher with 13 and hit another double. Altrock had set the chances record in 1904.

"Eleven batsmen smote the ball at or near Walsh, and he scored two putouts at the bag. The bounders could not come too fast or too slow for the agile giant. He whacked them down with either hand or dug the ball out of the dirt, and every grab meant the downfall of a helpless athlete."[3]

On April 26 Big Ed won his third straight start, beating Cleveland 2–1 in Cleveland. He gave up six hits, struck out eight and walked one. He continued his torrid batting, knocking in the winning run with a single in the ninth. Writing in the *Chicago Tribune* Charles Dryden said Walsh threw a new variation of the spitball, "the suds ball," against the

Naps. "Oozy Ed was framed up to win on a new and improved spitter of his own invention. Just before the start the word went round that the big one would not pitch. He damaged an elbow shoveling chewing gum in to his hopper, but that was only a bluff to divert suspicion from the real dope. The new suds incentive is shaving soap which the boss hurler eats prior to the game. Walsh's control of the new suds ball was perfect, and therein lies the secret of his third straight win."[4]

The next day, after Smith stopped the Naps 6–2, the Sox caught a train back to Chicago to play one game, a makeup against the Tigers. Big Ed made his first relief appearance of the season. Jones brought him in with no outs in the eighth with the Sox leading 3–1. The Tigers' McIntyre and Bill Coughlin were on second and first and the league's two best hitters, Sam Crawford and Ty Cobb, were coming up.

Crawford hit back to Big Ed and he forced McIntyre at third. Cobb did the same, but this time Big Ed took the out at first and Coughlin went to third. Now there were two Pennsylvania breaker boys over at third. Coughlin was a former miner from Scranton, and he had two missing fingers to prove it, and Hugh Jennings, who came from Pittston, a Plains border town, was the Tigers' manager and third base coach.

Jennings was in his first season as the Tigers' manager and as the "Ee-Yah" man, he kept up a constant series of yells from the box meant to distract Big Ed and jazz up the Tigers. "His mouth was never closed," wrote Dryden. "Game young advocate, that Jennings."

Big Ed got Rossman, the next batter, to swing at a spit-

Hugh Jennings was a coal country neighbor of Big Ed's. They had a lot in common, but clashed on the field. Jennings liked to get Big Ed's goat.

ball so viscous Sullivan couldn't handle it and Coughlin scored. Big Ed finished the strikeout on Rossman and set the Tigers down in order in the ninth with two more strikeouts. Though Big Ed and Jennings had a lot in common as the sons of Irish immigrants born just five miles apart who both rose from the mines of Northeastern Pennsylvania to baseball fame, they were not friendly and often clashed on the field. Jennings enjoyed getting Big Ed's goat. After the 1907 season a spitball pitcher anonymously accused Jennings of doctoring the baseballs in Detroit to make the spitball ineffective. The accusation was made in the *Washington Post*.

"At the winter meeting a prominent American League ballplayer made the claim that Detroit manager Hugh Jennings doctored balls to make the spit ball ineffective. 'Jennings has a doctor prepare a lotion which is not visible to the naked eye, but which prevents the fingers from slipping on the moistened spot on the ball and consequently makes the spit ball impossible.'

"It is charged that the seals of the boxes in which the balls come are broken, the lotion applied on the ball, which is then resealed in the box so cleverly that the umpire cannot detect that the box has been tampered with. The prominence of the player involved gives the story a rather truthful tinge."[5]

Use of the word "prominence" suggests the source of the story may have been Big Ed. In 1907 he was the most prominent spitball pitcher in the American League. Big Ed pitched three games in Detroit in 1907. He won one, lost one and one ended in a tie.

After that one game in Chicago both the Sox and Tigers went over to Detroit for a four-game series. In the first game, on May 1, the Sox scored three in the first inning for Doc White. The Sox led 3–2 in the fifth when, after White gave up two singles with one out, Jones brought Big Ed in. He got an out and would have gotten out of the inning, but Davis booted a grounder to short to let in the tying run. The game went on for 14 innings and ended in a 3–3 tie. Big Ed pitched to the end. In the 14th, after he struck out Davy Jones for the third out with the winning run on third, the game was called by darkness. In the third game of the series Big Ed batted for Jones in the 9th and struck out. In the final game on May 5 he started and the Sox got a scare when he was injured participating in a triple play so freakish even Jennings was speechless. In the fourth inning with Rossman on third and Schaefer on second, Schmidt grounded to Davis at short. Davis threw home and Rossman ran back toward third. Sullivan chased him, caught him near third, tagged him out, then threw to second where Schmidt was tagged out by Rohe. Schaefer, seeing the plate was uncovered, ran right past Sullivan for home. Big Ed ran in to cover. The ball, Schaefer and Big Ed reached the vicinity of the plate about the same time. Schaefer lowered his shoulder and sent Big Ed sprawling, knocking the ball loose. But Davis ran in from shortstop, picked up the ball and tagged Schaefer as he tried to crawl to the plate. The play went 6-2-4-1-6. None of the outs was a force-out. Big Ed did not get up and Dryden wrote that it was the first quadruple play in baseball history with three Tigers and Big Ed being put out.

"So severe is the injury sustained by Walsh that he may not be able to play for a month. The overlapping muscles in the right side of his neck and shoulder are wrenched. On the advice of a physician, Manager Jones left Walsh behind when the team started for home tonight. The pitcher was too lame to be moved. Dr. Kirby, who has charge of the case, suggests that the patient be taken to the baths at Mount Clemens, Michigan, and the suggestion may be carried out tomorrow."[6] Doc White finished the game.

But Big Ed's injury was not as serious as it seemed. He was back on the slab on May 12 in Chicago. He beat the Athletics 10–3. He struck out eight and hit a two-run double to right with the bases loaded. He was tagged out when he ran with his head down trying to make a triple, only to find Quillin had stopped at third. It was the Sox' third straight win over the A's. Walsh was 4–0 and the Sox were 5–0 in Walsh starts. The Sox were 17–7 on the season and led the A.L. by 3½ games over Cleveland. Five days later Big Ed lost for the first time 4–1 to Patten and Washington in Chicago. He struck out eight.

On May 26 Big Ed won a five-inning no-hitter 8–1 against the Highlanders in a game shortened by rain, lightning and hail. Leading 4–1 in the fourth, the Sox tried to retire themselves intentionally, hoping to get to the fifth and make the game official, while the Highlanders manager Griffith tried to stall. He pulled starter Al Orth and put himself in. It was one of only four appearances by Griffith as a player that season. He walked the bases loaded then grooved one to Walsh, who knocked in two runs. Sullivan, who was on first, stopped between third and home and was tagged out. With two outs Griffith refused to pitch to Jones until umpire Jack Sheridan threatened to forfeit the game to the Sox. The Highlanders got their run in the first when Big Ed walked two and threw two wild pitches. He retired the next 13 batters.

On the 29th Big Ed was a winner in relief over St. Louis 6–5. "Ed Walsh had the eel ball better subdued than in his last public appearance, when he finished out a game for Doc White." The "eel ball" was the pet

8. Sox Are Tamed by the Tigers

name for Walsh's spitball as dubbed by Charles Dryden, a reporter for the *Trib* who covered the Sox. In contrast to 1906 when the spitball was rarely mentioned in game accounts, in 1907 Dryden and other writers referred to the pitch a lot with colorful names like the "eel ball" and the "Vapor Float."

Two days after Big Ed shut out the Browns, the Sox finished a 22-game homestand 15–7 and left on a 15-game Eastern swing with a 22–12 record and a two and one-half game lead over the second-place Naps. On June 3 Big Ed beat the Naps and Addie Joss 2–1. Again he had the spitter under control and Dryden came up with still another nickname. "Walsh never had 'Spitz,' his trained eel under more perfect subjection. He used it constantly, yet did not issue a pass all day, and he struck out eight of the Naps' sluggers in five innings."

In Philadelphia on June 5 he lost to Rube Waddell 3–0. Waddell pitched a 3-hitter with 11 strikeouts. Big Ed struck out eight. On June 10 after Big Ed beat the Senators 2–1 in Washington, the Sox were 30–15 and in first place by one-half game over the Naps and five games over the third place Tigers.

His next start was in the rain in New York on June 13. Though he was a winner, 4–3, he was far from sharp. He gave up five hits and walked five and struck out only three. He was saved by some slick fielding in the ninth. After Davis knocked in the go-ahead run in the top of the ninth, he threw out a runner at the plate for the second out in the bottom of the inning. With two outs Griffith sent up Branch Rickey to pinch hit. The man who would one day make history by signing Jackie Robinson hit a shallow fly ball to right center. Jones slipped and fell as he went for the ball, got up, made a headlong dive, caught the ball and ended the game with a somersault.

After the game Big Ed went home to Meriden to visit his wife and two young sons, telling Jones he would be back on the 17th to pitch the final game of the New York series. But when the day came he wired Jones from Meriden claiming his arm was sore and asking to be excused from the start. Jones relented and Walsh stayed in Meriden until the Sox got to Boston. He reported there and started on the 19th. This was a recurring pattern for Walsh. Over the years when the Sox were on eastern swings, he would leave the team and go home, claiming that either his wife or one of his kids was sick or that he was injured. The injuries were bizarre and the treatments were mysterious, as this account of his start on the 19th recounts. "Ed Walsh, some eel tamer, was opposed by two of Manager McGuire's stable of twirlers and won an easy victory, despite the lameness which disabled him on his return to the club on Monday.

"Walsh's lameness descended from his arm to his right ankle during the night, and it proved a fortunate decision, for with the aid of a leather stocking, illustrated oil, and some rubber bandages Prof. Bardell was able to fix up the ankle so it would stand the strain of pitching a full game without injury."[7]

The cure must have worked because two days later Big Ed relieved Altrock in the final game of the Boston series and pitched the last six innings of a 4–4 tie. On the way home the Sox stopped in Detroit for one game and White beat the Tigers 4–3. So the Sox survived their Eastern swing with an 8-6-1 record and were still in first place with a 35–18 record, one and one-half games ahead of the Naps and three and one-half ahead of the third place Tigers. Back home, Big Ed started the first game of a series with Cleveland and struck out six in the first four innings. In the third Big Ed led off with a triple to left center, but was stranded. That ended up costing him and the Sox as the game went 12 innings and the Sox lost 7–5. Big Ed's own error in the 12th, on an easy roller by Elmer Flick, led to the winning runs for the Naps. The Naps beat White 3–2 in the second game. Big Ed pitched two innings in relief in the third game, a win in a seven-inning game shortened by rain.

After the third game the Sox went to St. Louis for a four game set. Big Ed started the second game and for one of only nine times in 46 starts in '07 did not finish. After giving up 10 hits in six innings and striking out only one, he was relieved by Altrock in the seventh and the Sox lost 7–4. The game marked the only time in Big Ed's career that opponents scored as many as seven runs in consecutive games he started. As he worked a paltry six innings in the second game, Jones came back with him on one day's rest for the fourth game of the St. Louis series on June 29 and the result was a six-hit shutout and a 9–0 win. "While Walsh was blanking the Browns with wide sweeps of the moist brush which he daubed in the whitewash bucket every inning, the Sox had considerable fun with Fred Glade."[8]

The Sox caught a train back to Chicago that night for a two-game series with the Tigers beginning the next day. Doc White started the first game, and kept Hugh Jennings quiet with a six-hit shutout and seven strikeouts. Cobb hit two singles, but got no farther than second and the Sox won 2–0. June ended with the Sox on a three-game win streak and in first place with a 40-21-2 record. They had a two and one-half game lead over the Naps, five over the A's, and six and one-half over the fourth place Tigers. The Sox made it four straight on July 1 when Smith beat the Tigers 4–2.

8. Sox Are Tamed by the Tigers

In Cleveland on July 2 Addie Joss beat Big Ed and the Sox 4–0. When Cleveland won again the next day, the Naps caught the Sox atop the A.L. standings. The Sox needed a double header sweep to regain first and got it on the Fourth. Smith won the morning game 3–2. Big Ed won the matinee 7–1. The morning game drew 16,522 and the afternoon game 11,781, including a "bevy of high school girls" in the outfield grass who were guarded by a police officer. Big Ed gave up seven hits, three in the third when the Naps scored their run, and struck out three without a walk.

After the double header on the Fourth, the Sox went home to begin a 20-game homestand against the Eastern clubs, including four double headers. The Sox won 10 of the 20 games and lost seven. Three ended in ties. They were three of the six tie games the Sox played in 1907 which were not made up. By the time the eastern invasion was over on July 22, the Sox had increased their lead over the Naps to three games, but the Tigers, who had gone 12–4 against the east during that same time, had moved into third, just three and one-half games back. Big Ed started six of the 20 games. He won three and lost three. In the three losses the Sox scored a total of one run. In the second game of the stand against the A's he had one of his best outings of the season. "With Eel Walsh pitching almost impregnable baseball, the White Sox trimmed the Athletics yesterday without working overtime to do it and by the decisive verdict of 6 to 0. Until near the finish it looked as if Walsh was going to pitch a hitless game." Walsh had a no-hitter until the seventh when Oldring hit a hard smash which caromed off Rohe's glove to Davis, who threw to first, but Oldring beat it out. Big Ed allowed two more hits in the eighth. He struck out four and did not walk a batter.

In his fourth start of the homestand on the 16th against New York, Big Ed won 3–2 in 13 innings and upped his own record for fielding chances for pitchers to 15, handling 12 assists and three putouts. He struck out four. On a day's rest he tried to salvage the second game of a double header against New York after the Sox were hammered in the first game 11–2. He and Orth both pitched one-hit ball through five, but the Highlanders won 4–0. In his last start of the homestand on July 21, Big Ed was a 3–0 loser to Boston's George Winter.

The next day the Sox left Chicago for Philadelphia to start a 19-game road trip against the Eastern clubs. The trip got off to a disastrous start. Waddell beat Patterson 2–1 in the first game. The next day the Sox failed to score in a third consecutive Big Ed start and he was beaten by Bender 2–0 in the first game of a double header. They also lost the second game and lost again the next day. Big Ed finally stopped the four game slide with a 7–2 win in the fifth game of the Philadelphia series. Though the Sox would go 4–1 in Walsh's starts on the Eastern swing — one of the wins was a 3–0 four-hit shutout of Washington — they were 4–10 in the other games and when they got back to Chicago on August 11 they had fallen to third place, one-half game behind the A's and one full game behind the Tigers, who went 11–5 in 16 games on their Eastern swing.

In the last series of the Eastern trip, a five-gamer in Boston, Jones used Big Ed in three of the games. On August 7 Altrock was hooked up in a pitching duel with Cy Young. The Sox held a 1–0 lead in the ninth, when Boston's first baseman Bob Unglaub led off with a triple. Jones brought Walsh in to save it. Altrock stomped off the mound and threw his glove under the bench in disgust. Big Ed got two strikes on Hobe Ferris, but the Boston second baseman singled to center to tie the game. In the 14th, with night falling, Big Ed gave up a single to Ferris, a wild pitch and then a game-winning single to Henie Wagner. Young, then 40 years old, pitched all 14 innings. He struck out four and induced 24 infield ground outs. In six innings Big Ed struck out four and walked one.

The next day Big Ed started and went seven innings in a 6–4 win. He was losing 4–0 after seven, but the Sox batted around in the top of the eighth and scored six, the big blow a bases loaded triple by Isbell. Doc White pitched the eighth and ninth innings to preserve the win. After a day's rest Big Ed relieved in the last game of the Eastern swing, pitching the last two innings in a 4–2 loss in Boston on August 10. After the game both teams caught a train for Chicago, where Boston was to be the Sox' first opponent in a 14-game homestand.

The long road trip was tough on the Sox physically. Nearly all the key players got injured or sick, but very few games were missed. A writer for the *Tribune*, who went by the moniker "Hek" in his "In the Wake of the News" columns, set the Sox' health problems to rhyme.

> Fielder Jones has bowed a tendon,
> Dougherty's picked up a nail.
> Tannehill is slowly mendin'
> Altrock's simply out on bail.
> Jiggers has appendicitis,
> Sully's threatened with the grip.
> McFarland's took with badarmitis,
> And typhoid camps in Walsh's hip.
> Rohe has the yellow fever,
> Doc White has a pale blue streak;

8. Sox Are Tamed by the Tigers

> Poor Hub Hart, the tub receiver,
> Has a cold sore on his beak.
> Isbell's joints are getting creaky,
> Soon we'll hear the last of him.
> Truth comes on us slow and sneaky:
> Hickman's chance is mighty slim,
> Redolent of every lotion
> Science lends the healing sores;
> Hampered by their locomotion,
> Baseball exudes from every pore,
> Charley-horsed, ringboned, and spavined;
> Coughing, wheezing short of breath —
> You can't make a dose they haven't
> Twixt an ambulance and death.
> Buffaloed, perhaps, they may be.
> Deeply stung at every fall,
> But never once to play the baby!
> All the time a-playing ball.
> So let us all be up and rooting.
> They'll win the pennant on three legs.
> Here's to the good, game, fighting cripples.
> Drain it, drain it, to the dregs.[9]

Jones called on Big Ed to start the first game of the homestand on August 12. It was his fourth appearance in six days, all of them against Boston. He was solidifying his reputation as a tireless workhorse. He gave up seven hits and two walks in eight innings and had another busy day in the field handling 12 chances, but he lost 5–3. Washington came into town after Boston and Big Ed stopped them 3–2 on the 16th, striking out six without a walk, and the Sox passed the Tigers for second place. Big Ed used the spitter to get out of a jam in the second. "Walsh slid out of a hole in the second with the aid of his highly productive salivary glands."

The first place A's came to Chicago on August 20 sporting a 12–5 record for the month. Big Ed cooled them off in the first game. He beat Eddie Plank 4–1 and was involved in a collision at third base with A's second baseman Danny Murphy, who got the worst of it. "Murphy sprinted around to third when Nicholls bunted to Tanny for the first out at first. Walsh hustled over to cover third. He leaped for Donahue's high throw and came down on top of Murphy, crushing him like a hired man stepping on a potato bug."

Nig Smith beat the A's 1–0 the next day and created an odd circumstance at the top of the A.L. standings, with the first place team one-half game behind the second place team. The A's were considered to be in first place with a winning percentage .001 better than the Sox' percentage. Yet calculated by games the Sox were one-half game up. The next day, August 22, Big Ed came back on one day's rest with first place on the line and lost 2–0 to Waddell, who pitched a two-hitter and the A's got out of town with a better winning percentage and a one-half game lead.

New York followed the A's into Chicago and was greeted by Doc White with a 4–0 shutout while Big Ed rested for a day. The next day he relieved Smith in the sixth and finished off a 5–2 win over the Highlanders. The next day he started the last game of the Highlanders series and the last game of the homestand. Big Ed won it 3–2 but it took a three-run bottom of the ninth rally to get the win. The winning runs scored on a throwing error by Highlanders shortstop Kid Eberfeld. Hundreds of the 10,000 fans rushed the field after the winning run scored to mock Eberfeld and congratulate Davis who had hit the ground ball. In the clubhouse the White Sox did what the fans wanted to do to Hahn, who had started the rally with a one-out single. They stood him on his head. The thrilling win put the Sox into first place, but it took long division to get them there. The White Sox were 70–47. Carried out to five decimals that was a .59829 percentage. The A's were 67–45. Their five decimal winning percentage was a mere .59821.

The Sox were 9–5 on the homestand against the eastern teams and had picked up two and one-half games on the A's. Big Ed pitched 22 innings in the last four days of the series, prompting Dryden to make this prediction: "The Sox will carry but three pitchers on the trip to Cleveland this week — Walsh, Ed Walsh and Mr. Walsh."

He wasn't far from wrong. Big Ed pitched two of the three games in Cleveland, a 5–0 loss and a 2–2 tie, the Sox' fifth unfinished game of the season. The game was called after eight innings by mutual agreement so the Naps could catch a train to St. Louis. Now the Tigers, who won their seventh straight that day, were in first place, one and one-half games ahead of the A's and two and one-half ahead of the Sox.

As it happened the Tigers and Sox were scheduled for a four game series in Chicago beginning the next day. If the Sox could sweep, or at least win three of four, they could regain first place, but they wound up splitting the four games, which suited the Tigers. The four-game series included a Labor Day double header which drew about 20,000. Big Ed pitched the second game and beat the Tigers' ace, Wild Bill Donovan, 4–2. It was one of only four losses all season for Donovan who finished 25–4. Big Ed was thrown out of the game in the sixth inning by umpire Tim Hurst, a Pennsylvania coal country compatriot. "A bad play, in which

Donahue and Rohe were about equally culpable, in the sixth made opportunity for a close play at the plate, which Tim Hurst gave in Detroit's favor at imminent risk of being torn limb from limb, and there was a disorderly lot of kicking during which Walsh pushed Hurst about, compelling the umpire to chase him off the lot." Big Ed had struck out six in 5⅔ innings before he was run. When Ban Johnson heard about the incident the next day he suspended Big Ed for five days. While he was out the Sox won two of three in St. Louis. When he came off of suspension on September 8, the Sox were in third place three games behind the A's and one behind the Tigers, who were back in Chicago for a two-game set.

Though here it was September and the Tigers were only one game out, the scribes and fans outside Detroit were having a hard time taking the team seriously as pennant contenders. After all, the Tigers had finished 1906 71–78, in sixth place and 21 games behind the Sox. But those 1906 Tigers didn't have Hughie Jennings. The first year manager dismissed the team's critics as the two-game series opened in Chicago. "The man who calculates the Tigers have no chance to win the pennant is dead wrong."[10]

Big Ed started the first game, which turned out to be a microcosm of the Tigers' 1907 season wherein things just seemed to go their way. He had a 3–2 lead with two outs in the ninth with a Tiger runner on third and an 0–2 count on Tigers second baseman Red Downs. "Walsh thought it best to waste a ball on the batter, and he did. Like Chesbro's famous wild pitch, it was the inevitable eel ball and it wiggled itself slimily through 'Hub' Hart's mitt, just far enough back of the plate to let in the expiring Tiger, who suddenly became decidedly alive. That tied up the knot—then Downs struck out, instead of being the final victim, two more innings were required to settle the argument."[11] The "argument" went to the Tigers 6–3 in 11. Big Ed struck out six, including Cobb, but gave up a long home run to Sam Crawford. Though White beat the Tigers the next day, the Tigers got out of Chicago with their two-game lead over the Sox still intact.

The Sox left Chicago for St. Louis that evening, except for Big Ed, Sullivan, and Dougherty, who went to Cincinnati to participate in Garry Herrmann's field day. Big Ed entered the fungo hitting contest and Jones predicted he would win it. "Jones says he believes there are few men in either of the major leagues that can out-hit Walsh in long drives."

Big Ed finished second to Cincinnati's Mike Mitchell, who hit one 413 feet, eight and one-half inches, which was considered a record, but Big Ed lived up to his manager's prediction three years later. He broke Mitchell's record during a Chicago field day on September 30, 1911, with a 419 feet and one-half inch drive. The record lasted five years. It was broken by Cincinnati pitcher Peter Schneider before the last game of the season in 1916.[12]

After the Cincinnati field day, Big Ed caught up with the Sox in St. Louis, starting the third game of the four-game series on September 12 and winning 3–2. The next day was Friday the 13th and, as crazy as it seems, the superstitious Jones tried to counter the bad luck by using 13 players. "The combination of the 13th of the month and Friday proved too strong for the White Sox today, although Manager Jones pressed thirteen world's champions into the game in an effort to offset it. Walsh worked in the seventh all right, but was succeeded by Patterson in the eighth, so as to produce the correct number of players to offset the hoodoo."[13] It didn't work. Jack Powell shut out the Sox 3–0.

On the 16th the White Sox went to Detroit for a crucial four-game series. Both teams were three games behind the A's and tied for second place. This was the series where the Tigers went from pretenders to contenders. The Tigers won three of the four games. Big Ed pitched the last game of the series, the second game of a double header, on September 18. The Sox had already lost two of three and the importance of the game was evident to Big Ed. It was reported that he went to bed at 7 o'clock the night before and that he received a wire from a friend in Wilkes-Barre who had a premonition that Ed would win. The Wilkes-Barre friend was wrong. Ed Killian and the Tigers beat him 3–2. The series was the beginning of a monumental hot streak by the Tigers. Beginning with the three of four wins over the Sox the Tigers won 14 of 17 including 10 consecutive from September 21 to October 5. They ascended into first place to stay on September 24.

The Sox didn't quit during the Tigers' hot streak. They got as close as one game out as late as September 24 when Big Ed beat Waddell and the A's 8–3 in Philadelphia with his bat and arm. He hit a double and a triple. The next day Plank shut out the Sox 5–0. On September 26, Jones, feeling desperate, pitched Big Ed again. "Believing that it was his only chance to beat the Athletics and thereby stay in the race, Fielder Jones sent Walsh back today." It didn't work. Big Ed gave up seven hits, and for one of the few times in 1907 was wild. He walked six, hit a batter and threw a wild pitch.

That night Big Ed went home to Meriden for a visit and a short rest. He caught up with the team in New York and as the Sox were at least mathematically alive, Jones started Big Ed on October 1 and 3. Both games were losses, but as the Tigers refused to lose it didn't matter. The Tigers clinched

8. Sox Are Tamed by the Tigers

on October 5 in St. Louis. The season ended on the seventh with the A's in second place and the Sox in third place, six games out. As though losing out on the pennant weren't bad enough, Big Ed also lost his wallet while shopping in New York. He didn't get any sympathy from his teammates. As the wallet was alligator, Nick Altrock said, "it probably crawled out of your pocket."[14]

Big Ed led the league in games, 56, a major league record he would break the next year; starts, 46; complete games, 37; innings pitched, 422.3; saves, four, ERA, 1.60 and was second to Waddell in strikeouts with 206. He walked 75 batters, an average of 1.6 per nine innings. Big Ed also led in assists by a pitcher with 227, a major league record. For all that, his won-loss record was just 24–18.

So how does a pitcher lead the league with a 1.60 ERA and lose 18 games? Answer: lack of run support. The Sox were shut out in eight of Big Ed's 18 losses, including three consecutive shutouts in Walsh starts on July 18, 21 and 25. They scored one run in four of the Walsh losses and two in two others. Average run support in the 18 losses was 1.27 per game.

Just how anemic was the Sox batting in 1907? Though the Sox, as they had in '06, led the A.L. in walks by a wide margin and were third in runs scored, two of their players had the lowest batting averages in the league among regulars—Sullivan .191 and Tannehill .216. Their best hitter, Jiggs Donahue, batted .295 with 68 RBI. Consider that Big Ed was the second leading home run hitter with one. George Rohe hit two. The team hit five. Big Ed had 11 extra base hits in 154 at-bats. Catcher Sullivan had 12 in 329 at bats and Ed Hahn had 16 in 592 at bats.

Meanwhile the Tigers had the league's two best hitters in Cobb, who led in hits, doubles, triples, RBI, batting average and slugging, and Sam Crawford, who was the second to Cobb in each and led in home runs. The Tigers led in runs scored by 75 and batting average by 24 percentage points over the Naps, who were second in both. The Naps' manager, Napoleon Lajoie, played in every game and was third in the A.L. in batting average and fourth in RBI. Another problem for the Sox was their top heavy pitching. Walsh, Smith and White won 74 games, the rest of the staff won 13. The Tigers had five pitchers with 12 or more wins—Ed Summers, 24–12; George Mullin, 17–13; Bill Donovan, 18–7; Ed Willett, 15–8; and Ed Killian, 12–9.

No wonder then that the Sox' 1906 pennant-winning season was increasingly seen as a fluke and that the Tigers would be installed as prohibitive favorites in the A.L for 1908.

9

Big Ed: Ironman

"When Charley Comiskey's special car of baseball players comes rolling into San Francisco it will usher in a boom for baseball in California and particularly the bay cities. The coming of Comiskey's players is the greatest event in baseball history in the state. Fans will get a chance to see Ed Walsh the premier pitcher of the American League." So wrote T.P. MacGilligan in the *Oakland Tribune* in January 1908 when it was announced that the White Sox would take spring training in California in 1908. MacGilligan may have been a little ahead of the curve on his assessment of Big Ed as the best in the A.L., but it wouldn't take long for Walsh to show that MacGilligan was a prophet.

Fittingly, Big Ed started the 1908 season as the closer one day and the starter the next. On April 17 in Chicago he relieved White in the ninth of a 0–0 game versus the Browns, gave up a hit and a run and was tagged with the loss. Waddell won it on a one-hitter. The next day Big Ed was the starter and hurled a shutout of his own, a three-hitter with four strikeouts in a 3–0 win versus the Browns.

Thus began the most amazing single-season statistical pitching performance that baseball had ever seen or ever would. By the standards of later eras, Big Ed's 1908 numbers seem super-human. He started 49 games, 31 percent of the White Sox' games, and completed 42. He appeared in 66 games, 42 percent of the team's games, and pitched an all-time record 464 innings, one-third of the available innings. One statistic is more stunning than the next: 40 wins, 11 shutouts, a 1.42 ERA, but most stunning of all was the 56 bases on balls. Throwing a pitch almost no other pitcher could control, he walked 1.08 batters per nine innings. But the overall statistics don't tell the whole story of Walsh's 1908 season. Many of his best performances came when the pressure was the greatest. In the heat of what would become known as the greatest pennant race ever, he pitched in 13 of the Sox' last 16 games and in seven of the last 10.

Big Ed pitched the second of his 11 shutouts on May 3 versus the Naps in Chicago. He struck out nine batters, five in succession in the sixth and seventh innings, including three of the Naps' best hitters, Nap Lajoie, "Nig" Clarke, and Joe Birmingham. On May 9, after a win over Waddell and the Browns in Chicago, Walsh was called home when his brother Thomas was injured in an explosion at the Woodward mine shaft in Plains. Four days later Big Ed met the team in Philadelphia and hurled a four-hitter with six strikeouts and one walk in a 2–1 win over the A's, a day after the A's had scored eight runs against Owen. "Ed Walsh came on this morning from the bedside of his disaster-stricken brother at Wilkesbarre [sic] and made the Athletics forget all about the swatting lesson they learned yesterday."[1]

While he was in Plains the local paper made note of his visit. "Edward Walsh is in town and you can feel it in the air. All his friends were around to give him a glad hand."[2] His brother survived, but almost exactly a year later another brother would not be so lucky.

In a series in New York in May Big Ed pitched two games and a funny thing happened. The Sox scored runs for him. He won on May 21 9–2, and on the 25th 9–3. On May 28 in Boston he knocked in one of the runs in a 2–1 win. At that point the Sox were 16–16 and in sixth place, though only two games back of the Highlanders, who led with an 18–14 record. The Tigers were in third place, one game out at 17–15.

On Decoration Day, and the next day, the Sox and Tigers played back-to-back double headers, first in Detroit and then in Chicago. Big Ed pitched the last of the four games. He threw strikes at the knees inducing 21 infield outs as this colorful passage in the *Chicago Tribune* by Charles Dryden describes: "Mr. Walsh shut the Tigers out with four safeties spread far apart like the berries in a South Clark street shortcake.

"An idea of how the Tigers did not pester Walsh's spitter may be gleaned from the circumstance that Donahue had twenty-one putouts and Walsh figured in seven assists. That is what might be called keeping the batted ball close to one's place of business."

After Big Ed lost the second game of a double header 2–1 in St. Louis on June 4, the Sox went home for a 17-game homestand against the Eastern teams. They played single games every day for 17 consecutive days from June 6 to June 21 and won 16 of them, including the first 13. On

June 8 Walsh and the Sox beat the A's 10–0 for their sixth straight win on the stand. Moxie Manuel, in one of his 16 appearances on the season, pitched the ninth for Walsh and struck out the side. With that win the Sox went into first place by two percentage points in what was already being called the "Greatest Race Ever" by the scribes, and why not? Three teams were tied for first place at the end of the day and all eight teams were within six and one-half games. The standings looked like this:

Chicago	24	20	.545	
St. Louis	25	21	.543	
Cleveland	25	21	.543	
New York	23	20	.535	.5
Philadelphia	23	22	.511	1.5
Detroit	22	23	.489	2.5
Boston	21	27	.438	5.0
Washington	18	27	.400	6.5

Big Ed beat New York on June 12 5–1, and again on the 16th 3–2, when he struck out eight and walked one and knocked in a run with a sacrifice fly. On the 20th he beat Boston and Cy Young 1–0. It was his 29th appearance of the season and his 16th win. "Cy Young and 'Big Ed' Walsh fought out a remarkable pitching duel on the South Side grounds today, and the White Sox star came in a winner.

"The pitching by the two stars was as near alike as two peas. Each struck out half a dozen batsmen, each passed only one man and neither allowed two hits to come in the same inning."[3]

The next day Manuel beat Boston 7–3 in the last game of the homestand. The 16–1 homestand put the Sox up by two and one-half games over the Naps and the Tigers, who were tied for second, and three over the third place Browns.

With that the Sox got on the train for a six-game trip to Detroit and Cleveland and went straight to baseball hell. They lost all six games, with Big Ed dropping two of them, 6–1 to the Tigers and 4–2 to the Naps, who moved ahead of the Sox into second place and dropped the Sox to third, while the Browns took over first. At the end of the day of the sixth loss on June 28, the Sox headed back home to start an eight-game homestand against the Tigers and Browns. If they cared to look in the newspapers they saw this:

St. Louis Browns	37	25	.603	
Cleveland Naps	36	25	.581	.5
Chicago White Sox	35	27	.556	2.0
Detroit Tigers	33	28	.548	3.5

The Sox could not recapture the home magic as they went 3–5 in the eight games, with Big Ed winning two and losing one. After beating the Browns 5–1 on July 2, he pitched in both games of a July 4 morning-afternoon double header which drew 26,000 for the two games. He pitched the last three innings of the first game, an 8–4 win, struck out four and hit a home run, one of three hit by the White Sox all season. He was hammered in the second game for 10 hits and eight runs in the first three innings. The next day the Tigers came in for a single game and the Tigers' Ed Killian beat Nick Altrock 7–5. The Tigers passed the Sox for third place and the Sox dropped to fourth three and one-half back.

The next day Clarke Griffith resigned as manager of the Yankees and it was rumored that Comiskey was going to make a deal to send George Davis to New York as a player-manager. Comiskey adamantly declared he was going to stand pat with the Sox team as it was. "I have not a single deal for players or an exchange of any players on. I know no more about the Davis proposition than I read in the papers. I'm pretty satisfied with the team as it is. It's too bad we got kicked out of first place, but I am not discouraged for a minute. Anyone who thinks the Sox are on the toboggan has got another think coming."[4]

Having won the pennant in 1906, Comiskey did stand pat with the team. The only change was at third base where George Rohe and Lee Quillen replaced Tannehill. Tannehill, injured most of the season, got in only 49 games.

On July 6 the Sox boarded a train for Washington to start an 18-game road trip against the Eastern teams, but, as Comiskey said, they did not board a toboggan. They went 11-6-1 on the trip. Big Ed was 5–0 in starts but strangely didn't pitch between July 5 and July 10. On July 11 in what was to be the first game of a scheduled double header in Philadelphia, Big Ed was matched with the A's starter Harry Vickers, a Canadian who pitched 317 of his lifetime 458 innings in 1908.

Big Ed blew a 4–2 lead in the bottom of the ninth when the A's scored two. The game went 16 innings and three hours and 17 minutes, timewise a major marathon for the deadball era. Both Big Ed and Vickers went all the way and each walked one batter and struck out nine. Vickers gave up 11 hits and Walsh 15. The Sox scored in the top of the 16th. Jones doubled with one out and went to third on Isbell's ground ball to first. Vickers failed to cover first base and the Sox used the extra out to get the winning run on a sacrifice fly by Dougherty. In the bottom of the 16th the game ended on an unassisted double play by Tannehill, who grabbed a hot liner and beat the A's runner to third. Big Ed had asked Jones before the game to let him pitch both games of the double header, but umpire Connolly called off the second game. On July 15 in the first game of a doubleheader at Philadelphia, Big Ed again defeated Vickers, this time 3–1. On the 18th he beat the Red Sox 7–2. He struck out five, drove in a run with a sacrifice fly, and took a verbal shot from Isbell. "Sullivan and Isbell allowed Cravath's foul to drop between them in the sixth. Isbell called Walsh down for not calling, and then Walsh got angry and fanned Cravath."[5]

In New York Big Ed beat the Highlanders with complete games twice in three days. He won 6–3 in the first game of a double header on the 21st and hit a double and scored a run. He walked one and struck out eight. On the 23rd in the first game of another double header he won 6–2. He struck out seven and hit another double and a sacrifice fly. Manuel won the second game of the double header, the last game of the Eastern swing, 7–3.

The Sox headed home after the double header on the 23rd. Though they did win 11 of 17 on the trip, they lost ground to the Tigers, who followed the Sox through the east and won 14 of 18 to take their turn on top of the A.L.

Standings At Close of Play on July 23, 1908

Detroit Tigers	52	34	0	.605	
St. Louis Browns	50	37	0	.575	2.5
Chicago White Sox	49	38	1	.563	3.5
Cleveland Naps	46	39	0	.541	5.5

The Sox got back to Chicago and opened a 16-game homestand, four games with each of the Eastern teams, on July 25 versus the A's. This stand was not nearly as productive as the earlier 16–1 monster. The Sox had to win the last three of the stand over the Highlanders to get over .500 at 9–7. Big Ed started five of the games and relieved in one. He was 3–2 in the starts. The best of them were a 7–0 shutout of Boston on August 7 and a 2–1 win over the Highlanders on the 10th, when he faced just 29 batters. From the *Trib*'s account of the Boston game: "Big Ed Walsh and his salivated slants put the White Sox back in third place today. The spitball king applied the brakes with reckless abandon, allowing only three hits, and was at no time in distress."

The Sox did pass the Naps for third place during the stand, but lost ground to the Tigers and were five back when they started an 18-game road trip by losing four of seven in Washington and Philadelphia. Walsh got the only win, 5–3 at Washington on the 15th. He drove in two runs himself with a single and scored one. He also pitched in the only other game the Sox didn't lose of the seven when he preserved a 4–4 tie in relief in Washington on the 17th. "White was knocked out of the box in the fifth inning, but Big Ed was unhittable in the gloom of the gathering storm, which necessitated the calling of the game while the locals were at the bat in the eighth inning."[6]

After a 6–5 loss to Plank on the 18th in Philadelphia — when Big Ed walked two batters, hit one, threw a wild pitch and committed a balk — he said his one-year-old son, Bob, was sick and went home to Meriden to be with the boy, promising to rejoin the team in Boston. He did, just in time to save games on successive days. On the 21st he saved an 8–7 win in relief of Smith by striking out the side in the ninth. The next day he relieved White, shut Boston out for three innings and had a hit and run scored in a 6–4 win. After a day's rest he started the last game of the Boston series and won 2–1, knocking in the winning run with a sacrifice fly. The next stop was New York for a pair of double headers on the 29th and 30th. The Sox won 3 of 4. Big Ed won one of the games 2–1. They finished up the road trip in St. Louis by splitting a four-game series. Big Ed split, too, losing the first game 4–0 to Waddell and winning the third 4–1.

The Sox got back to Chicago on September 4 in third place, three back of the Tigers and one-half game back of the second place Naps. The Sox had 33 games left, 21 against the two teams ahead of them, the Tigers and Naps, and 24 at home.

Cleveland came in first for a six-game series including two double headers. White won the first game and Big Ed won the second one 7–0 on September 5 in his 51st appearance of the season. He drove in two runs with a double and a sacrifice fly and struck out eight. The Sox made it three straight in the first game of a double-header the next day when Smith won 7–1. The second game was stopped by darkness after nine, tied 1–1.

The next day Big Ed pitched on a day's rest and lost to Addie Joss 6–0 in the first game of a double header. In the fifth he did something he hated to do: he gave an intentional walk. He gave the pass to Bill Bradley to load the bases and get to the little-known Wilbur Good, a backup outfielder who played in only 46 games that year. Good promptly cleared the bases with a triple. The Naps also won the second game and now the Sox were in second place. They were three back of the Tigers, a half-game ahead of the third place Browns and two and one-half ahead of the Naps in fourth.

The Sox went over to Detroit for a four-game series starting the next day. The first two went extra innings and the Tigers won both by a run. Big Ed pitched the third game and it, too, went extra innings. He went all 11 innings and won 4–2. In the top of the 11th singles by Jones and Isbell, with Dougherty's triple sandwiched between, won it.

After the game the Sox caught a train back to Chicago, where they would play 20 of their last 22 games, starting with a double header with the Naps on the 13th. After the Naps won the first game, Big Ed came back again on a day's rest in the second game for his fifth start in nine days and won 1–0. He held the Naps to five scattered hits, struck out five, didn't walk a batter and knocked in the only run with a sacrifice fly. Only two of the Naps reached second base. For the third time in 1908 Walsh hit a double and a sacrifice fly in the same game. But the Sox dropped the next three games to the Naps, with Big Ed losing the second one 3–0 to Glenn Liebhardt on September 15. Big Ed struck out nine and hit a triple, but was left at third. By winning again the next day, the Naps moved into second place, two behind the Tigers and one and one-half ahead of the Sox in third. Big Ed got two days rest then beat the visiting Nationals and Walter Johnson 1–0 in a game where he tagged out a runner at home and caused a near riot.

"With one gone in the eighth, Ganley got a free ticket. Unglaub singled into short right. Warner went up for Cates, and hit sharply to Walsh. Ganley was run down after a lively skirmish on the lines. Unglaub thought he saw an opening and dashed for home. Walsh got the ball and plunged at him. Bob bumped Ed hard, and sent him on his neck, but he held the ball and the decision was 'out.'

"A riot ensued. Walsh wanted to fight, and threw off his glove. Unglaub was about to apologize for bumping Ed, when Jakey Atz ran up and called Unglaub 279 things, all highly uncomplimentary."[7] Big Ed gave up four hits, walked three and struck out seven.

That was the second of six straight wins for the Sox over Washington and Philadelphia. Big Ed beat the A's 2–0, with a two-hitter with five strikeouts, for the fifth of those wins a day before Smith beat them 3–2 on September 23. At the end of the day the Sox were in second place, but now two behind the Naps, winners of nine straight, and one and one-half games ahead of the Tigers, who slipped to third. The Highlanders came in for two games on the 24th and 25th. Big Ed lost the first one 1–0. The next day, inexplicably, the Sox scored 12 and won for Smith. It was only the fifth time all season they scored over nine runs.

Boston came in next for four games, two single games on the 27th and 28th and a double header on the 29th. Big Ed pitched and won three of the four games, including both games of the double header, allowing a total of one run. He won 3–0 on the 27th in a steady rain. "Rain, which was falling when the game started and continued to drizzle down all through the contest, didn't seem to affect Walsh in the least. It was pouring rain in the ninth and Walsh wound up striking out the last two men, Speaker and Hoey."[8] He struck out eight and walked one.

In the double header Big Ed won 5–1 and 2–0 in his 61st and 62nd games of the season. He pitched all 18 innings, struck out 15, 10 in the first game, and allowed seven hits, three in the first game and four in the second. After Walsh's double header wins the standings looked like this. Note that the Sox had played four tie games which were not made up.

Detroit Tigers	86	61	.585	
Cleveland Naps	86	62	.581	0.5
Chicago	85	62	.578	1.0

So the stage was set for what many baseball historians call the greatest game ever pitched. It happened in Cleveland on October 2. Big Ed, pitching for the fourth time in five of his team's games and in the third straight, faced Addie Joss in Cleveland. The pair of future Hall of Famers padded their Cooperstown credentials that day in the heat of a pennant race. Joss pitched a perfect game. Walsh pitched a one-hitter and struck out 15.

"Chicago's White Sox went down to defeat today in what undoubtedly was the greatest and most sensational battle of pitchers in modern baseball. Between them Addie Joss and Eddie Walsh tied one world's record and broke one season's record and one catcher's finger. Cleveland's star hurler won out, 1 to 0, while Chicago's king of pitchers lost on a cross between a

Addie Jones and Big Ed hooked up many times in memorable pitching duels. The greatest was on October 2, 1908. Joss pitched a perfect game and Big Ed pitched a one-hitter with 16 strikeouts.

passed ball and a wild pitch which will become almost as famous in history as Chesbro's 1904 wild pitch."

Ossie Schreckengost, who caught Walsh that day in one of only six games he played all season, said he never in his life saw anything break the way Walsh's spitball did.

"Considering the fact that it broke one of Ossie's fingers off so cleanly that only the skin kept it from falling off, that spit ball certainly did some record breaking.

"Even before Cleveland scored, the crowd of 10,000 chilled fans realized what was in store for them and began cheering Walsh. Before the game was half over the applause which followed each half inning was almost equal, the home rooters yelling for Walsh almost as hard as for Joss. When Eddie struck out his fifteenth man in the eighth inning the roar which followed was only surpassed by that which tore holes in the atmosphere when Addie retired the twenty-seventh consecutive Sox [sic] in the ninth round."

The Naps scored in the third inning. Birmingham led off with a bloop single. Before he threw a pitch to the next batter, Big Ed wheeled and threw to first and caught Birmingham napping way off first base. Birmingham couldn't get back so he took off for second.

"Issy pegged hurriedly to second and nailed Birmingham squarely on the reverse side of his koko. The ball then bounced off the runner's skull with a resonant whack into left field and without pausing to rub the sore spot Birmingham dashed on to third in safety."

Walsh struck out the next two batters and had two strikes on the third when a pitch got away and Birmingham scored. In the eighth Joss struck out on a wicked spitter which broke Schreckengost's finger. He was replaced by Shaw. The Sox came close to getting a runner on twice. In the third Parent grounded to Perring who threw wildly to first. Stovall dove for the throw and held the bag. Batting for Walsh in the ninth, Joss Anderson grounded to Bradley. "Bradley in his anxiety to throw perfectly pegged badly. At risk of colliding with Anderson Stovall reached far to his left for the throw, caught it but toppled over and fell flat on top of Big John who slid under to duck a collision." It was close but O'Loughlin called him out. Stovall had 16 putouts.[9]

Though Big Ed would pitch a no-hitter of his own in 1911, the 15 strikeout one-hitter opposite the Joss perfect game is often considered the best game he ever pitched. In later years, though, whenever he was asked which was the greatest game he ever pitched, he always said it was the game after the Joss perfect game, a game in which he pitched only 2⅔ innings. Of the 10 batters Big Ed faced in that game on October 3, it was what he did to the second one he faced that made it, in his mind, the greatest game he ever pitched.

In Big Ed's own words from a magazine story over 30 years later: "It was a Saturday and it was said to be the biggest crowd ever in Cleveland to that point. The Sox were leading Cleveland 3–2 in the ninth. Nig Smith the starter got one out in the ninth, but then the Naps loaded the bases on two errors and a walk."

Walsh warmed up hurriedly and was brought in.

"The first batter I faced was Bill Hinchman. Bill wasn't a champion hitter, but he was a tough guy in a pinch. I knew his weakness was a spitball on the inside corner. I told Billy we'd have to get close on him. And I did. Bill got a piece of the ball and hit a fast grounder to Tannehill and we forced Perring at the plate.

"So there were two out and Lajoie at bat. If the Frenchman had a weakness it was a fastball high and right through the middle. If you pitched him inside he'd tear the arm of the third baseman and if you pitched him outside he'd knock down the second baseman. I tried him with a spitball that broke to the inside and down. Lajoie hit the ball hard down the third base line and it traveled so fast that it curved 20 feet, I'd guess, over the foul line and into the bleachers. Strike one.

"My next pitch was a spitter on the outside and Larry tipped it foul. Sully signed for another spitter, but I just stared at him. I never shook him off with a nod or anything like that. He signed for the spitter twice more, but still I just looked at him. Then Billy walked out to the box. 'What's the matter?' Bill asked me. 'I'll give him a fast one,' I said.

"Billy was dubious, but finally agreed. I threw Larry a fastball that rised and he watched it come over without even an offer. 'Strike three,' roared Silk O'Loughlin.

"Lajoie sort of grinned at me and tossed his bat toward the bench without ever a word. That was the high spot of my baseball days, fanning Larry in the clutch and without him swinging."[10]

Like other of Big Ed's memories, this one is a little off. He recalled that he came into the game with one out in the ninth. He didn't. He came into the game with one out in the seventh. After he fanned Lajoie he pitched two more innings. He struck out four batters in all and gave up two hits but no runs as the Sox won 3–2. Meanwhile the first-place Tigers rolled to their 10th straight win, as Wild Bill Donovan shut out the Browns 6–0. After their games both the Sox and Tigers went back to Chicago for a season-ending three-game series which would decide the A.L. pennant. As the first game of the three-game series began, the standings looked like this:

Detroit Tigers	89–61	
Cleveland Naps	88–63	1½
Chicago White Sox	86–63	2½

The Sox, in order to win the A.L. pennant, had to win all three games and hope the Naps lost in St. Louis. For two days things worked out. As Big Ed had pitched 28⅔ innings combined in the Sox' four previous games, Jones gave him the first game of the series off and started Doc White, who beat the Tigers 3–1. In St. Louis the Naps-Browns game ended in a 3–3 tie. The next day the Naps lost the opener of a double header to the Browns and were eliminated. So it was left to the Sox and Tigers to decide things. Big Ed went against the Tigers' 24-game winner Ed Summers. Despite Hughie Jennings' efforts to distract Walsh with his usual grass pulling and signature yells, Walsh struck out nine and gave up one meaningless run as the Sox won 6–1. "Manager Hughey Jennings who alternated from the coaching box at first to that at third was as usual a source of joy for the fans, his first appearance being greeted with a volume of 'Ee Yahs.' Hughey could not resist sampling the grass at both stations and as the tide of battle veered against the Tiger, he was urged to try a little more grass."[11]

It was Walsh's 40th win and the American League pennant race was forced to the final day. Here's how they stood:

| Detroit Tigers | 89–63 | |
| Chicago White Sox | 88–63 | ½ |

Never before had so many fans watched baseball in one city on one day. While some 22,000 saw the White Sox-Tigers game, 30,247, the largest crowd ever at Chicago's West Side Grounds, saw the Cubs beat the Pirates. The Cubs appeared to wrap up their third straight N.L. pennant with that game, but were ordered to play one more game in New York to make up the so-called "Merkel Boner" game. The makeup game was played on October 8 and the Cubs won to clinch.

Fans lined up early in the morning to get into the South Side Grounds for the last Sox-Tigers game on October 6. The gates were opened at noon and by 2 P.M. every available space was filled and the gates were closed. The Tigers had Wild Bill Donovan, 17–7 with 25 complete games in 28 starts, available on two full days rest. As an extra precaution Jennings and trainer Harry Tuthill sat up until four in the morning putting hot towels on Donovan's arm.[12]

Fielder Jones, on the other hand, didn't have a clear choice as starter. White, Smith or Big Ed had started the Sox' 16 previous games and Big

Ed had pitched in 13 of them. Big Ed had no rest, White had one day's rest and Smith two. Jones decided to go with White, a decision Big Ed would second guess for years.

"Fielder Jones pulled one of the few boners of his career by pitching Doc White. Not to say White wasn't a great pitcher. He was all that, but not once that year had White been able to repeat against Detroit and Jones was asking him to repeat. In a way I blame myself more than Jones. I should have pitched that game myself. Had I offered to pitch, I would have pitched. I was overworked and about gone, but if I had decided to pitch, Jones would not have refused me. You see I could ask Jones for permission to pitch, but under the conditions Jones could not order me to pitch."[13]

The 22,000 fans came armed with noise makers of all kinds, but the Tigers silenced them early. White lasted only four batters and all four scored. After Crawford doubled into the roped off crowd and Cobb tripled, Jones brought in Big Ed. For the only time in that '08 stretch he wasn't effective. Though charged with only one run — Cobb scored and was charged to White — Walsh gave up six hits in 3⅔ innings. He was relieved by Smith, who pitched the last 4⅓ and gave up two runs.

For the Tigers Donovan pitched the game of his career considering the stakes. He hurled a two-hit shutout with 10 strikeouts. The Tigers won 7–0 and were A.L. champs again. Unplayed games figured in the race. In those days tied or postponed games which could not be made up during the season were not rescheduled.

In the last 19 days of '08 Big Ed pitched in 10 games, starting eight. He pitched 77 innings and gave up only two earned runs and pitched both ends of a double header winning both. He was the losing pitcher only twice and both were 1–0, including the Joss perfect game.

He led the league in games (66), IP (464), K's (269), complete games (42), saves (6), shutouts (11), and winning percentage (.727). His ERA was 1.42.

Jones said nothing after that final game, but the next spring, in March of 1909, defended himself. "We were up against a tough proposition" Jones said. "A victory meant everything. Walsh never pitched a harder game in his life than on Monday. It was a question whether he could come back, willing worker that he is. So I decided to see how they warmed up, for, with Bill Donovan against us, a run or two either way probably meant victory.

"Walsh did not warm up well. White felt fair. There was still Smith. He might or might not pitch a great game. So, in view of White's work on Sunday, he was sent in with Walsh or Smith in reserve in case he weakened. The Tigers had one of those irresistible batting streaks and White and Walsh both succumbed. All talk about Big Ed's sulking because he was not put in at first was bosh. Frank Smith pitched good ball after the game already was lost. Perhaps it would have been better if he started. I don't know. If we had won the White Sox would have been the best bet, but we didn't. That's one of the chances a manager takes."[14]

Part of the blame for the Sox' failure to win the pennant in 1908 had to go to Smith. During another of his paranoid fantasies about being disrespected, he jumped the team for most of July and missed at least six starts.

10

The Holdout

Ring Lardner's first writing job was covering the White Sox for a Chicago paper. Lardner — who would later gain fame as a fiction writer of such stories as "You Know Me Al," "Haircut," "Some Like Them Cold," "The Golden Honeymoon," and "Alibi Ike" — introduced himself to manager Fielder Jones. Jones said they'd get along fine if he didn't pester him about who was going to pitch the next day. "Anything drives me crazy it's newspaper guys all the time wanting to know who's gonna pitch tomorrow," Fielder said.

"My paper," Lardner said, "will be satisfied if I'm right half the time. I'll just pick Walsh everyday."[1]

It's a funny line and it illustrates how Big Ed was regarded after his monumental season in 1908. Though he got a $3,500 bonus from Comiskey after the season, which may have doubled his salary, Big Ed still thought he was underpaid and while some people agreed with him, some did not. Just how much he was paid at any point during his career with the White Sox cannot be known with certainty. There are reports that he got as much as $10,000 per year beginning around 1908. Other accounts say he never had a salary for a season that was half that, not counting post season bonuses. In 1910 the *Washington Post* said Walter Johnson would sign for $6,000, making him the second highest paid pitcher after Big Ed. In 1916, after Big Ed left the White Sox once and for all as a player, another *Post* article had this to say: "His salary averaged $10,000 for many seasons. Comiskey refused to cut it when Big Ed lost his skill. Comiskey told him he could remain on the club's payroll as long as he lived as a reward for his loyalty. But Walsh prefers to retire to a private life."[2]

Sportswriter Grantland Rice in his Sportlight column disputed that contention. "Dick Kerr, one of the best of the last few years, is still out of the game due to a salary dispute with the White Sox, a ball club noted for never overpaying a player. Ed Walsh was worth $20,000 a year, but we doubt he ever got half that."[3]

In an article in Big Ed's Hall of Fame file, former Hall director Ernest J. Lanigan wrote that Big Ed's salary in 1904, '05, and '06 was $1800. Lanigan claimed Big Ed was paid $3,500 in 1908 and given a $3,500 bonus after the season, but his highest season salary ever was $6,000. In a story after Big Ed's death in 1958, *New York Times* writer Arthur Daley said his top salary was only $3,000.

Big Ed came up in a 1925 story about escalating salaries after Rogers Hornsby signed a three-year deal for $100,000. "There are men in the big leagues whose careers hark back to the days when a $5,000 a year player was a rarity. Charles Murphy of the Cubs, managed by Frank Chance, didn't haggle much over salaries. When his great team was at its peak the annual payroll was $90,000 and that led all the rest by far. 1908 was the high water mark of the now gone Cub machine. Then $5,000 was a record amount. One or two Cubs were paid that much. At the same time Ed Walsh was working for far less, yet no one thought he was underpaid."[4]

To say "no one" thought Big Ed was underpaid wasn't right. Big Ed, for one, thought so and he had allies at the *Washington Post*. In early December in 1908, *Post* writer Ed Grillo said Big Ed was making Comiskey rich. "A pitcher of the Ed Walsh type is invaluable. It was due to his efforts that the White Sox were contenders last season and he individually made Comiskey every cent of the profits his books showed last season."[5]

Big Ed went public with his salary demand on December 22, when he told the *Chicago Tribune* he wanted $6,500 for 1909 and would hold out until he got it. In January the *Post* said he was worth it. "If Comiskey's great right hander had never done anything else he made a record for the 1908 season which is one of the prized memories of baseball," the story gushed. Then it posed a question: "Where would the Sox have finished without the aid of the real iron man? It's safe to say they would have had to do some tremendous fighting just to stay in the first division."

In the story, Nationals manager Joe Cantillon called Big Ed "one of the freaks of baseball" and manager McAleer of the Browns said his men would rather face any other pitcher. Surely, the story concluded, both competitively and at the box office, Big Ed was worth more than the $4,500 to $5,000 Comiskey had paid him in 1908.[6]

Four days later Walter Johnson went public with discontent over his salary in this telegram to the *Post*: "I received my contract several days ago, but I have returned it to Cantillon because the figure named is not what I think it ought to be."

Then the *Post* speculated that Johnson thought he was worth more money because of what Big Ed had done in '08. "Perhaps, too, Johnson realizes that when he reports next spring it will be for a hard season's work, for Cantillon intends to use him as often as the White Sox do Big Ed Walsh."[7]

Comiskey said nothing publicly about the holdout and Big Ed wasn't heard from again until January 22 when it was announced he was joining the Yale University baseball staff as pitching coach. He said nothing about the White Sox except that he didn't intend to quit. A day later the *Boston Globe* reported that Big Ed told the paper "it will take about $6500 to induce him to play with the White Sox this season." The story concluded that "Comiskey will doubtless have to come across with the money or lose his chief star."

But even as he reported to Yale, Big Ed wasn't hinting that he would sit out the season, which was his only option other than signing with the Sox on Comiskey's terms. At Yale in late January he told the *New York Times* that he didn't expect to be with the Elis beyond April 1. It was noted that Yale's chief rival, Harvard, also had a pitching coach that winter from Pennsylvania hard coal country, Christy Mathewson.

When Comiskey hadn't responded, publicly or privately, to Big Ed by February 3, Big Ed upped the ante and went on the offensive. In an interview with the *Washington Post* on the Yale campus in New Haven he said, "Make it as strong as you please and as stiff as you like that I don't sign with Chicago again unless I get $7500. I think the people of Chicago feel I earned a much bigger salary last season than I received. I think that they feel I am worth to the nine all that I ask."[8]

Will Cohen, another *Post* writer, wasn't buying Big Ed's threats and said so in a poem he called "But don't you believe him."

> Same old story, same old stuff,
> Each year you hear the same old bluff:
> Ball players cry, "I'll not play at all,"
> But in the spring they all play ball so don't you believe them.
> Christy Mathewson has quit the biz,
> He'll pitch again, no, gee whiz!
> For writing policies he's undertaken,
> And baseball has forever shaken —
> But don't you believe him.

> Writes Frank Chance, the Chicago player,
> Who this winter has been a layer:
> "I'll not play ball this year because
> Murphy won't let me be the boss"—
> But don't you believe him.
> Big Ed Walsh, of spitball fame,
> Claims he's no longer in the game
> With the fleet White Sox will be
> Unless Comiskey raises his salary—
> But don't you believe him.[9]

The poem went on for 10 more stanzas, two of them about Evers and Chesbro who were also threatening not to play in 1909.

Around this time, Yale head coach Tad Jones suddenly and unexpectedly resigned and it was speculated that Walsh might take a permanent job at Yale and leave the Sox. Yale wanted a professional coach for the entire season. But Big Ed denied it. "I have no disagreement with Comiskey except over salary. I shall insist on the terms named. Comiskey has not written me since I sent him $7500 as my terms. I expect these will be accepted and that I will be joining the White Sox in time to pitch the opening game if needed. Until then I expect to coach Yale, but no longer."[10]

Big Ed remained out of touch. When the team left for California on February 26 Comiskey didn't even mention his name. Big Ed was represented by his older brother Martin Walsh. Martin said he wouldn't venture a guess as to whether or not Ed would come back, but hinted his brother was stubborn and usually stuck to whatever he said.

In late March Big Ed was still with Yale and sticking to his $7,500 demand. A story in the *Washington Post* subtitled "Is He Worth This Amount?" discussed the issue. While admitting that Walsh meant several times $7,500 to the owner of the White Sox in '08, the story didn't conclude that Walsh was necessarily worth $7,500. From the story: "A big league club owner could very easily explain why he would have to turn down a demand for a salary of $7,500, or $8,000, in the case of Mike Dolin.

"In the first place it would wreck the ball club, for every other player would go on strike in a holy minute. One player has to be paid in proportion to what his teammates get. By paying men like Walsh, Lajoie, Cobb and Donlin in proportion to the amount of money they draw through the gates, the salary list of any ball club would soon be way above any reasonable limit and the club owner wouldn't be able to get a return on the money invested; in fact, he would go broke."

10. The Holdout

The story went on to say the average major league salary was about $3,200 and that the public was on the side of the magnates, as the owners were called.

"There have been so many phony holdouts, retirements and threats to jump to outlaw leagues by players who never intended to do anything but jump right into the band wagon, that the dear old public has switched its sympathies to the owners, who have out grown the position of slave owners and barterers in human chattels."[11]

As the *Post* was widely circulated and respected this couldn't have helped Big Ed, especially given the quote of Joe Tinker of the crosstown Cubs. "When I think of the way I used to work as a lather for $18 a week before I became a professional ball player I have to stop and shake hands with myself for my luck in being able to draw major league money. I couldn't earn the money the Chicago club pays me doing anything else. Being paid a good salary for doing the pleasantest task on earth is what I call a pretty fine arrangement."

Big Ed wanted to believe that the fans were on his side. The fans did love his work ethic and knew the Sox couldn't win without him. On the other hand Big Ed's salary demand was 10 times the average salary of an American worker in 1908, when most industrial workers worked a 10 to 12 hour day in unsafe conditions and there were no paid holidays or vacations. And this was happening at a time when baseball was only 40 years removed from a time when it was considered crass behavior to accept money to play. It didn't help Big Ed that while Comiskey was considered a tightwad when it came to players' salaries, he was also considered a fans' owner. It was many years before he gave into a modern system of bookkeeping. "That's not what the fans want," he said in a magazine article. "They want seats and good ball games. I never saw a popular auditor."

In the early years Comiskey operated the Sox without a bookkeeper. "The day's receipts were tossed in a leather suitcase. Settlement was made with the visiting club by check. Commy took what money he needed for his personal expenses until the next day's receipts. Charles Fredericks, a nephew who acted as secretary and treasurer, did likewise. Then the contents of the suitcase were deposited in the bank. Fixed charges and salaries were paid. The balance remaining in the bank at the end of the season represented the profits for the year."

When Comiskey spent $750,000 of his own money to build a concrete and steel park in 1911, it was suggested he could cut down the number of 25 cent seats and add 50 and 75 cent seats. He wouldn't do it. He said, "Those bleacherites made this big new plant possible. Never while I am living will their space be cut down. The fellow who can pay only 25 cents to see a ball game always will be just as welcome at Comiskey Park as the box seats holder."

When it rained he opened the gates and let the bleacher fans enter the sheltered higher price sections for free. It was said he sat among the fans rather than in his private box. He was also popular with newspaper writers. Comiskey was never too busy to treat a cub reporter with the same courtesy as a seasoned veteran. A saying among the writers: "Print it first, then ask Comiskey to confirm it. If you don't he will tip off the other papers."

He let the field be used for amateur and benefit games more than any other field in the country. "How can I help it. Either they are my friends or it's for some worthy charity."

Once he let the field be used for an experimental game called auto polo. Two cars raced around the field with a driver and a mallet man. He charged no rent and had to shell out $400 to repair the damage done to the field. While Comiskey was tight when it came to players' salaries, a fact that helped create the 1919 Black Sox, in other ways he was free with his money. He paid for lavish post season hunting trips for 30 to 40 men. In 1914 he took the White Sox on a world tour and paid $30,000 for Sox expenses. In 1906 he threw $15,000 into the Sox World's Series winnings. He gave Walsh that $3,500 bonus after the 1908 season and another $3,000 for his sons' educations a few years later. Even at that he undervalued Big Ed considering he made much of his fortune during Big Ed's heyday. But there is evidence that Comiskey was furious with Big Ed over the 1909 holdout more because he went public with his demand and hired a lawyer than over the demand for the $7,500 itself.

"So Walsh has a lawyer, now, has he. He didn't need a lawyer during the three years I was paying him to sit on the bench and learn something about pitching." Comiskey shut down all communication with Big Ed and the lawyer. "We'll get along fine without Walsh," Comiskey said publicly.[12]

On April 1 the Yale baseball team went to Washington, D.C., to play Georgetown, but Big Ed was not with them. He had been fired over a disagreement with head coach Billy Lush, who would not explain what happened. In Chicago Comiskey maintained his hard line. "I have not written Walsh and will open no communication with him, as I'm through with him. We have a splendid string of pitchers and Walsh's return would make it harder to choose among them. Walsh has been treated pretty good by the White Sox and he has forgotten the years we carried him along on the

10. The Holdout

payroll at a comfortable salary just to sit on the bench and learn how to pitch which is why everyone else thought it was a joke to carry him. He was paid well for all the grand work he did for us last year in addition to his salary, but somebody is giving him some bad advice and if he wants to take it he has only himself to blame."

Walsh wasn't Comiskey's only personnel headache that spring. Fielder Jones had quit after the 1908 season and moved to Portland, Oregon, where his brother ran the family's engineering business and where the Jones family also owned a walnut company and timber and oil rights in eastern Oregon and other states. Comiskey sent an envoy to Portland to try to convince Jones to come back to the Sox. Jones said only one thing could lure him back and it was the one thing Comiskey couldn't countenance — part ownership of the team. Still Commy held out hope that Jones would return, and started spring training without a manager. It wasn't until April 12, two days before the season, that Commy gave up on Jones and named Billy Sullivan manager. Comiskey had heard nothing from Big Ed "and could not care if he had heard less."[13] Also on the 12th Comiskey sold Big Ed's brother Martin to Pueblo, Colorado, in the Western League. Big Ed fought back by hiring his friend and lawyer from Meriden, Cornelius Danaher, to petition the National Commission to declare him a free agent on the grounds that Comiskey did not send him a contract for the season within the time specified by baseball law. Big Ed said he got it on March 2. The commission's rules said contracts should be sent on or before March 1. He also said his request for $7,500 was met by an offer lower than last season.

Comiskey: "We sent Walsh his contract as the rules require and in proper form some days before starting for California, so he has nothing to stand on to make his claims. He can hire all the lawyers he chooses. I am not worrying over him and he can do as he pleases. He is getting a lot of bad advice and when he has left all that foolishness behind him he will come back to the team a wiser and better pitcher." Big Ed missed one payday on April 21, but it was speculated that his legal advisor covered it.[14]

On April 21 Cap Anson, then 56 and playing first base and barnstorming with his semipro Anson's Colts, made a symbolic gesture in support of Big Ed. As the Colts' train passed through Plains, Pennsylvania, where Big Ed was born, Anson stopped the train and took off his cap. "He said the tribute of uncovering was because he believes Walsh is the king pitcher of them all."[15]

In April the Naps offered three pitchers — Glenn Liebhardt, 15–16 with a 2.20 ERA in 1908; Henie Berger, 13–8, 2.12; and Cy Falkenberg, 6–2, 1.96 — for Big Ed. It would take three pitchers to replace him. Combined, the three had pitched only 79 innings more in '08 than Big Ed had. Comiskey denied rumors that there was a trade in the works.

Two weeks into the season, with Big Ed and Comiskey still at an impasse, the *Chicago Tribune* speculated that Comiskey was taking a financial hit far greater than the $7,500 Big Ed was demanding. "Walsh's absence has cost the club a fortune and the season is not two weeks old. If he stays out the whole season the club will have lost more than Walsh's weight in gold. It seems rather poor business to refuse to come to terms with the best pitcher in the country today, when the team's standing as well as financial success depends on his work. All because Walsh declared his intention to demand $7500 in a newspaper before telling Comiskey."[16] The *Trib* was right. In the end the Sox attendance fell by 158,000 in 1909 to 478,400, 153,000 less than the Cubs drew.

Meanwhile nothing was heard from Big Ed, who was back home in Meriden, though one report said he was distraught and having trouble sleeping. Then on April 29 came the news that the men had reached an agreement. Big Ed wired Comiskey that he was leaving Meriden for Chicago and Comiskey said his salary would be adjusted. The report of an agreement was premature. Big Ed did go to Chicago, arriving on April 30. The next day he met privately with Comiskey, but the men came out of the meeting saying they didn't have a deal after all. Big Ed denied a lawyer caused the holdout. "I haven't been taking the advice of anyone but myself," he said. "The Meriden and New Haven correspondents have been busy with stuff about me and it was mostly stuff. I haven't said a word about staying away since February when I wrote President Comiskey telling him what I wanted."[17]

Big Ed and Comiskey went at it again the next day, May 2. They talked all morning. They came out of the meeting and said nothing to reporters. Big Ed went down to the field where the Sox were getting ready for a game that day with the Tigers. He went to Manager Sullivan on the field before the game and said he was ready "to get in the wagon." Sullivan produced a contract and Walsh signed. Comiskey came by and signed it separately. The signatures were reproduced in the *Tribune*. Everyone agreed that Big Ed got a raise, but how much? There were conflicting reports. H.W. Lanigan, the sporting editor of the *St. Louis Times,* said Comiskey's offer was $4,500.[18] But the figure was kept a profound secret, though Walsh appeared happy. The *Tribune* said he "was like a cheerful kid once the deal was signed."

Big Ed wasn't allowed to play right away. Because he had reported late he had to apply to Ban Johnson for reinstatement and pay a $100 fine.

10. The Holdout

That took another couple of days. On May 4 Big Ed officially joined the White Sox for 1909. Over 70 years later, Newark sportswriter Howard Roth said that as an old man Big Ed told him that he asked Comiskey for $10,000 in 1909 and Comiskey threw him out of the office and threatened to blacklist him for life and that in the end he settled for $4,600, a $2,000 raise. This story appeared in the *New York Times* on July 27 in 1981 during a players strike. Other things in the story call its credibility into question. The story says Big Ed pitched three complete games in the 1908 City Series. There was no city series in 1908 as the Cubs were in the World's Series. The story says Big Ed was living in Pennsylvania and working as a night watchman in the 1950s. He lived in Connecticut all of his adult life after getting married in 1904. He moved to Florida just a year before he died.

At whatever price, Big Ed was prepared to pitch on May 5, but a wire from home with news of a tragedy put his debut on hold. The wire said his younger brother David had been seriously injured in a mine accident and was near death. The *Washington Post* reported David was killed. A local Wilkes-Barre paper had the real story. "David Walsh, a mule driver boss, was hit by a trip of runaway rail cars at the Henry Colliery of the Lehigh Valley Coal Company in his hometown of Plains. He and mine foreman O'Malley were together as the trip approached, the latter jumped just in time to save himself. Flying coal from the cars is thought to have caused the injuries to Walsh. O'Malley went to his aid and he was unconscious. His condition is critical and it is feared he may not recover."[19]

Big Ed caught the first train east. He stayed at his brother's home in Plains two days, but when David didn't regain consciousness, Big Ed went back to Chicago. He arrived the morning of May 9 and made his first start of the season that day in the first game of a double header. He was given a loud reception when he took the slab to start the game. He was a little wild by his usual standards. He walked four and hit a batter, but he beat Cleveland and 42-year-old Cy Young 4–2. In the second he struck out Young with the bases loaded and two outs. He struck out five and gave up four hits. As a batter he had two hits and even stole a base. Ring Lardner wrote in the *Trib*: "He proved he was worth at least what he got last season, what ever that may have been." The win evened the Sox record at 9–9.

On May 11 the Sox beat Washington and went over .500 11–10. Between the 5th and 19th they lost six in a row to fall to 11–16. They didn't get back to .500 until July 31 when Burns and Smith beat Washington in a double header. At that point they were in fifth place 12½ out. They never got any closer.

A more mature Big Ed, probably about 1909 when he was 27. He held out for $6500 and didn't pitch until May.

A few days after that first start Big Ed got a sore throat. It rapidly grew worse and he was sent to bed with suspected tonsillitis. Reports said he fought it off and by the 15th "he was able to sit up and take copious nourishment."[20] On the 17th he got his second start of the season and pitched all 13 innings in a 1–0 loss to Jack Coombs and the A's. Each pitcher gave up just six hits and each walked just two. Big Ed had three strikeouts. For nine innings from the second to the 11th he allowed only two base runners, on a hit and a walk. In the 12th he hit a double but was thrown out trying to go to third by Collins on a ground ball to second. The A's won it on doubles by Davis and Ira Thomas in the 13th.

The next morning Big Ed went back to Plains to be with his family at his brother's bedside. He stayed for a week, but David lingered on in a coma. Back in Chicago on the 24th he was given a start versus the Highlanders. He hadn't seen a baseball in a week, but he beat the Highlanders 7–3. As a batter he hit a triple that hit the fence in left center on a line and broke one of the fence boards. Sullivan scored on the play, was knocked unconscious, but was all right.

On June 1 Big Ed was back in Plains for his brother's wake and funeral. The local newspaper called David one of the best amateur baseball players in the area and said the cause of death was a fractured skull. He was survived by a wife and five children — the oldest was 12 — two sisters, and six brothers including "Brother Edward (Duck) the famous pitcher with the Chicago American baseball team and Martin a pitcher with the Pueblo, Colorado baseball team."

After the funeral Big Ed caught up with the White Sox in Washington on June 7. On June 10 in New York he threw a second straight shutout, beating the Highlanders 1–0. On June 16 in Boston he pitched the eighth and ninth innings. Sullivan came back with Big Ed on two days rest in the third game of the New York series, but it didn't work. He was pulled in the fourth in a 7–5 loss. On the 16th in Boston he pitched the eighth and ninth innings in a 6–4 win. The game was an unremarkable one in an unremarkable season, except for four words that appeared in a story about the game. It was written that Walsh pitched "despite a lame arm." That was the first reference to arm trouble for Walsh, but it would be far from the last. More bad news on June 23: Big Ed's brother Martin was released "on account of wildness" by Danville of the Virginia League, which had bought him from Pueblo.

In 1909 Big Ed pitched in fewer than half as many games, 31, and almost exactly half as many innings, 230⅓, as he had in 1908. He was 15–11 with a 1.41 ERA and a league-leading eight shutouts. It was a disastrous season for the Sox. After four seasons from 1905 to 1908 when they played .600 ball and finished first once — and one and one-half, two, and five and one-half games out the other three seasons — they finished in fourth place 78–74 and 20 games behind Jennings' Tigers, who won their third consecutive A.L. pennant. The Sox were getting old and their run as A.L. contenders, at least during the Walsh era, was over.

The team had started to unravel when Fielder Jones quit. Frank Isbell, 35, also retired after '08. George Davis was 39 and was replaced by Freddy Parent. Nick Altrock and Jiggs Donahue were traded to Washington in May of '09. Donahue never played again after '09 and within four years was dead from venereal disease. Tannehill was only 29 in '09 but his skills were diminishing. He wasn't nearly the player he was when he led A.L. third basemen in assists and double plays for three seasons. Hahn, 34, had his role reduced to part time. Doc White was 30 in 1909. He hung around until '13, but '08 was his last great year. Nig Smith had the best season of his career in '09, leading the league in complete games and strikeouts and winning 27, but at 31 it was his last good season. He was traded away in 1910.

Despite the team's failure, there were some memorable games and happenings during the second half of the 1909 season. On July 2 the White Sox stole 12 bases in the 15–3 win over St. Louis, including three steals of home in the 6th inning, a major league record. Big Ed got one of the steals of home. On July 29 N.L. president Henry Pulliam shot himself in his New York City office. He died the next day. August 2, the day of his funeral, was declared a day of mourning and no games were played. The Sox were in Philadelphia and Big Ed's wife and youngest son were with him. They went to Atlantic City for the day with some of the other players. The boy got sick. A doctor said it was from too much hotel food. Rosemary took the boy home to Meriden.

On July 15 Big Ed beat the Highlanders 3–1. He wouldn't pitch again for a month because of a sore shoulder which was destined to become the most famous, and most denied, sore shoulder in America in the years ahead. When Big Ed came back and pitched again on August 14 the opponent was again New York, which was now being called the Yankees. Big Ed pitched a six-hitter and won 4–3. As a batter he hit a ball described by Lardner as the longest single ever. "It would have cleared the bleachers and most fences in the league, had it not struck the top of a sign board on top of the left field fence. It bounded so far back into the field Walsh had to stop at first." [21]

The next day George Davis, who had been injured most of the season, played shortstop. It was only his 28th game of the season and, coming eight days before his 39th birthday, it would prove to be the last of his career.

On August 28 Big Ed had a no-hitter going through six and finished with a three-hitter to beat Walter Johnson 1–0. He walked two and struck out six. On September 1 he made the shortest start of his career versus Philadelphia — three pitches. He threw two balls and a strike to A's lead off batter Heitmuller and strained something in his rib cage. On September 13 he hooked up in another beauty with Addie Joss and the Naps. It was his best game of the season. He won 2–0, pitching a three-hitter with seven strikeouts and two walks and knocking in both runs with a two-run single in the fifth.

The next day in a rain-soaked game the Sox were losing 4–0 with two outs and the bases loaded in the third inning. Pat Dougherty was batting with a 3–1 count. He hit a ball over first base, which was called foul by umpire Bull Perrine. Dougherty argued the call and was tossed from the game. Sullivan sent Big Ed up to pinch-hit. With the 3–2 count and two outs, he hit the first pitch to center. The ball hopped by center fielder Elmer Flick. Three runs scored and Big Ed landed on third, from where he scored the tying run on an infield single by Altzinger. Big Ed played the last three innings in left field until the game was halted by rain in the sixth. No balls were hit to left field during the last three innings. Lardner, writing in the *Trib*, knew why. "The Naps showed their respect for him by refusing to hit in that direction."[22]

Just a day later in Boston Big Ed came in to close a game with one out and two runners on in the ninth. He struck out Jake Stahl — who had a single, double and triple — to end the game. The next day he started and pitched a six-hit shutout in a 7–0 win.

The City Series resumed after the 1909 season after having been interrupted by the World's Series for two years. Big Ed started and completed three of the five games, but the Cubs won, 4 games to 1. When the Cubs beat Big Ed 4–0 in the first game, they made no secret of the fact that they considered the win revenge for what Walsh had done to them in the '06 World's Series. "Chance's men bit off large and juicy portions of sweet revenge," Lardner wrote. Orval Overall threw a five-hitter with five strikeouts for the Cubs. Mordecai Brown beat Frank Smith 5–2 in the second game at West Side Grounds the next day. The third game was played in the rain. Big Ed was brilliant. Winning 2–1, he gave up the run in the first inning. He retired 15 consecutive batters from two out in the fifth through two out in the ninth. He beat Ed Reulbach, who balked in the winning run brushing a raindrop off his nose in the ninth inning with the bases loaded.

The fourth game was postponed for three days, so when the series resumed, in weather no better than it had been during the postponed days,

Sullivan came back with Big Ed. It was another 2–1 game, but a loss to Overall. Only 9,000 paid due to the weather. In the fifth game on the 15th Brown hurled a one-hitter to end the series, beating White 1–0. The announced attendance was only 3,142, the weather described as raw and gloomy without a ray of sunshine. Total attendance for the series was 74,512. Each Cub took home $717.32. The Sox got $455.44.

Meanwhile the World's Series between the Tigers and Pirates was being called the greatest postseason ever. It was the first to go the limit, seven games. It broke records for attendance, receipts, and payouts to players. There was also a series between the Boston Red Sox and New York Giants. Combined, all three post season series drew one-quarter million fans and grossed over one-quarter million dollars, more than any 17 games in any 10-day period ever. The players of the six teams made over $100,000 and the club owners made $125,000.

11

Big Ed Opens Comiskey Park

The 1910 A.L. baseball season was notable as the first one started by a president of the United States. William Howard Taft became the first U.S. president to throw out the ceremonial first pitch on April 14 at Washington's League Park. The Senators' Walter Johnson pitched a little better than the president. He hurled a one-hitter and beat the Philadelphia Athletics and Eddie Plank 3–0. The 1910 season was also a notable one for the White Sox, not for how they played on the field, but for the field they played on. The Sox finished 1910 68–85 in sixth place 35 games behind the pennant winning A's, but opened their spanking new, concrete-and-steel, three-quarter-million-dollar ballpark, Comiskey Park, on July 1.

Back in March Big Ed had hopes for a much better season than 1909. He was one of the first to report in 1910. He got to Chicago on February 23. He was described as "bigger and pinker than ever" and said he expected to pitch enough, and well enough, to make up for what he missed in 1909. He claimed that missing spring training and the beginning of the '09 season had hurt his arm. "He tried to pitch before he was ready for work, with the result of a lame arm, which clung to him the better part of the season."[1]

Two days later 36 players and a total party of 68 were on the train when it left Rock Island Station for California. Big Ed made his first game appearance of the spring in Los Angeles against the local team on March 19. He faced six batters and struck out three. The locals were impressed. "He made such an impression on J.W. Brooks in two innings that the Vernon director wanted to give Comiskey $25,000 for him, but Comiskey merely smiled. The three that struck out missed the ball by several feet every time they swung at it. Walsh throws the ball 243 miles an hour."[2]

Big Ed pitched his last exhibition in Kansas City on April 10. He pitched seven innings, then left for Chicago to have his back examined, saying he felt there was a tendon or something loose. Though Big Ed described his injury as being in his back, it was likely the back of his shoulder that was bothering him

By opening day the dismantling of the 1906 world championship team was all but complete. The only players left from that team were Walsh, Smith, White, Sullivan, Tannehill, Dougherty and Hahn. Of those only Dougherty was a full-time starter in '10 and Tannehill was the only position player to play in more than 60 games. Instead the Sox lineups in 1910 were peppered with largely unknown and easily forgettable players like rookie first baseman Chick Gandil, who batted .193; Rollie Zeider, who batted .217 as the everyday second baseman; William Billy Purtell, who hit .223 in 102 games at third; Russell "Lena" Blackburne, who batted .174 platooning at shortstop with Tannehill; and outfielder John "Shano" Collins, who batted .197 in 97 games. Not even Comiskey's new manager, the already legendary Hugh Duffy, who batted .440 for the Boston Nationals in 1894, could save this crew.

The day President Taft threw out the first pitch in D.C., Big Ed started the Sox' opener in Chicago versus the Browns. He lasted 5⅔ and gave up eight hits, but was hurt by six errors in a 5–4 loss. On April 20 Addie Joss threw another no-hitter at the Sox, this time beating Doc White 1–0.

In Big Ed's second start on the 21st in St. Louis, the Sox got a run in the first and for seven innings Big Ed made it hold up. Showing his old form he twice struck out two batters in a row with the potential tying run at second. In the seventh first baseman Gandil made a throwing error trying to get the ball to Big Ed covering first, and shortstop Blackburne booted a cinch double play. The Browns scored four in the inning and won 4–1. Walsh struck out seven and gave up five hits. Big Ed's hard luck continued as he fell to 0–3 in Cleveland with a 3–2 loss on April 27. He had three hits as a batter, half the Sox' total and only two fewer than the Naps. In the sixth the Naps scored a run on three strikeouts. Graney struck out, Kruger struck out but reached on a passed ball and stole second. Turner then struck out but Krueger stole third and scored on a wild throw to third. These games were more typical than odd during Big Ed's starts in 1910.

11. Big Ed Opens Comiskey Park

On April 29 in the *Chicago Tribune,* in the "In the Wake of the News" column, the writer who called himself Hek set Walsh's plight to poetry.

> You can see the curl on Ed Walsh's lip,
> The frown on Ed Walsh's brow.
> As he poses with hand upon hip
> With the wilt of a pensive cow.
> You can see him look with mute appeal
> That should get to the heart of stone,
> As much to say "It's a rotten deal;
> I can't win it all alone."[3]

On May 1 in Chicago Big Ed pitched a game reminiscent of his iron man years of 1907 and '08. He took a 3–1 lead into the ninth, but Cobb beat out an infield hit, Hahn dropped an easy fly ball and Blackburne booted two balls at short and Detroit tied it. The game went 15 innings before the Sox won 4–3. Big Ed pitched all 15. He struck out 13, Cobb twice, and walked only one. That performance again moved Hek to poetry:

> G____S
> The quality that Ed Walsh showed in that nerve shredding game —
> What is the word you would like to use in bestowing on it a name?
> 'Tis a short and homely common noun that takes the place of all
> The euphemistic terms applied to liver, and heart, and gall,
> And all the inner human works that make up the grand machine —
> It shoots them all with a single breath both forcibly and lean.
> "Sand?" That doesn't do at all; it's a painfully poor excuse
> For the virile term that's on every tongue, but is barred from printed use.[4]

Thanks to Big Ed's "guts" the Sox were 5–5. It was the last time they would be at .500 all season. They won only five of their next 21 games and by May 29 they were in seventh place with twice as many losses as wins at 10–20. It wouldn't get much better.

On May 14 Big Ed lost 4–3 in 11 in Philadelphia. On May 18 with Halley's Comet clearly visible in the daylight sky, he lost the fourth game of the series in Philadelphia 4–2. He struck out six. May 22 the Sox played an exhibition in Providence. The whole team went, except Big Ed. He went home to Meriden for a day, then went to Boston and pitched still another extra inning complete game which ended 4–3. This time he was a winner. He struck out 11. He took matters into his own hands with a bat. He scored a run in the third after hitting a triple, and knocked in the winning run with a sharp single to center in the 15th. After the game he went back home to Meriden and met the team in New York on May 25.

As the team collapsed around him, Big Ed kept battling. At home against Boston on June 1 he pitched a one-hitter and won 1–0. He faced just two over the minimum, hitting one batter. He struck out five, Speaker twice, and only four balls were hit to the outfield. The rest of the outs were ground outs, including seven hit back to Big Ed. On June 15 he pitched still another extra inning complete game that ended 4–3. This one was a win against the A's in Chicago. He struck out six, walked one, gave up eight hits, and would have won in nine but for second baseman Zeider, who was charged with five errors. Big Ed was 2 for 5 batting. He doubled and scored in regulation and in the 14th knocked in the winning run with a base hit to left. On June 19 he pitched a two-hitter and beat Eddie Plank and the A's 4–2 in Chicago. He struck out six, walked two, had a hit and scored a run. On June 22 he pitched still another complete extra inning game, losing to the Naps' rookie pitcher, Fred Harkness, 3–2. Big Ed took a 2–1 lead into the ninth, but an error by Blackburne led to the tying run. He struck out six and walked two. Lord knocked in the winning run with a fly ball off the right field wall as it was getting dark.

On July 1 Comiskey Park opened at 35th Street and Shields Avenue. Though ground was broken in February, work didn't start until March. The park was built in four months, including five weeks of stoppage by a steel workers' strike. Automobile owners of the city led a monster parade to the park. There were 12 ticket windows and 14 turnstiles at the corner of Thirty-Fifth and Shields leading to the pavilion and grandstand where seats were $1.75 and 50 cents. Box seat holders had their own entrances. Mrs. John Edwards had the honor of being the first woman to pass through the gates for a seat in the grandstand. Miss Alice Cann was the first female holder of a box coupon, no. 23. Mrs. Comiskey had the front third base box with several guests. Gerry Hermann, chairman of the National Commission and president of the Cincinnati ball club, was host to a party of 40. The presidents of the St. Louis Browns, St. Louis Cardinals, Pittsburgh Pirates, and Chicago Cubs were there. So was Ben Shibe, president of the Philadelphia A's, who built the first concrete and steel park. Cap Anson had a box in the second deck. The old flagstaff was moved to the new park and painted white. Four military bands played and thousands of soldiers under the command of General Frederick Dent Grant stood at attention as the flag was raised.

From a story in the *Chicago Tribune*:

> One of the perfections of the new plant is that there is not a seat of any denomination from which a clear view of the field cannot be obtained. This is due to architect Davis. He had the advantage of inspecting all the other

baseball plants of the kind before completing his plans for the Sox park and was able to obtain the exact pitch and elevation required to give the last row in any part of any stand as clear a view of the proceedings as can be had from anywhere else.

The cantilever form of construction eliminated all obstructions except a single row of uprights halfway between the front and rear of the stands and these steel uprights carry their tremendous load without seriously obstructing the view from anywhere behind.

It was said that the size of the enclosed grandstands dwarfed the field making it look smaller than what it actually was — the biggest playing field in the Major Leagues. Attendance was over 28,000, not all of whom were happy. Comiskey received complaints that patrons at the opening game were charged 10 cents for pop. Comiskey said he would give a season's pass as a reward to any patron who reported future attempts by peddlers to bilk the public.

That night there was a party at the Chicago Automobile Club, where 150 guests "drank toasts to the Old Roman's continued good health and prosperity." A.L. president Ban Johnson was the toastmaster. After it ended Comiskey ordered that all leftover food from the banquet be sent to the Newsboys' Home with his best wishes. Oh yes, there was a game. Big Ed, of course, pitched it and lost 2–0 to Pelty and the Browns. He struck out six and walked one.[5] Though the fans went on calling the new park the South Side Grounds, its name was Comiskey Park. Its subtitle might have been "The House that Walsh Built."

After the park opening Big Ed, with Duffy's blessing, left the team and went home to Meriden, promising to meet the team in New York on July 7. He was a day late. On July 9 in New York he pitched the ninth inning of the first game of a double header which the Sox won 5–2. He started the second game and, as was becoming a habit, pitched a complete extra inning game. He lost 3–2 in 11. He allowed just seven hits and struck out five but walked five and hit a batter. It was the start of an 11-game losing streak for the Sox. July 10 was a day off. Most of the players went to beaches and Walsh went back to Meriden to be with his wife and young sons.

After Boston beat Big Ed 5–1 on July 13, a cartoon in the *Globe* showed Walsh as a giant scarecrow. Two Boston players with bats stood looking at him, one saying, "He doesn't look so fierce when you get used to him." After the Boston series the Sox went to New York where Big Ed got in trouble for accusing the Yankees of stealing signs. Frank Farrell, owner and president of New York, asked President Johnson to require that

Big Ed prove his charge or be punished for the accusation. Big Ed chose the former. A few days later a member of the Sox anonymously said, "Five members of the White Sox and one Red Sox stand ready to make affidavit in regard to what they know of the signal work. The first indication we had was when Lee Tannehill saw something moving to and fro on one of the signs in center field. The next day Ed Walsh with the aide of a pair of strong field glasses could plainly see the slides in the signboard move as each rival batter came to bat."

The alleged statement by Big Ed was that the signaling device was a panel four by two inches 700 feet from home plate. Farrell said the Highlanders would ruin their eyesight even trying to find a panel at that distance. Johnson investigated and on July 23 said he could not find evidence of the signal stealing nor could he find evidence that Ed Walsh had accused the Yankees. Still, he offered a $500 reward to anyone who could prove sign stealing was going on. On the 26th Farrell added $1000 to Johnson's reward pot. On the 30th Johnson, still insisting there was nothing to the signal-tipping plot, called Duffy to his office. Johnson said if he wasn't satisfied with Duffy's statements he would call Ed Walsh. He never did and the matter dropped.[6]

On July 21 in Philadelphia Big Ed stopped the team's 11-game losing streak and the team ended a 32-inning scoreless streak when they scored three in the eighth to win 3–2. Big Ed gave up six hits including a strange homer to Berry. The ball went through the fence slats. The Sox were 32–48 and in seventh place ahead of only the Browns.

In Washington on the 25th Big Ed beat the Nationals 4–2 thanks to a goat home run as described by Ring Lardner. "Dougherty started off with a single. Mullen laid down a nice sacrifice then came Purtell's goat home run. Bill hit one down the left foul line and the ball disappeared. Mr. Perrine and some of the athletes rushed to the scene to collect evidence and it was discovered the sphere had struck the spinal column of a pet goat grazing in that pasture and caromed into the stand."

The Sox got home on July 29. They had been on the road since July 6 and lost 16 of 21 games in six cities. Big Ed pitched the opener of the homestand on two days rest against Summers and the Tigers, losing 1–0. Cobb scored the only run. He singled, went to second on a fly ball, and with two outs scored from second on a slow roller to third by Lathers. Purtell fielded it with his bare hand and threw to Gandil at first. Lathers was called safe. Big Ed argued vehemently with the umpire and was tossed from the game.

On August 1 Big Ed was scheduled to pitch against the A's. He was warming up when he got word that he had been suspended for three days for his "flow of words in the middle of Sunday's game with Detroit," as the *Trib* put it. On August 3 Big Ed and Jack Coombs hooked up in one of the classic pitching duels of all time. They both went all the way in a 16-inning 0–0 game which was called by darkness at 7 o'clock. Coombs allowed just three hits and struck out 18. Walsh gave up six hits and struck out 10. In the 16th inning the A's put runners on second and third with no outs on a walk and a throwing error by Big Ed, but he got foul outs to first and catcher and then a ground ball to third to get out of it. In the Sox 16th Coombs struck out the side, including Walsh, who was the last out of the game. It was a game worthy of another poem by Hek:

> On a sixteen inning split
> O pitcher with the moistened ball.
> O, would I could your praise extol
> With all the swell poetic slants
> Of Horace or Poeta Pants — Ed Walsh
>
> O twirler of hard luck sublime,
> You're there with it most of the time;
> You hold 'em in your magic spell
> You pitch and pitch — but wotinel? — Ed Walsh
>
> O hurler with the heart of steel,
> You grind 'em neath your iron heel,
> The hits are scarce when you're about,
> But no one helps you with a clout — Ed Walsh
>
> O pitching bear, O twirling whale.
> O hurling mastodon — all hail!
> The throbbing geeks your praises sing.
> But, shush! That don't get anything.[7]

Big Ed got hot in early August and pitched two consecutive gems. On August 7 at home against the Nationals, he pitched a three-hitter and faced just 30 batters in a 4–0 win, a game which was billed as a heated battle for sixth place. He struck out 10. On the 11th he pitched a three-hitter in a 1–0 win over Boston. He ran his scoreless streak to 35⅔ innings and struck out 15, just one less than Rube Waddell's record for nine innings.

On August 14 a record crowd of 32,498 paid to see a double header with the Yankees, despite the Sox being in seventh place. Big Ed lost the second game 5–1. It was said there were probably bigger crowds at World's Series games in 1908 and 1909 where free passes were issued, but this double header gate was considered the biggest paid crowd.

On August 17, during a 27-hour train ride to Philadelphia, the Sox stopped in Wilkes-Barre. "Walsh gave his teammates a tour of his home area. They saw where he got his start, where he went to school at Plains, where he was a miner and mine boss and where he pitched his first game of ball. There is a nice crop of corn in that ball yard now."[8]

On August 23 in Washington, Big Ed beat Walter Johnson 1–0. Johnson struck 12 and walked one. Walsh struck out six and walked one. It was the third consecutive time that Walsh beat Johnson 1–0. Afterward, Big Ed had pain in his shoulder which was dismissed as merely a cold "which settled in his arm."

The next day, August 24, Big Ed, Doc White, Sullivan and a couple of other players went to the Washington Monument. Sullivan wanted to try to catch balls dropped from the monument as Gabby Street had famously done in 1908. Walsh and White dropped balls off the monument from 542 feet. It was windy and it took until the eighth attempt, a ball dropped by Big Ed, for Sullivan to make the first catch. He caught the next one dropped by White. Sullivan used his catcher's mitt and said it didn't hurt at all. According to a *Chicago Tribune* correspondent, Sullivan caught three of 11. The *New York Times* reported that it took 23 tries before Sullivan caught one and that he caught five. The *Times* estimated speed of the balls at 161 feet per second. The *Times* said White threw the ball as far as he could, rather than just drop it. The *Washington Post* also reported Sully caught three of 11 on the eighth, ninth and 11th tries.[9]

On August 9 Comiskey finally got Nig Smith out of his hair by trading him and Billy Purtell to the Boston Red Sox in exchange for third baseman Harry Lord and second baseman Amby McConnell. Smith, who also threw a spitball, made his debut for Boston against Big Ed on August 31. "There was nothing to this meeting of a pair of spitball artists but the coal miner from Wilkesbarre [sic] who struck out 10 Boston men and scored the easiest kind of shut out. Walsh pitched a masterly game, always on the mark, making it easy on his catcher and working Boston batters to perfection with his control."[10] He walked three, and gave up five hits. For once the hitless wonders supported him with eight runs. Smith gave up eight hits, walked four and hit a batter.

Big Ed was on his game on September 9 when he beat the Browns 8–1, and Ring Lardner was on his in his description of the game and his shots at the Browns manager. "Jack O'Connor sent in a bunch of alleged young wonders against Walsh. They did manage to score, but it was not their fault. It is the opinion of many persons that the institutions which are opposing cruelty to animals, child labor and kindred evils should go

11. Big Ed Opens Comiskey Park

after Jack O'Connor for his share of the day's doings. It was a mean piece of work to push such innocent lambs as Corridon, Graham and McDonald into the clutches of the monster."[11]

On September 13 in Chicago Big Ed pitched a three-hitter with 13 strikeouts, but lost 1–0 to Red Nelson and the Browns, who scored a run in the first on a walk, passed ball and single. In Chicago on the 18th Walsh, aided by a triple play, beat Boston 6–0. On September 21 Big Ed pitched the last four innings in relief of Jack Scott, a big game hunter from Wyoming, as the Sox beat New York 6–4. He didn't allow a hit or run and struck out four. It was way too little, way too late, but it was the Sox' seventh consecutive win.

The next day he pitched one inning in an exhibition game at Battle Creek. The star was "Little Alec" Zwilling, who played at Battle Creek and was given an ovation each time he batted. The Sox won 10–1. Big Ed's last start and appearance of the season was a 3–1 loss to the A's, on September 25 in the first game of a double header at Philadelphia, appropriately, in 14 innings. Plank started and Coombs pitched the last six innings, extending his shutout innings streak to 53. The Sox stopped his scoreless streak in the third inning of the second game, which was called by darkness. Coombs won 18 of 19 starts in July, August, and September, and finished the season 30–9 with a 1.30 ERA. He pitched 13 shutouts, an A.L. record, and in 12 other games gave up one run.

Big Ed had an even lower ERA. He led the league with a 1.27, completed 33 of 36 starts and lost 20 games. He won 17. It was the only time in baseball history that an ERA leader lost 20 games. The average run support in his 36 starts was 2.41. Throw out three freak games where the Sox scored eight, eight and six runs and the run support in the other 33 starts was 1.96. He also led the league in saves with five and assists, 154, and pitched 369⅓ innings. Big Ed batted .217, six points higher than the team average, and equal to or higher than position players Zeider, Gandil, Blackburne, Parent, and Collins.

Hek compared him to a Civil War general. "Ed Walsh, the conspicuous hero of a lost cause, the Robert E. Lee of the White Sox, will take formal leave tomorrow and retire to the quiet of his New England home. This should be a good time for the White Sox fans, who are nothing if not emotional, to trot out the music and flowers and betoken their appreciation of the brilliant but in large measure futile performances of a game and willing performer."[12]

In the National League the Cubs ran away with the pennant, winning 104 games and finishing 13 games ahead of the second place New York

Giants. It didn't help the Cubs that the A.L. season ended a week earlier than the N.L. season. While the Cubs played out a string of meaningless games, the A.L. champion A's tuned up with a five-game series against an A.L. all-star team, which included Big Ed, Ty Cobb, Tris Speaker, Doc White, and Walter Johnson. The A's lost four out of five games to the all-stars. Big Ed started two of them. He won 5–1 on a five-hitter and lost the second one 3–0, the only loss by the all-stars in the five games. Connie Mack didn't care that his team lost and said, "Those games, more than anything else, put the Athletics in a condition to outclass the National League champions." The A's won the 1910 World's Series 4 games to 1.

12

Big Ed Owns the Cubs

Two stories about hunting dogs were all that was heard of from Big Ed during the winter after the 1910 season. After the World's Series he invited Harry Lord and Cy Young on a hunting trip to Maine, which turned tragic when Big Ed mistakenly shot and killed Poor Richard, a fox hound who had been loaned to them by a local. Big Ed replaced the dog and acquired two more. On December 10 he sent Comiskey the two hunting dogs who were named Balls and Strikes. It was suggested by one writer that they ought to have been named Saliva and Strut.

Sick of the "hitless wonders" tag, Comiskey tried to get some batters for 1911, starting with the trade he made in August of 1910 that brought Amby McConnell and Harry Lord to play second and third. In January he bought outfielder Matty McIntyre from Detroit for cash. He also signed his old friend James "Nixey" Callahan, who had been a pitcher, outfielder, manager and second baseman for the Sox from 1911 to 1914. Perhaps Callahan, at 36, had given up his hard living ways which had caused him to split with Comiskey and the Sox after the 1905 season. Callahan hadn't played in a major league game in five seasons, but he didn't disappoint the Old Roman in 1911. He would bat .289 with 60 RBI and lead the team in steals with 45.

In March Comiskey acquired center fielder Ping Bodie from the San Francisco Seals. The 23-year-old rookie's real name was Francesco Stephano Pezzolo, and he was one of the first Italian-Americans to reach the major leagues. It was Bodie who famously said years later when he roomed with Babe Ruth, "It was like rooming with his suitcase." After his baseball career, Bodie worked as an electrician and extra in the motion picture industry in California. The name Bodie came from the California Gold Rush town where he lived and Ping came from the sound the ball made hitting his 52-ounce bat. He had made a lot of noise with it in 1910, hitting 30 home runs for the Seals.[1]

Led by Bodie, who hit .289 with 97 RBI, the new lineup produced for Comiskey, Duffy, and Big Ed in 1911. From 1910 to 1911 the Sox went from seventh in the A.L. in runs scored, 456, to third, 716, an increase of 1.7 runs per game. The team batting average went up 58 points from .211 to .269 and from eighth to third in the league. As amazing as those numbers seem, they were indicative of a dramatic league-wide trend. The overall league batting average went up 30 points from 1910 to 1911 from .243 to .273 and 1,084 more runs were scored. All the batting boosted the league ERA from 2.52 to 3.34. The Sox pitching staff's ERA went up almost a run per nine innings from 2.03 to 2.97. But that was still third in the league in 1911. As the Sox were third in runs scored and third in ERA in 1911 they won more games, going from 68–85 to 77–74, but they improved only one position, from sixth to fifth. They finished 24 games behind the pennant-winning A's who batted .296, scored 861 runs and won 101 games.

Big Ed, despite occasional reports of problems with lumbago in his back and shoulder and other aliments, put in another ironman season, leading the league in games, 56; innings, 368⅔; and strikeouts, 255. He was second in wins, 27; losses, 17; shutouts, five; and complete games, 33. Coombs won 28 and Johnson had six shutouts and 36 complete games. Big Ed's ERA of 2.22 was a little high by his standards, but was sixth in the A.L. after the Naps' Dave Gregg, a 6–1, 180 pound rookie southpaw, and Johnson, Wood, Plank and Bender.

On May 18, after a five-game winning streak, the Sox were four games over .500 at 16–12, though already eight games behind the Tigers, who went off to a sizzling 26–5 start. On June 27 the Sox got to six over, 31–25, after Big Ed shut out Detroit 3–0, but were down to fourth place. That was as good as it got for the Sox who hovered around .500 all season. The low was on September 4 when, after six consecutive losses to the Naps in a pair of home and away series, they were 61–66. They had to win 11 of their last 15 to pass the Red Sox by percentage points for fourth place. It was a disappointing season, but with Big Ed pitching in 56 games there were plenty of personal highs and lows.

Big Ed started the opener on the road in Detroit on April 13 and lost 4–2. Crawford and Cobb hit a home run and triple back to back in a three-run first inning. Big Ed gave up six hits in the first three innings, but only two in the last five. He walked one and struck out five. On the 16th he started in St. Louis and won 7–1. He struck out eight without a walk and was 2 for 4 batting with a double. In the eighth inning McIntyre went into the overflow crowd and made a sensational catch of a long drive by Clarke. His first home start on April 20 must have been embarrassing for Big Ed. He gave up 14 hits to the Tigers and lost 6–3 to unknown rookie Ed Lafitte. That wasn't the embarrassing part. That Hugh Jennings "nearly died laughing" was.[2]

On April 27, after Comiskey complained that the White Sox still weren't hitting despite the roster changes, Ping Bodie said, "You want some hitting, put me in the lineup." Duffy did and Bodie had a double and a triple as Big Ed beat the Browns 14–4. On the morning of May 3 in Cleveland Big Ed woke up complaining of sickness and a sore arm. That afternoon he pitched one of his classic games. He pitched eight shutout innings in a 7–1 win and struck out 11, including Joe Jackson twice and Lajoie once. He must have been feeling much better that evening at the hotel. "Tonight he was bold enough to sing his latest song composition in the dining room."[3] A few days later he told Sam Weller of the *Trib* that he had changed his delivery against the Naps. "He says he put a slight pause in his windup, then let the ball go with a snap, and it fooled them." Why would Big Ed suddenly change his delivery, unless it was because of a sore arm?

On May 10 in Chicago, four days before Big Ed's 30th birthday, 18,000 fans came to see a matchup between Big Ed and the Big Train, Walter Johnson. They were disappointed. Johnson was knocked out in the second inning and Big Ed lasted three. The Sox won 9–6. On May 23 the Yankees came to town and sent Russ Ford to the mound in the opener. The 28-year-old phenom was 26–6 in 1910 with a 1.65 ERA and was on his way to another 20-win season, but nobody knew how he was doing it. "The young fellow has something that no other pitcher in either big league possesses. Even Eddie Sweeney, the Chicago boy who is catcher for the New Yorkers, will declare to his friends that he doesn't know the secret of Ford's delivery. All he knows is the sign he gives for the young pitcher to throw it, and he shoots it over with as much speed as a spitball and a quicker break. Ford is keeping the thing a secret, although all of the American league pitchers are trying to learn it." Ford, as was discussed in chapter four, was throwing a ball he scuffed with an emory board hidden in the lining of his glove.

Big Ed was pitted against Ford. The game went 12 innings with the Highlanders winning with three singles in the top of the inning. Ed gave up 11 hits, walked seven and struck out seven. Once again there was a hint that all was not quite right. "Big Ed was not at his best by any means. He has not fully recovered from his recent illness, which no doubt taxed his strength a bit."[4]

On May 28, Bodie saved Big Ed from defeat before 20,000 fans with a bases-loaded triple in the bottom of the ninth. It was getting dark when Bodie hit the smash, which Joe Jackson might have lost in the gloom. The game ended in a 5–5 tie. On June 1, Big Ed was sick again, or still. A doctor came to the hotel in the morning and treated him for a stomach aliment. He moped around the lobby the rest of the morning, complaining to anybody who would listen. When he got to the park, Duffy, probably remembering the last game he pitched after a morning sickness when he struck out 11, told him to warm up. He won 10–3. Big Ed gave up 11 hits, but four of them, and two of the runs, came in the ninth with the game in hand and Big Ed pitching nothing but dry fastballs. "Duffy is hoping the big fellow will be just as sick next week in New York and all summer when it's his rung to do the slabbing."[5]

June 8 in New York brought another Ford-Big Ed matchup. By this time the *Tribune* writer decided that Ford was throwing a spitball as he billed the game's pitchers as ""two masters of the saliva service." This time Big Ed was the winner 7–2 in one of his best outings of the season. He gave up five hits, walked two and struck out 12. With the weather warming up, Big Ed warmed up as well and stopped complaining about his health. After the 12-strikeout game against Ford, he pitched equally well in Philadelphia on June 13, but lost 2–1 in 10 to Chief Bender. He struck out nine. "Never did Big Ed look better than today for the first nine rounds. He fanned nine of the slugging champions. His spitter was breaking beautifully and he could put it over under any conditions."[6]

While still in Philadelphia on the 16th, Big Ed put on a fungo hitting show for the fans during a pre-game rain delay. He hit several balls over the fence and two over the buildings across the street from the outfield. He pitched the last game of the Philadelphia series on the 18th. He gave up four runs on five hits and his own throwing error in the first inning, but gave up only two hits the rest of the way and won 8–6.

After an all-night train trip to Detroit the Sox played the Tigers the next afternoon and Big Ed became part of a negative all-time record that would last 90 years. He was the loser in the biggest blown lead in major league history. Leading 13–1 after five and one-half innings, the Sox let the Tigers make up the 12-run deficit and come back to win 16–15. Ty Cobb, who had five hits and five RBIs, scored the game winner in the ninth when

Crawford hit a drive over Bodie's head off Big Ed, who had relieved in the eighth. The Philadelphia Athletics matched the record when they came back from 12 down against the Indians on June 15, 1925. On August 1, 2001, Cleveland set a new comeback record coming from 13 runs down to beat the Seattle Mariners 15–14.

In a 4–2 win in St. Louis on June 21 there was evidence that Big Ed was losing his fastball, which over his career he used maybe 25 percent of the time, or less, to set up the spitter. "Ed was in good form and if he hadn't tried to slip a straight one over on 'Nig' Clarke for a first strike in the seventh inning he might have possessed a shutout victory. 'Nig' hit it for a double to left center and opened the way for the Browns two tallies. Ed stuck to the spitter after that."[7]

On the 27th at home the spitter was breaking down and away consistently and Big Ed shut out the Tigers 3–0 with eight strikeouts. He gave up just four singles, one an infield hit by Cobb, who was cut down stealing. He walked one, Crawford, who was also thrown out in a rundown. It was the Sox' sixth win out of seven and it was at that point that they were 31–25, which would turn out to be their best record of the season.

On July 4 the temperature was in the 90s in Chicago just as Big Ed liked it. In the morning game of a double header Walsh beat the Tigers again 7–3 and stopped a 40-game hitting streak by Cobb, though neither the Detroit nor Chicago papers mentioned the streak. Cobb had hit .491 since the streak began on May 15.[8] The Tigers won the second game 11–10, but slipped out of first place one-half game behind the A's, who won an Independence Day double header in New York. Big Ed survived allowing 18 base runners, 10 hits and eight walks, by throwing the spitball in all the tight spots. He struck out four.

On July 6 Big Ed was angry over stories that appeared in California papers where Fielder Jones was given credit for Big Ed's phenomenal 1908 season when he won 40 games. One of the stories said, in part, "That Big Ed isn't nearly so effective as he was in 1908 is unanimously agreed over the American league circuit. The secret to Big Ed's 1908 success was due largely to Fielder Jones' long baseball head. Big Ed had to pitch as Jones ordered when he was at the height of his power, while now he is using his own judgment."

Big Ed accused Jones of planting the stories. "If Fielder Jones is not the author of these stories about me then he owes it to the fans to deny them before they are accepted as coming from him for a certainty. The story sounds very much like a Jones yarn. It is a piece of fiction. The story says that I need Fielder Jones and says my greatest success was due to the fact that Jones made me win. The reverse is true. I made Fielder Jones a name for himself in the baseball world. He came near ruining my arm in order to win another pennant in 1908. I admit Fielder Jones has brains, but he didn't make me a pitcher and didn't make me win. Charlie Comiskey and Billy Sullivan taught me everything I know about pitching that I didn't work out myself. Jones simply used me."[9]

The Highlanders, or Yankees as they were increasingly being called, came in for a five-game series on July 7. Big Ed pitched and won the first game 5–3. The Sox also won a double header the next day. The following day was a Sunday and with splendid weather and the Sox on a three-game win streak a crowd of 22,000 came out to see if the Sox could make it four straight over the Yankees. Duffy was out sick and Lord, the team captain, was manager for the day. He considered coming back with Big Ed on a day's rest to oppose Ford, but decided to go with 23-year-old left hander Irv Young, hope for the best and come back with Big Ed for the series' final game on Monday. It didn't work. Young lost to Ford 5–2. Big Ed pitched the ninth inning after Young was lifted for a pinch hitter, and struck out the three batters he faced. The next day Jim "Hippo" Vaughn and the Yankees beat Big Ed 5–2 in 11, dropping the Sox from third to fifth place.

Later in the month, in New York, Big Ed pitched two complete games against the Yankees on two days rest, winning one and losing one. He had an easy time beating Vaughn 10–2 on July 29 and lost 4–3 on August 1. Big Ed took four days off after the August 1 game to recover from an "attack of lumbago." He got back on the mound in the second game of a double header on August 5 in Washington versus rookie Jay Cashion. Cashion beat Big Ed 3–2 and knocked in the winning run in the ninth.

In the first game Washington's Germany Schaefer, a renowned practical joker who once batted with galoshes on to protest that a game was being played in the rain, stole first base from second base. "Weird base running by Germany Schaefer set a problem for the umpires that will keep the experts guessing all summer. Washington started in the last of the ninth as if it would surely put the winning run over in a hurry. Milan began with a double and when Schaefer bunted a play was made at third base, but it was too late to get a man. With none out Elberfeld popped to McConnell and then Schaefer stole second. Gessler fanned, making two out, then Schaefer was sorry he was on second, so with Walker at bat the Dutchman took a lead off second on the other side and stole first base.

"This brought Manager Duffy out on the field, right out by the pitcher's box, where he argued with Umpire Parker for permitting the play,

12. Big Ed Owns the Cubs

and while this argument was going on Schaefer thought it would be a good time to steal second again. He started down and allowed himself to be trapped between the bases, then Milan began edging from third for home.

"Finally the latter made a dash for the plate and Collins shot home to Payne, who tagged the man three feet away. Umpire Connolly called him out and immediately it seemed all the ball players in uniform surrounded him, the Washington players protesting that the play shouldn't go because Chicago had ten men on the field. Manager Duffy having stayed out in the middle of the diamond during it all."[10]

Big Ed complained of a backache after the loss to Cashion, but pitched two complete games in the next series in Philadelphia, losing 3–2 on August 7 in 10 and winning 5–4 on the 10th. He was 2 for 3 batting and scored three of the five runs in the win. The next day the Sox stopped in Detroit for one game and won, to conclude a 20-game road trip 8–12. The Sox were 51–52, mired in sixth place and 16½ games behind the first place A's, who led the Tigers by two and one-half. If there was going to be a miracle run for the pennant it would take a 1906-style 19-game winning streak. The time was at hand as the Sox opened a 21-game homestand on August 13 with four-games sets against the Tigers and A's. The Tigers came in without Ty Cobb. Hugh Jennings said Cobb had left the team on his own without explanation for an indefinite time. The Sox managed a split with the Tigers. Big Ed won one of the games with a one-hit, 2–0 shutout. The only hit was a slow roller up the middle which Big Ed just missed fielding. A no-hitter remained elusive for Big Ed, but not for long. The A's came in to Chicago next, took three of four and ended any dreams the Sox may have had for a miracle race for the pennant.

The pennant may have been out of reach, but a personal achievement that had eluded Ed throughout his career was not. Against the Red Sox on Sunday, August 27, with 18,000 fans cheering as though a pennant were on the line, Big Ed pitched the one and only no-hitter of his career. He came within one batter of a perfect game. A walk in the fourth inning to Art Engle was the only base runner he allowed. He struck out eight. Big Ed had pitched five one-hitters before hurling the no-hitter. He had two one-hitters in 1906, one in 1909, one in 1910 and the one exactly two weeks before the no-hitter.

> It was not until the fifth inning that the big Sunday crowd began to realize the possibilities of the situation. Then in different parts of the stands people discovered that the visitors had not made a hit off Big Ed.
>
> Like a blaze in tinder dry grass spread the knowledge that Big Ed had a no hit game within reach again and immediately the crowd forgot every-

thing else. They paid little attention to what the White Sox did while at bat. Forgotten was the fact that the home team was winning the game and with it a possible berth in the first division; forgotten was everything except the magnificent performance the great slabman was giving. As each out was registered a great yell went up, and the game resolved itself into a series of sharp spasmodic yelps with breathless silences in the intervals.

To eight other men Big Ed owes part of his laurels, for no team ever worked harder to back up a pitcher than those Sox did yesterday. Their defense was perfect and toward the end when every nerve was tense with the excitement the players extended themselves beyond the normal limit.[11]

The final out was a ground ball toward third base. Big Ed dove on it, bounced up and threw to first before third baseman Harry Lord could get near it. A play like that didn't spring just from Big Ed's exuberance over finishing off a no-hitter. He played the field like that every time he pitched. Though he did at times forget to cover first on balls hit to first base, he went after everything hit anywhere near him to the point where his third basemen feared him.

In his next start after the no-hitter Big Ed lost 2–1 to the Naps, who pulled off a hidden ball trick to tag out little-used utility player Felix Chouinard several feet off second base. Big Ed pitched one more notable game before the 1911 regular season ended. On September 27 in Boston he helped the White Sox beat the Red Sox 3–0 with his arm, glove and bat. He pitched a five-hitter with six strikeouts and one walk. He picked Speaker off first base and ran over and made the putout himself. He also tagged Gardner out at home by blocking the plate after a passed ball and knocked in a run with a sacrifice fly.

On September 30 at a field day in Chicago, Big Ed hit a fungo 419 feet and one-half inch, beating the previous record, a 413 foot eight and one-half inch drive by Cincinnati's Mike Mitchell on September 11, 1907. Some sources say Big Ed's record lasted until 1931 when it was broken by Babe Ruth who hit one 421 feet. But in 1916 the *Chicago Tribune* reported Big Ed's record was broken by Cincinnati pitcher Peter Schneider before the last game of the 1916 season.

After the 1911 season the Chalmers Automobile Company awarded an automobile to an MVP in each league as voted by the baseball writers in each city using a point system. The 36-horsepower cars were considered status symbols and were so popular the company couldn't make them fast enough to fill orders. In 1910, the first year of the Chalmers award, the award autos were given to the batting average leaders in each league. This led to a controversy in the American League. Ty Cobb and Nap Lajoie

12. Big Ed Owns the Cubs

entered the final day of the season in a virtual tie. In St. Louis, Lajoie beat out seven bunt singles in a double header and won the title. St. Louis was accused of laying down and Cobb protested. Chalmers wound up giving automobiles to both players and for 1911 asked the writers to select MVPs. Big Ed was second in the voting in 1911 to Cobb. Cubs outfielder Frank "Wildfire" Schulte won the N.L. car. Christy Mathewson was second in the voting.

But the 1911 Chalmers announcement on October 11 did not drop the curtain on the 1911 baseball season for the White Sox or the Cubs. Two days later on Friday, October 13, the City Championship series was revived after a year's absence because the Cubs had been in the World's Series in 1910. As they were in every city series in the era, the Cubs, who won 92 and were second in the N.L., were heavy favorites. The Cubs had won handily in 1909, when they claimed revenge against Big Ed for his beating them in the 1906 World's Series. But 1911 was Big Ed's series for revenge. The Sox won the series in four straight. Big Ed won two and saved one.

The crowd of over 22,000 came out for the first game at Comiskey Park to see Big Ed and Mordecai Brown. But hundreds, if not thousands, of them missed the ending. White Sox fans streamed out by the hundreds when the Sox, trailing 3–1, failed to score in the bottom of the eighth. The fans who stayed saw the Sox win with a dramatic three-run rally in the ninth. Bodie, Callahan and Zeider singled to make it 3–2. Zeider was sacrificed to second and then Ralph "Redhead" Kreitz, who was catching in place of Sullivan, ended the game with a two-run single to right field. That hit off Brown that made a winner out of Big Ed was Kreitz's 15 minutes of fame. His entire major league career consisted of seven games he played for the Sox that season.

The Sox made another comeback the next day on the West Side to win 8–7. Doc White started but was pulled in the first inning in favor of Jack Scott. The Sox trailed 6–3 after four, but scored one in the fifth and two in both the sixth and eighth to win 8–7. Walsh pitched a scoreless ninth inning and was saved by Amby McConnell, who made a sensational running catch of a drive by Hofman. "To Ambrose McConnell of Utica, N. Y., the whole south side of Chicago owes the great wave of joy which swept it from river to lake and back to river last night."[12]

Game three back at Comiskey Park on Sunday drew the biggest crowd ever for a game in Chicago. The gates were closed two hours before the game. Paid admissions were 36,308, but more snuck in and 5,000 were turned away. The biggest crowd at a World's Series game that year between teams from the country's two biggest cities, Philadelphia and New York, was 38,241. In another tight game White started and won with a complete game five-hitter.

Three days of rain put off the fourth game until Wednesday, October 18. It was a rematch of Big Ed and Brown, each with four full days rest and it drew 22,986. The Sox won 7–2. The game ended this way according to a newspaper account: "Edward Artist Walsh shot a perfectly nude strike across the heart of the plate and Heine Zimmerman cut a third straight gash in the circumambient ozone with two out in the last half of the ninth inning yesterday."[13]

The 1912 season was a replay of 1911 for Big Ed, the White Sox and the Cubs. Big Ed put in another ironman season; the Sox won one more game, 78, than they had in 1911; the Cubs won one fewer, 91, than they had won; and the city series games were more popular than any of the regular season games.

But while the Sox did wind up with a nearly identical record in 1912 as they did in 1911, there was a big difference in the way they got there. In 1911 they hovered around .500 all season. With a revamped lineup in 1912 they got off to a sizzling start, winning 20 of their first 25. With Nixey Callahan elevated to manager; Morrie Rath, a Cleveland castoff who had been out of the majors in 1911, at second base; and Buck Weaver, a 20-year-old rookie from Pennsylvania coal country, at short, they were in first place alone every day from April 24 to June 9. The Sox were 9–3 in Walsh starts during their time on top. Their biggest lead in that time was five and one-half games over Boston on May 19. On June 10, after losing a four-game series at home to Washington, the Sox slipped into second place behind Boston by percentage points. They never got back on top.

On May 8 in Washington the White Sox broke a five-game Walter Johnson win streak and Johnson broke Lee Tannehill's arm. A Big Train fastball ended Tannehill's 10-year career right then and there. Big Ed pitched the last 5⅔ innings, Lord and Bodie hit home runs off Johnson and the Sox won 7–6. But the Sox would lose 13 of 22 games to the Senators, who were one of the most improved teams in baseball history. The Senators went from 64–90 and seventh place in 1911 to 91–61 and second place in 1912. Johnson was the biggest factor in their rise. He won 33 games and led the league in ERA, 1.39, and strikeouts, 303. The home runs he gave up to Lord and Bodie on May 8 were the only home runs he gave up all season.

After the White Sox fell behind the Red Sox in mid–June, Callahan guessed (correctly as it turned out) that there was an urgency to stay with

12. Big Ed Owns the Cubs

the Red Sox. His solution was to start Big Ed in three consecutive games. On June 12 he started in Chicago against the Yankees. When the Sox piled up early runs — they went on to win 11–2 — Callahan pulled Walsh after three innings saying he wanted to rest him for the Red Sox, who were coming in next for a four-game series. Big Ed got a new nickname that day. *Chicago Tribune* writer Cy Sanborn dubbed him "the Big Reel." Though he might have been called that before in the clubhouse, that may have been the first time it was used in print.

The next day, June 13, over 10,000 fans came out in the rain to see the White Sox christen the 1911 City Championship pennant and to see if the Big Reel could reel in the streaking Red Sox. The Woodland Bards band performed eight numbers and then marched the team, and 230 Illinois National Guardsmen, to the flagpole where the pennant was raised. After the game was delayed by rain for an hour, the Big Reel had one of the more memorable games of his career. He pitched a three-hitter to win 3–2 and knocked in two of the three runs, including the game-winner with two outs in the ninth. "Enough sawdust to supply a five ring circus was worked into the mud and play resumed. The players slipped, slided and skated through the rest of the rounds."[14]

The rain postponed the game the next day, so Callahan came back with Big Ed on the 15th on one day's rest. It didn't work. "Big Reel attempts too much and is driven from mound" read the headline in the *Tribune* the next day. Big Ed lasted only two innings and gave up five hits and all four runs in a 4–3 loss. Boston won the next day and Callahan, desperate to at least split the four games, gave Big Ed the ball for the fourth game on the 17th on two days rest. He was tagged for 13 hits in a 4–1 loss. Speaker had a triple, two doubles and a single. "Walsh was as effective as of old in spots and several times pitched himself out of deep holes with honor. But when not in trouble he resorted to the side arm stuff and the Red Sox were laying for it."

That was a curious observation. Why was Big Ed, who almost always threw three-quarter arm or straight up overhand, throwing sidearm? It was a likely indication that his arm was hurting from all the work, but nobody said anything.

By losing those three straight games to the Red Sox, the White Sox dropped below Washington into third place. The three straight wins were the first three of nine straight wins for the Red Sox. By July 4 the Red Sox were in first place by seven games and the Sox were all the way down to fourth. In the end the Red Sox finished 105–47 and won the pennant by 14 games over the Senators.

Ed wound up leading the league in games, 62, for the fifth time in six seasons and innings pitched, 393, for the fourth time in six. He also led in starts, 41, and saves, 10. Saves was not a statistic in 1911, but Retrosheet, a popular baseball Web site, credits Ed with 10 in 1911 and according to Retrosheet it was the first time an A.L. pitcher had double figures in saves. Ed was 27–17 with a 2.15 ERA. He struck out 254 and walked 94.

For once someone predicted that the White Sox would win the City Championship series which opened on October 8 at Comiskey Park. Sanborn, writing in the *Tribune*, wrote that the outfields were even and the Cubs had a superior infield, but the Sox would win because "there is only one Ed Walsh in captivity."

Doc White agreed. "All South Side fans expect Walsh will be called on to do most of the work. The big fellow is a glutton for work and is always willing to do more than his share. He can pitch whenever Callahan wants him to, which will be whenever any of the other pitchers are in trouble."

Cubs manager Frank Chance said Walsh was an advantage, but he was only one man. "I'll have a strong fresh pitcher for each of the next three games. The only advantage they have is one pitcher—Ed Walsh."

At a meeting on October 7 a comprise was worked out concerning A.L. and N.L. warm up rules. A.L. pitchers were not permitted to warm up at the start of each inning, while in the National, pitchers were. Given that the weather was likely to be cold, it was agreed to allow the pitcher to throw five balls before each inning and when relieving in the middle of an inning.

Despite the prediction of fair weather the first game was postponed by rain at 11:50 that morning. That didn't sit right with Stewart W. Hunter, a fan from Logansport, Indiana, who bought two tickets for $6 from scalper J. W. Felder with the understanding that he would get a full refund if the game was rained out. But Felder refunded only $4. Hunter filed suit. "I didn't mind paying $6 to see the game, but I did object to giving him $2 for nothing."[15]

The weather was wretched the next day, but the game was on. In wet, winter-like conditions which usually didn't suit him, Big Ed was practically unhittable. But the Sox couldn't solve Cubs rookie Jimmy Lavender, who had been 16–13 with a 3.04 in the regular season. The teams played to a 0–0 tie. Sanborn wrote that it was "0–0 in favor of the Cubs." Such was the effect of Big Ed. The Cubs didn't lose to him so it was as good as a win. He pitched a one-hitter and faced only two over the minimum.

12. Big Ed Owns the Cubs

Tinker got the hit, a double. A batter reached on an error, the only other base runner. Attendance was 16,000 and scalpers took a hit. They walked through the streetcars taking fans to the game first asking for $1.50, then $1.25 and finally face value of $1. Even at that there were few takers. Fans who had advance tickets were going, but for others it was just too wet and cold. At the ballpark just before game time scalpers took a loss at 50 cents.

The second game on October 11 was a 3–3, 12 inning tie. Big Ed pitched the last inning, his 10th consecutive scoreless inning. The next day a game finally produced a winner as the Cubs won 5–4. Lavender pitched again for the Cubs and survived giving up 14 hits and five walks. Doc White took the loss.

The Cubs released Mordecai Brown after the game, five days before his 35th birthday, though he was allowed to dress and collect a full series share. Brown had won 20 plus games for six consecutive seasons from 1906 to 1911 when he averaged 288 innings. But in 1912, hampered by a knee injury, he appeared in only 16 games and was 5–6.

The next day the weather moderated and 30,393, the biggest crowd ever at the West Side Grounds, saw Big Ed face the Cubs' Ed Reulbach. The game was nearly forfeited several times as the overflow crowd broke through the helpless line of bluecoats and onto the field. In the second inning the crowd caused a 20-minute delay before they were pushed back. Left and center were so short that five ordinary fly balls went into the roped-off crowd for doubles. Walsh hit one of them and scored the first run of the game in the sixth. The Sox led 2–1 into the Cubs' seventh when Schulte tied it with a line drive home run that dented the right field scoreboard. The Cubs scored two more in the inning, one when Walsh missed a throw back from Sullivan that rolled into center field, and won 4–2.

Having survived two games pitched by Walsh with a tie and a win and with a two games to zero series lead, the Cubs were all but crowned city champs. When Larry Cheney, 26–10 in the regular season, beat the Sox 8–1 at Comiskey to take a three games to zero lead the next day, the scribes wrote the Sox epitaph. "That practically settled the local argument," wrote one.

But then there was that "only Ed Walsh in captivity" fellow. On just one day's rest he pitched the next day in game four back at the West Side Grounds and beat Lavender 5–4 in 11 innings. In game six the Cubs led 5–4 in the ninth with one out when Sox reserve outfielder Wally Mattick hit a bases-loaded triple to the fence in left center. He scored on a ground out and the Sox won 8–5. Walsh came in to pitch the ninth. Vic Saier grounded to Rath on the first pitch. Evers singled. Archer struck out.

Downey, pinch-hitting for Lavender, tapped back to Walsh to end the game. Today that would be called a save. Then it was described in the *Tribune* as "like eating cherry pie with a spoon."[16] Before long Walsh would need help to do even that. But at the time he seemed invincible, and with the series now tied at three, an invincible pitcher was just what the Sox needed.[17]

13

What's the Matter with Big Ed?

It was only the third inning, but Charles Comiskey was well-satisfied. With his Chicago White Sox leading the rival Cubs 11–0 in the third inning of the seventh and decisive game of the 1912 City Series, the Sox president went to his office in the two-year-old steel and concrete ball park which bore his name, sat at his desk, wrote out a check, and went back to his private box.

Down on the pitcher's mound, as Big Ed took his five warm up tosses to start the fourth inning, he saw a frantic movement in Comiskey's box. He looked up and saw his boss smiling and waving a piece of paper. Big Ed laughed and waved back. He knew that his name was on that piece of paper and that it was a check for $1,500. Before the game that day, on October 21 in 1912, Comiskey had said to Big Ed, "go in there and beat the Cubs and I'll hand you $1500 out of my own pocket."[1]

Comiskey, a notorious tightwad, was often out of character as it regards Big Ed. He was sometimes generous toward him and treated him like a son. He once gave him $3,000 for his sons' college educations. But it didn't dawn on Comiskey, or Nixey Callahan, that a seat on the bench might have been a better reward than money. But Big Ed was a man who finished what he started and Comiskey and Callahan never considered taking him out of that game, or almost any other game for that matter, not even after he was hit in the throat with a one-hop batted ball in the fourth, not even when he batted in the eighth with the Sox leading 16–0, not even considering he had pitched the ninth inning the day before.

When Big Ed got the last out in the final game, completing a miraculous White Sox comeback from a three games to zero deficit to a four games to three series win, he had pitched 41 of the possible 83 innings. In that 16–0 win in the seventh game, he gave up five hits in the first five innings and none after. He struck out five batters, two consecutively in the third when pinch hitters Lavender and Sheckard whiffed on six pitches.

Adding the 41 innings Big Ed pitched in the City Series to his regular season 393 innings gave him 434 innings pitched in 1912. As staggering as that number seems, 1912 was a typical Big Ed season. In '12 and the previous five seasons combined he had averaged 56 games and 376 innings per season. In two of those seasons he had pitched over 400 innings. But if his arm was hurt after the 1912 City Series, as he would much later admit it was, his $876.58 winners share added to the $1,500 from Comiskey must have killed the pain, for he said nothing at the time.

After the 1912 season *Chicago Tribune* writer Hugh Fullerton called for an Ed Walsh poetry contest. The winner was identified only as "Cal."

> When the score is in a knot —
> Call Ed Walsh.
> When the game is getting hot —
> Call Ed Walsh.
> When the pitcher starts to quiver,
> And the fans begin to shiver,
> Who is it saves the life? —
> Eddie Walsh.
>
> When the pitcher starts to waver in the pinch,
> Who is it to the rescue? — It's a cinch
> It's the great big noble Eddie —
> Yes, it's he, the ever-ready —
> He's Johnny on the spot in a pinch.[2]

Comiskey, in another fit of generosity, arranged for a hunting trip to Lake Superior in Wisconsin. Big Ed left with the Old Roman's son, Louis Comiskey, right after the City Series and already had two days of hunting and fishing in when the rest of the party — Comiskey and 32 other men, including Callahan, A.L. president Ban Johnson, President McAleer of the world champion Red Sox, Cubs' treasurer Williams and a chef — arrived in two sleepers and a private dining car. A trainload of provisions had been shipped to camp ahead of the party.[3] When the chef, a New England native, spotted McAleer he approached him with hat in hand and grabbed the hand extended to him and with tears in his eyes and a choking voice stammered, "I'm so proud of you." McAleer said none of the thousands of congratulations he received was more sincere.

After the hunting trip, Big Ed went home to Meriden and spent a leisurely off season hunting, fishing and resting his arm. In January 1913 he sent a letter to Callahan. On January 15 Callahan told the *Tribune* all was fine with the Big Reel. "In his letter Ed said he was feeling fine this winter and thought he would be at his best. Of course I'm always banking on Ed Walsh going at the same old pace."[4]

That was the public stance, but by February there were hints that all was not fine with Big Ed, now 31 years old. The *Los Angeles Times* reported on February 5 that "Callahan and Gleason plan to give Walsh more rest this season and believe he will win a larger portion of his games as a result."[5] On February 18 Callahan and the White Sox trainer, Buckner, got ready for the spring trip to Paso Robles, California. Because Callahan wanted to present his players in clean uniforms for the exhibition games, 72 uniforms, more than twice the normal amount, were packed in four big trunks. There were enough uniforms for two complete teams to have clean uniforms for the games and another for morning practices. Buckner packed soccer balls, a medicine ball, eight tennis rackets and two dozen tennis balls. "There will be some real baseball practice in the 10 days at the California resort," Buckner said, "but most of the exercising will be done in other ways."

Jim Scott went ahead to California with instructions to build a court for a new game of rackets invented by Callahan. The game was similar to handball, a popular pastime, but a tennis racket was used instead of the bare hand. Callahan's schedule called for each day's practice to wind up with a 15-minute soccer game. It was an idea tried for the first

James "Nixey" Callahan played for the Sox in Big Ed's first two seasons in 1904 and '05 and managed them in Ed's last good year in 1912 (Library of Congress).

time the season before and because the soccer sent the players to the baths exhausted, Callahan liked it. The deluxe special train wasn't scheduled to leave Chicago until Thursday, February 22, at 8:30 P.M.[6] On February 18 Big Ed walked into the Comiskey Park office, the first White Sox to arrive in Chicago. Wearing a blue business suit, an elegant black chinchilla coat, and black derby hat, he declared his right arm was feeling strong and his health was splendid. Asked what he did all winter, he said, "just hunting, fishing and resting."[7]

Over 2,000 fans gathered at the train station for the Sox getaway. Outfitted with two Pullman cars with lower berths for each player, dining car, and a lounge-observation car, the train carried 23 players, Comiskey and his family, five baseball writers, scout Ted Sullivan, and 50 well-heeled fans. Two players were picked up along the way and 12 others were to meet the team in Paso Robles. After spending the night in Cheyenne, Wyoming, the train arrived in Paso Robles on the 23rd.[8] Once settled in camp, Big Ed went through workouts with the rest of the team. He threw only lightly, though, and didn't try the spitter. There were conflicting accounts of his condition. From a newspaper story: "Ed Walsh is in better trim than any of the pitchers for the heavy grind of the season. He has kept in perfect shape all winter and has been systematic in his training here. Walsh is a marvel of humanity — an argument against the decay of strength and stamina."[9]

But in a letter home Big Ed talked for the first time about life after baseball. "I wrote a letter to Mrs. Walsh and told her to make preparations to leave the east for good. I'll sell my home down there and build a home in one of the Chicago suburbs. The boys will be almost in the country and still find good schools. I feel now that I belong in Chicago. When the time comes that I can't pitch any longer, I would like to go into some business right there."[10]

Rain and cold kept the team indoors and limited what they could do the first week of camp. Sam Weller, a *Chicago Tribune* writer who was with the team, put it this way: "The hotel advertises the place as one of sunshine, sulfur and mud. So far there has been plenty of sulfur and mud." To keep busy the team played Callahan's racket game and tossed Buckner's medicine ball. Big Ed and Davy Jones, a former Tiger who had been the Detroit team handball champion, played a game and Big Ed won 21–9. On March 10 the White Sox played their first exhibition games, a morning-afternoon double header against Oakland and the San Francisco Seals in San Francisco. Big Ed pitched the second game. He went four innings, and though he gave up five hits, nothing seemed amiss. He was clearly the main attraction to the 10,000 who came to the second game. "Big Ed seemed to have all his speed and was able to stick over a regular spitter when the occasion demanded it. In the fourth two batters got on with scratches and he got the side out without the runner reaching third. Two were forced at third and one popped out. Attendance was 10,000."[11]

What Big Ed said to Callahan after that outing isn't known, but eight days passed before he pitched again. What happened on March 18 illustrated what Callahan was up against in California that spring. On the one hand he wanted to use Big Ed only sparingly and save him for the regular season; on the other hand the California fans demanded to see the Big Reel. On March 18 he was supposed to pitch against Portland of the Pacific Coast League in Visalia. Businesses closed for the afternoon and schools were dismissed. A crowd of 1,500, huge for the small town, came out. When Big Ed did not pitch as advertised the fans booed. Lord, who as captain was in charge of the team that day, "brought Walsh out as a trophy so the crowd could take a peek at him." That didn't appease them. When he did not pitch by the sixth inning the fans started chanting "Big Ed" and kept it up for two innings. When he didn't come out in the eighth, the county sheriff, a burly man a head taller than the 6-foot-1 Walsh, and wearing a long mustache, climbed out of the grandstand and strode across the diamond to the visitors' dugout. As the fans lustily cheered him on, the sheriff walked over to Big Ed and ordered him to go to the slab and pitch.

"Lord didn't care to disobey the law," said a newspaper account, "especially as it was laid down by that particular lawman, so he told Ed to warm up and pitch the final inning.

"The game was the most notable event since gold was discovered in the mountains east of here. The town boasts 4000 population and 1500 of them paid 50 cents and $1 to see big leaguers in action. A feature was the number of automobiles. It seems that nearly every other man in the section of the state owns a car and all within 40 miles of the burg were driven to the ballpark. Automobiles were lined along the right and left field lines as thickly as they would stand and more than 100 were parked in the streets and lots outside."[12]

It was another six days before Big Ed pitched again. On March 24 he pitched the second game of a four game series with the Los Angeles Angels. He went seven innings, gave up two unearned runs, five hits, struck out just two, walked one, and won, 5–2. The outing was encouraging, but in what would become an ever-increasing pattern, he took a long break before his next appearance. It was 90 in the shade for a game in Yuma,

Arizona, on April 1. It was perfect weather for Big Ed, who always pitched better in the heat, but his only appearance in Yuma was at a nearby farm where he gathered a handful of ostrich feathers. The fans accepted that Big Ed didn't pitch, as they knew little of baseball and were appeased by other entertainment. The Alabama Minstrels sang between innings. Several hundred Indians were in town. "They wore long hair, had paint and feathers in plenty and were all bare footed. Baseball is still novel in this town. The field was marked out for the game with a chalk line that went all around the infield." After the game the mayor took the team in a car caravan to a hill from where they could view the reclaimed Imperial Valley, a desert made green by irrigation.[13]

Finally on April 3 Big Ed pitched again in Amarillo, Texas. It was hot but the sun wasn't visible due to a rampant dust storm. Conditions were bad but cowboys and ranchmen came 100 miles in motor cars to see a game and Callahan was afraid to cancel. Big Ed pitched three innings in a 12–2 Sox win over the local amateurs. The locals got two hits off him. For those bored by the baseball, champion rough riders broke wild horses for entertainment.[14] From Amarillo the Sox made their way East, stopping in St. Joseph, Missouri, on April 6 for a game against the local team. Callahan decided it was time to find out once and for all if Big Ed was ready for the American League Championship season, which was just five days away. Over 5,000 fans came out to see Ed pitch and for six innings he gave them their money's worth. It was 1–1 going into the seventh, when St. Joe's suddenly erupted for six hits and three runs. He finished the inning, but that was all. He walked four and struck out four in the seven innings.

Weller spoke to Big Ed in the locker room and wrote, "This was to have been the final workout for the star before sending him to the mound for the opener Thursday at Cleveland. He had intended to work nine innings, but after his experience in the seventh felt he had enough for one day. Walsh will not change his plans for opening day. Walsh said he will be the man to open unless his right arm drops off before Thursday."[15]

Big Ed's arm didn't drop off, but, as Weller wrote, his plans for opening day changed the next day. "After he was bombarded in the seventh inning against the St. Joe team, Walsh admitted he had a sore arm and Callahan made up his mind right there that Walsh was not ready for the opener," Weller wrote. Callahan was worried about Big Ed, whom he called his "Big Moose," but believed he would come around as he had in the past. "You have to remember," Callahan said, "Walsh wasn't ready last spring when the season opened and wasn't much help to us at any of the

13. What's the Matter with Big Ed?

A rare close up look at Big Ed. His eyes look a little tired. Maybe he was feeling the effects of all the worrying over his arm about 1912.

time we were in first place. Walsh finally did come around when the others fell down. There isn't anything the matter with Walsh. He just needs more time and warmer weather and the way the other fellows are pitching it may be just as well to let Ed go light on the pitching for the first month."[16]

Either Callahan's memory of how Walsh had started the previous season was faulty or he said what he said hoping everybody would buy his theory and not remember what really happened in 1912. In fact, Walsh did pitch opening day in 1912, took his regular turn thereafter and started 7–1.

The day before the Sox' 1913 opener in Cleveland the *Tribune* broke the news. "It will be a remarkable opening for Comiskey's team because Ed Walsh will not be on the slab for Chicago when the gong rings. Callahan announced the Big Moose was not ready and he would not be asked to pitch a game until he was ready."[17]

Scott pitched the opener and lost 3–1. Benz pitched the next day and won 13–3. The Sox then went to St. Louis for a three-game series. In the first game the Sox were leading 7–2 in the ninth when Lange, the Sox starter, walked the first three batters. Loath to let the game slip away, Callahan brought in Big Ed. In his first appearance of the 1913 season he faced three batters, each as the potential tying run, and struck them all out. Emboldened by the three strikeouts, two days later Callahan gave his Big Moose his first start of the season. He pitched a complete game, gave up nine hits, and beat the Browns 5–3. In the seventh, working with a 4–1 lead, he walked the lead off batter, then gave up a double and single and suddenly it was 4–3 with a runner on first and no out. Then the old Big Reel emerged and fanned Williams, Pratt and Stovall in succession. It was noted that he didn't seem to be letting go with the spitter except when he had to, as in that spot in the seventh. Even so it was believed that Big Ed was back. "It looks as if manager Callahan need not hold his big star back any longer. From now on he can be counted on to pitch at least every fourth day and be counted on to save a game or two in between."[18]

Big Ed's second start came at home on April 21 after a full four days rest. Over 20,000 fans came out to see the Big Reel make his home debut, but they saw him for only three innings. Cleveland started the game with a double and seemed to have no fear of him after that. Though he gave up just one run in three innings, he gave up six hits, two of them doubles. Lajoie was robbed of an extra base on a diving catch by Ping Bodie, the Naps popped up a bunt for a double play with two on, and two more runners were caught stealing, or it would have been worse. Walsh didn't come out for the fourth inning and was relieved by Cicotte, who gave up just one run over the last six innings. Cleveland won 2–1. The weather didn't help. The wind off the lake felt like it was coming off ice.[19]

The homestand lasted nine more days, but Big Ed did not appear again. The writers inquired, but nobody was talking. On April 29 — the day Comiskey announced he planned to spend $150,000 to expand the capacity of South Side Park to 45,000, making it the largest in the country — the Sox left for a five-game set in Detroit with 22 players. Big Ed was not one of them. It was said he had a bad cold. On May 11 before a home game against the Athletics, White Sox fans presented Big Ed with a six-cylinder touring car with oversized tires, selected for especially heavy touring. "Although fox hunting is a great sport, motoring has it all over it like a tent," Big Ed told Teddy Edwards, a friend from Hartford who was a manager of the Goodyear Tire and Rubber Company in Akron, Ohio. "I am going to get as much out of my car as possible this summer. It is going to go anywhere I can take it."[20]

As things turned out Big Ed would have plenty of time for motoring that summer. The day after he was given the car, though, perhaps as a reward to his generous fans, Big Ed pitched for the first time in almost three weeks. Though he pitched a complete game and beat the A's 4–3, it was clear he wasn't up to his old form. "The Big Reel was not right, as his four passes and two wild pitches make affidavit. He had to resort frequently to the slippery elm box and at times had to resort to heroic stops by Ray Schalk to cope with the loose chucks he made."[21] As was his new pattern, he let loose only when he had to. In the ninth with the tying run at third he struck out Rube Oldring to end the game. Despite that win it was clear something was wrong with Big Ed. But what? The White Sox team doctor, Dr. James H. Blair, had a bizarre theory — Big Ed's problem was not in his arm, but in his stomach. Blair said excessive use of the spitball was affecting Big Ed's digestion and making him weak. "The doctor said the saliva needed for Walsh's digestion has been used on the ball, but with care the pitcher may regain his old time form in a month."[22]

Big Ed didn't pitch again for a week after beating the A's 4–3. A rest like that was an indication that something was wrong. On May 18 he pitched a complete game and won 5–3. On paper that sounded great. In reality he looked terrible. It was a testament to his guile and guts, not his arm, that he held the Yankees to three runs. The *Trib* was merciless in its description. "A three-run triple by Harry Desmond in the third enabled Ed Walsh to add one more victory to his long string without pitching anything that would dent a wire screen. He gave up six hits and walked five. He breezed through the last three innings as nonchalantly as if he were sitting by an open fireplace in a smoking jacket and slippers inhaling a dollar perfecto. How Walsh got by with what he handed out was a mystery to everyone who watched him do it. He used nothing but a slow ball with an occasional lazy curve, a couple spitters and fastballs. When asked about how he pitched, Walsh made a noise like an Egyptian sphinx and with an immobile smile passed on to the shower. The only explanation was that the Yankees kept on hitting at Walsh's 1908 stuff and he kept feeding them mush balls."[23]

Six days later, on the day of his next start, Big Ed suddenly made public a plan to sell a mail order course for kids for $1 on the art of throwing the spitball. "I know when I was new in the game," he said of the venture, "I would have been glad for just such advice as I am going to hand out. I do not claim that my lessons will make stars out of those who follow them, but I know I have a lot of pointers that will get young fellows started in the right direction."[24] He had never been one to seek alternative incomes in the off season, now here he was doing so during a season.

Was the mail order plan one more hint that the end was near for the Big Reel's arm? He didn't suggest anything like that. He said he just wanted to help kids.

But his start that day belied his denial. He pitched just five innings in a 4–3 loss to Cleveland in Chicago and was lifted for a pinch hitter. Four days later he was back on the mound again for his most disastrous outing yet. In the second game of a double header at Cleveland, he didn't get out of the second inning. In the first inning he gave up two runs on two walks, a single and two wild pitches. In the second he gave up ringing doubles to the first two batters, the second one by the light-hitting pitcher Vean Gregg. "It was made plain to everyone that Walsh was not there or even thereabouts."[25]

After a five game series at home versus Detroit, during which Big Ed did not so much as warm up, the White Sox left for Boston to start a 16-game Eastern swing. On the way, Big Ed stopped home in Connecticut. He caught up with the team the next day, June 3, in Boston, but wasn't scheduled to face the Red Sox. It was cool in Boston and the official spin was that he had a heavy cold and would not pitch again until the weather warmed. On June 7 in New York, after nine days rest, Big Ed was given the ball. It was warm and humid. Clouds rolled in so thick the sky went dark and it was difficult for fans in the grandstand to see the outfielders. With one out in the third the deluge came. Everybody ran for shelter and hid for a half an hour while the downpour flooded the field. Conditions were not fit for ball playing, but when the rain slackened Yankee owner Colonel Ruppert, rather than sacrifice the gate money, ordered the game to continue. Another half-hour was spent trying to sweep lakes of water off the field and the game was resumed in a drizzle on a field of mud. Big Ed came back out after the delay and completed the game, losing 3–2.

After he lost to the Yankees in the rain, a week passed before he started again. In Washington he beat the Senators 6–4. "He started with nothing but his spikes and his half balk motion and the Big Reel had his troubles nearly all the way. He got through palpably in a posing mood. Had he not been replaced with Tex Russell in the eighth there might have been a different anecdote to relate."[26]

And so a pattern emerged. Big Ed could pitch, and even win, but he won throwing slop of a different kind. He threw the spitter, which required fastball arm action to be effective, only in desperate situations, and the more he threw it, the longer were his rests between games. He took regular turns after the start in Washington with starts in Philadelphia on the 18th and then back home versus the Browns in the second game of a double header on the 22nd. He pitched a complete game shutout against the Browns, winning 2–0. In the seventh he made a game saving play while covering first on a ground ball to first baseman Schalk. When Schalk threw wild, Big Ed made a diving stop and held the bag for the out.

Five days later he beat Cleveland 7–5, but then disappeared for almost three weeks. Big Ed didn't pitch for three weeks, but his brother Martin Walsh did. On June 24 Martin pitched a no-hitter for Tarrytown against Stamford. On July 3 Callahan bought pitcher Buck O'Brien from Boston. Was it another sign that Big Ed was not expected to regain his old form, or just insurance? On July 15 in Chicago it was flag-raising day and the Sox raised a Championship of Chicago flag. Big Ed was back on the mound and played like the Big Ed of old. He pitched a complete 10-inning game, walked just one, picked two runners off base, and batted in the winning run with a single in the bottom of the 10th. A large crowd was on hand for his reemergence. They cheered him lustily, but their joy would be short-lived — Walsh would make only three more appearances the rest of 1913.

He started on July 19 in the second game of a home double header against the Athletics. Over 30,000 saw him give up after five innings. Though at the time Big Ed said nothing about his arm, in an interview with *Baseball Magazine* in 1914 he described how he felt when he pitched in '13: "I could feel the muscles grind and wrench and it seemed to me it would leap out of the socket when I shot the ball across the plate, but I burned the ball just the same."

On July 24 the Sox left for an Eastern swing. Big Ed stayed behind. "It didn't seem natural at all to be starting away for an Eastern invasion without Ed Walsh. The last thing he said to manager Callahan before the boys left was that he would take the train to the East the very day he thought he could be of any help to the team." Though he tried to find a remedy, that day would never come. Left with nothing to do, Big Ed went upstate for some sulfur baths, a supposed remedy, and some hunting while waiting for an appointment with "Bonesetter" Reese on August 18.

Born in Wales in 1856, John D. "Bonesetter" Reese was 22 when he emigrated to Youngstown. He worked in a mill where he became interested in anatomy after observing, and sometimes treating, injuries from mill accidents. He studied anatomy and medicine on his own time. He hung around hospitals and befriended doctors who allowed him to witness operations. Because he made himself available around the clock, he became a physicians' apprentice of sorts. In time he put an MD after his name and saw patients on his own. After he treated some local ballplayers in the Youngstown area, he developed a word-of-mouth reputation as a doctor who could get athletes back on the field. It was believed he had a knack for placing his forefinger on the ailing spot and finding the patient's trouble with one poke. He worked for years without a license. Badgered by Ohio officials, he eventually took and passed the examinations to become a licensed MD, albeit one without a college or medical school degree. Among the notables who were treated by Reese were Hugh Jennings, Cy Young and Honus Wagner. He treated the athletes with manipulation, claiming to move misplaced tendons back into place.

While Reese was well known for treating athletes, he treated other injuries and was credited with saving a seven-year-old boy from being crippled. In 1912 Bernard Hill, the son of a mail carrier from Newark, fell off a bike. He was in bed nine weeks without improvement. His right foot and back were badly injured and he was thought to be paralyzed. His father took him to see Reese in Youngstown. Reese said a nerve in his foot was severed and a bone in his back was out of place. Under his treatment the child improved and returned home completely cured.[27]

While some athletes swore he cured them, it is likely his reputation produced a placebo effect, as few of the athletes regained their old form for more than a few days or weeks. Honus Wagner saw Reese for his knee after the 1913 season. After examining and treating Wagner, Reese declared him fit for duty, while creating a scapegoat for himself if Wagner failed. "He is far from being all in as a major league player. His leg is as strong as it ever was and there is no reason — unless the great player succumbs to the criticism of the masses — why Hans should not continue in the game for several years. His muscles show no sign of exhaustion, but there is grave fear in my mind that Hans will sink before the adverse criticism of the newspapers."[28]

So it was that when Wagner went from one of the game's all-around greats to a slow .250 singles hitter, it was the fans' and the writers' fault, not Bonesetter's. When Reese examined Walsh he diagnosed a misplaced tendon in his shoulder. On locating this it took exactly three minutes to "fix" the Big Reel.[29] "He doesn't looked particularly muscular, but his hands are like grappling irons," Big Ed said of Reese. "He dug his iron fingers into my shoulder and said there was a ligament displaced in my shoulder and in my arm where it was attached to the bone at the elbow. His remedy was a year's rest. I was looking for more immediate results. There may well have been a ligament out of place in my arm, I was perfectly willing to admit that, but I didn't want to rest a year or anything like it. However, that is about what I have done, if lack of successful work can be called a rest."[30]

13. What's the Matter with Big Ed?

On September 18 he pitched four innings in relief, his first appearance in two months, and gave up four hits and three walks. His last gasp of '13 was on September 23 when he coaxed five innings out of his arm in the second game of a double header in Boston. Though the White Sox won the game 3–2 they finished the day in fifth place, 21 games behind the first place Philadelphia A's. Big Ed called it a season and for the last week coached first base while the Sox played out the string. In 1913 Big Ed pitched in 16 games, 14 as a starter. He completed seven with an 8–3 record and a 2.58 ERA. The numbers proved one thing: Ed Walsh could be a fairly effective pitcher if he pitched just twice a month.

And things were about to get much worse. In the four seasons after 1913 Big Ed would pitch in fewer games, 16, than he would have by May in a typical single season before 1913.

Over the winter of 1913 and 1914 Comiskey took the White Sox on a world tour. When it was announced they would go, Big Ed told the *Tribune* he had other plans. "Not me, I'm going to work in vaudeville. I saw Jennings getting that money and decided I've been a fool. If a guy can go out and get $500 a week for kicking up one foot and yelling 'Ee-Yah' I see where I ought to get a fortune just to go and sing some songs."

Though by all accounts Big Ed was a fine singer, his threat to go on a vaudeville tour was more of a shot at Jennings than a serious consideration. He never did go on tour. Instead, while the White Sox were overseas that winter, he went to California to rehabilitate his arm for the 1914 season, insisting that 1913 had been a fluke. He was there waiting for the White Sox when they got to Paso Robles for their fifth annual spring there in late February.

Though at the time he said nothing about his arm, in an interview with *Baseball Magazine* in September of 1914 he admitted his arm was hurting that winter. "This year began like last year, only worse. The White Sox spent the winter in touring the world. I spent the winter in California hoping that I might sometime be able to do a little more work in my own chosen line, and most of the winter fearing that I was through. It was hard for me to realize and I fought off the admission even to myself. But appearances were all that way. I wasn't in the position of a youngster just breaking into the game who is merely delayed in his start. I was growing old. I had but little more time at my disposal, and what I did would have to be done quickly, if at all.

"I spent a long time in California trying to get into condition. So far as I could see I made no progress. It was very discouraging. And all the first part of the year I was practically useless."[31]

But that was not the party line coming out of Paso Robles at the time via the *Los Angeles Times*. "Ed Walsh has been working hard trying to overcome the ailment that kept him out of the harness last season. He took another stiff workout during the other day and the prospects for his coming back are brighter than ever. He pitched with tremendous speed and felt no ill effects in his shoulder."[32]

The *Chicago Tribune* was a little more cautious. The next day Sanborn reported that Walsh limbered up a bit and tested his arm gingerly and found he could get a lot of the old steam into the ball, but did not experiment with the spitter. On March 1 the *Atlanta Constitution* published shutout statistics and said Big Ed better come back "if he desires to retain his title of Monarch of the American League Whitewash Brigade." Eddie Plank threw seven shutouts in 1913 to Big Ed's one and was one behind Big Ed in career shutouts 56–55. It was noted that Walsh had blanked the Red Sox 15 times.

The team stayed together in Paso Robles for only 10 days and then split into two squads to play 78 scheduled games in seven weeks. On March 4, Big Ed pitched in a game for the first time since the last City Series game the previous October. He had little or nothing on the ball. He faced 13 batters in less than two innings and gave up seven hits. He hit a home run as a batter, which may have spurred the idea to have him go to Los Angeles with the second team, The Goofs, as an outfielder. In the first game in LA he hit two more home runs. The next day in Venice he was 3 for 5 with a double and a run scored in a 4–1 win. Before the game he pitched some batting practice and the *Los Angeles Times* took note. "Walsh apparently is in the best condition of the lot. He pitched batting practice for quite a spell and is feeling frisky as a two year old over the response of his veteran muscles. Ed Walsh is believed to be the only pitcher in America who can stand in the box and spit clear to home plate without winding up."

On March 8 he was the starting pitcher against the Salt Lake City Mormons in San Jose. He scarcely let loose and lasted six innings, before trading places with outfielder Ray Demmitt. Salt Lake won 5–2. That outing prompted rumors that he was through as a pitcher. Big Ed issued an immediate denial. "I was astounded to hear that I was through as a pitcher, that my comeback had been a failure. I have been pitching major league ball for 11 years and feel that I am good for a good many more. It is true there is a slight soreness in my arm, but that is a common ailment in the spring. Nine-tenths of the pitchers in the country are probably complaining about the same thing. I am not making any boasts or brags, but I do believe that I will be able to come back.

"It would be foolhardy for me to take any chances and for that reason I am nursing my arm along carefully. Just tell them that Ed Walsh doesn't think that he is through for a few years yet."[33] On March 14 he pitched three innings against Venice and gave up four runs. He didn't try to put much on the ball and the Gondoliers scored four off him in a 10–0 win.

In 1913 Big Ed's ironman role with the Sox had been filled by 21-year-old rookie Reb Russell from Mississippi. He pitched 316 innings in a league-leading 52 games and won 23. As the spring wore on it was speculated that if Big Ed came back the Sox would have best the pitching in the league. Neither Walsh nor Russell would have to be overworked. On March 24 came news that such a plan might really happen. Bill Gleason, a White Sox coach that spring said the Big Reel was right again, "with an upper 'R' on the Big Reel. He's carded to pitch in Los Angeles on the 28th. You can take it from your uncle William that Walsh is going to pitch some ball this year. I watched him work out yesterday and took the mitt myself to see what the big fellow has. He's there, I tell you, for he was spitting on the ball and putting the old break on it and there was steam behind that old pill. He has been nursing that wing of his all winter and spring like a baby. Only recently has he tried it out for the fair, but listening to the crack of the mitt and watching the ball yesterday, I know he's coming back."[34]

The good news kept coming. Big Ed pitched in Venice on March 28 and despite a 3–2 loss started to look like the Big Reel again. "He hurled five innings and found he had all his stuff when needed. The first batter poked a triple to right, but didn't score and it was the only hit he gave up. He did not exert himself too much, but turned loose good speed when he had to. Walsh also found his spitter would work as well as ever. After this test Walsh was as tickled as a six-year-old with a new railroad train to play with. He wore that famous old smile that had been missing from his Celtic physiognomy for many months."[35]

Big Ed pitched in the last spring exhibition game in St. Joseph, Missouri, on April 11. It was the same city in which he pitched the last exhibition the previous season and where he was exposed as not ready for the major league season. This time, though, he breezed through four innings, giving up just one hit.

When the season opened on April 14 in Chicago, Big Ed was on the bench without explanation. It wasn't until the Sox went on their first Eastern swing in mid–May that Callahan tried Big Ed out and even then it was in an exhibition game during a stop in Pittsburgh. It was quickly evident why Big Ed had not pitched sooner. He had no movement on his pitches and the Pirates battered him for 11 hits and seven runs, all earned, in four innings. It was not until June 30, in the Sox' 68th game of the season, that Big Ed got into a regular game. He was brought in relief of Russell in the seventh inning in a hopeless cause in Detroit.

> No battle scarred hero ever received a greater welcome from his home folks as Walsh was given by the hostile fans of this town when he broke back into the game. Before the megaphone man had his chance to announce the Big Moose, the rooters had spotted his familiar form striding in from the warming pan and began cheering.
>
> More than half the spectators jumped to their feet during this spontaneous welcome for an illustrious enemy and some stood on the backs of their seats to be better heard. They cheered him as he pitched a few preliminary balls and when he shot the first one across to Sam Crawford for a strike there was a yelp of joy as if it were the stockyard crowd rooting for Big Ed. As he retired the side in the seventh the fans cheered Walsh again and despite an awful eighth they were with him and jeered his erring teammates who were responsible for the runs made off him in the eighth.
>
> Walsh had practically his old speed and got his old time spitball breaking low. In addition he displayed a curve ball which he never had before.[36]

The line: no walks, one strikeout, two hits, one earned run in three innings. The Tigers won 8–1.

Encouraged by that outing, and by the reaction of the Tigers fans, Callahan gave Big Ed his first start of 1914 in Chicago on July 5 against the Naps. With 10,000 fans cheering him on every pitch, he went seven innings and won 6–3. He gave up three hits, three runs, three walks, and had three strikeouts. He was lifted for a pinch hitter in the eighth. On July 13 in New York even the skeptics had to admit that it looked like Big Ed was back. He pitched a complete game and shut out the Yankees 2–0. He gave up six hits, never more than one in an inning. He walked two and struck out three.

> Even the hostiles cheered Walsh when he demonstrated beyond all doubt that he is back. Right now Walsh is about all a person hears about on the White Sox team. The players showed how they felt during the game. Every man on the field was straining with every ball Walsh pitched. On the bench, too, no one sat down when the Sox were on the field. They moved about their coop nervously, shouting now and then to Walsh and assuring one another that the Big Reel would go through. Callahan hung on the edge of the dugout watching every move of the spitball king. After each inning as Walsh came from the slab he grabbed him and poured forth a string of encouragement.
>
> He used his new curve, but when the Yankees threatened in the later

13. What's the Matter with Big Ed?

innings it was the old spitball he fell back on and his fastball also seemed to travel much faster than in the earlier rounds. At the start the Yankee coachers yelled "He ain't got nothing." After the game they flocked around Walsh and congratulated him.

In the last three innings every ball Walsh threw had something on it that made the Yankees look foolish. The spitter was breaking as it used to break.[37]

It may have seemed to the fans that Ed was ready to return to his old form and to a regular spot in the rotation. But behind the scenes, Big Ed and Callahan knew better. He would get in only six more games the rest of the season and though he wouldn't admit it for another two years, he was through as a major league pitcher. He started again on July 18 in the first game of a double header in Philadelphia and lost to Plank 4–1. If nothing else he could still draw fans. Despite what was described as "boiling heat," 15,000 came to Shibe Park that day. Nine days later in Chicago he pitched a complete game against the Yankees in Chicago and lost 1–0 to Leonard "King" Cole. He allowed five hits, walked two, one intentionally, and struck out five, including Cree and Mullen, the last two he faced.

On August 2 he lost 5–2 to the A's in Chicago. "Ed Walsh went to the slab with considerable gusto. The fans cheered as if the honor of Chicago was in his hands. Ed toiled as if it were, too, but when the fourth round was over the 'Big Moose' hero of so many combats on the south side disappeared." The A's hammered him for four in the fourth. Baker hit a long triple to the wall. Big Ed left having walked four without a strikeout. On August 6 he pitched five innings in a 13–1 exhibition win in Waukegan, Illinois. He was cheered wildly when he went to the slab and when he went to bat.

By August the sporting press was getting sick of Big Ed's comebacks and turned from supportive to mocking.

> The new curveball is a 'loo-loo.' Some of Ed's teammates have told about it, but their description of it is just as lucid as most of the cables that describe the European war. The new curve first shoots to the left after leaving the hand and then shoots to the right. Half way home the ball stops for a second or two. If it is a warm day the ball pauses and cools itself off. If the day is cold the ball, after stopping, executes a few tangos and whirls as to keep itself warm.
>
> Providing the ball reaches the vicinity of the rubber safely it does several things. It loops the loop four times. Then it drops, or it doesn't drop, it shoots across the plate or it hits the player in the ribs or head, or on his manly buzzum, as according to Edward's aim.
>
> Sometimes upon arriving at the plate the ball doesn't do all those things. Sometimes, well, you know, Ty Cobb and them other fellows.[38]

When the Sox left for a 23-game Eastern swing on August 14, Big Ed stayed in Chicago. On their way back to Chicago on September 8 the Sox stopped in McHenry, Illinois, for an exhibition game. Though the town had a population of only 500, 2,000 came out upon the rumor that Big Ed Walsh would show. Many of them came from their summer homes in their motorcars and when play started there was a complete ring of motorcars around the field. Big Ed didn't disappoint. He drove from Chicago in his own motorcar and felt so good he insisted on starting the game. He pitched five innings gave up three hits, one run and struck out six. Part of the entertainment for the Sox was a motorboat ride down the Fox River. Their boat collided with a speedboat when the driver tried to pull alongside the players' boat.

Big Ed gave it one more shot. He appeared for two innings against the A's on August 26 in Chicago, one of three pitchers who gave up 17 hits in a 9–2 loss. "Ed toiled for less than two innings and the Macks hammered him, reputation and all."[39]

When the team left for Cleveland for the last series of the season, Walsh didn't go. He went with Comiskey to Camp Jerome in northern Wisconsin for a hunting vacation and ostensibly to rest before the City Series. But he didn't pitch in the series. Even without Big Ed, the Sox, who won only 70 games in the regular season, managed to upset the Cubs again for their third consecutive Chicago pennant.

In September of 1914 Big Ed gave a long and rambling interview to F.C. Lane in *Baseball Magazine* and the truth poured out.

> I date the beginning of the trouble with my arm to the city series of 1912. In the second inning of a game that I pitched against the Cubs I was hit on the jaw by a line drive which struck me so hard that the mark of the stitches showed in my face. It completely dazed me, but I went on pitching in a mechanical way and finished the game. I seemed to have as much stuff on the ball as I ever had, so they told me, and as the White Sox piled up a number of runs, I won without difficulty. After the game, when I had recovered from the shock of that blow and the general excitement, I noticed that my arm felt weak and sore, as though I had strained it. However, that was the finish of a very hard season. I had pitched in 62 games altogether, 393 innings in all, in addition to the hard work of the series, so I was through. And I thought little about it until the next spring.
>
> That spring I was treated to a novel surprise. For the first time in my life I was able to take things easy. Comiskey and Callahan told me to train lightly and not overwork, and I followed their advice. It would probably have made no great difference, anyway, in the result. At any rate, I continued to take things easy until I was slated to pitch an exhibition game at Venice. I went into the box with my old-time confidence. It had been a long time since

that game in the city series of the previous autumn. I had no intimation that the arm was not in as good shape as ever. And perhaps I was more surprised than anyone else in the park when that Venice club proceeded to hammer everything I had to all parts of the field. It was a most unwelcome surprise and I couldn't explain it. But I made up my mind to show better form on my next appearance.

Certainly the possibility that I might be even worse never crossed my mind. And yet that is exactly what happened. I went against the St. Joe team in Missouri, and, not content with hitting my best offerings freely, they batted me out of the box. It was a great humiliation to me and a crushing blow to my hopes. I couldn't understand what was the matter with my arm, for it had never acted in that way before.[40]

In the same interview he refused to blame Comiskey or Callahan for overworking him and he heaped praise on the Old Roman. "All I am in the baseball world I owe to Comiskey. If I am a good pitcher, he made me so. He took me in when I was awkward and green and had nothing but strength and a desire to learn. He showed all kinds of patience with me. He kept me on the payroll when my name on that payroll was all the world to me. He turned a deaf ear to the advice of friends who wanted him to let me go. He worked hard and faithfully with me and made a winner of me. He will always get my best so long as I have anything to give. He is the most generous, most popular and most likable man in baseball. He has thousands of friends. Everybody likes Comiskey."[41]

Everybody liked Comiskey in Chicago that winter, especially after he bought 1914 Chalmers MVP winner and second baseman Eddie Collins from the A's. He also bought rookie outfielder Oscar "Happy" Felsch from Milwaukee and hired energetic 33-year-old manager Clarence "Pants" Rowland. With that trio and other additions the 1915 White Sox would rise from sixth place and 70 wins in 1914 to third place with a 93–61 record. Big Ed Walsh would win only three of those games.

On January 10, 1915, under a new roster limit of 22 imposed by the A.L., 11 Sox were released unconditionally or sent to the minors. There was conjecture about how the Sox would handle Big Ed and Billy Sullivan, who was 40 years old, had been with the Sox since 1901 and was long beyond his effectiveness. It was speculated they might take minor league managing positions. The shoe dropped on "Sully" on February 8. Big Ed was kept on the roster and was with the Sox when they arrived in Oakland for spring training on February 21. He took on the role of a quasi-coach under Rowland. Some of the players went to a world's fair, the Panama-Pacific Exposition. Eddie Collins, who had never been to the coast before, and Big Ed were recognized.

At camp in Paso Robles, Walsh led the boys on 10-mile morning hikes through the hills around the camp. When the team was split Walsh was assigned to the Goofs as player-manager. But still some persisted in intimating that he would pitch again. The *Tribune* wrote this line: "The Moose plans to take his time getting ready for slab duties, but is adhering closely to the method of training which he believes will enable him to resume regular hurling."

On March 2 Rowland was asked point blank what he thought of the chance that the Moose was regaining his old form. "After the second team leaves Oakland and gets to the warmer climate of Los Angeles, I will put the big fellow to the test. The second team is not due in the southern end of the state until March 18 and by that time he will be in trim to show. I expect to send him through an entire game about that time. If Walsh shows any of his old form, he will lose his job as manager of the Goofs, because I want him to return East by the Southern route and take no chances with the possible chilly winds of the north. He has pitched a lot of batting practice, but never yet has he cut lose with anything like his old time speed."[42]

Big Ed kept quiet and whenever he was asked about his arm would say only, "It's feeling pretty good."

Manager Rowland had no explanation for the trouble with Big Ed's arm, but speculated the problem might be mental rather than physical. "I will admit that Walsh's case is a puzzler. Apparently there is nothing wrong with his arm. If there is any trouble he himself is unable to definitely locate it. He has no trouble getting it up above his shoulder and his action is free. I may be wrong but I am inclined to think the loss of confidence is the main trouble. When pitching he seems afraid to cut loose."[43]

It must have been lost on Rowland that when Ed "cut loose" it hurt like hell for six weeks. The *Tribune* had a funny take on Rowland's theory: "If this diagnosis is right many expect the trainer to quit massaging Ed's arm and begin massaging his head."

On March 29, 1915, the Sox left California for Chicago with Big Ed having thrown only in batting practice. Ed stayed behind to have his arm treated by a Los Angeles doctor. He was still there when the Sox opened the 1915 season on April 14 in St. Louis. That day the *New York Times* reported that Big Ed was about ready. "Ed Walsh was told today by the medical expert treating his arm that he would be in shape to return to Chicago in three weeks and take his regular turn in the box."

It got to the point where blisters were considered good news. The *Los Angeles Times* reported that Ed had blisters on the first and second fingers of his pitching hand and that meant he could grip the ball hard enough to create blisters, something he had been unable to do during the past two years. From that same story, "Walsh has been performing wonders in his workouts. As far as can be observed from throwing in practice he has 75 percent of his old stuff, if not more. How he'll fare against batters remains to be seen. But now he and his friends are hopeful. He will leave here on May 1 and be back in the harness three days later." [44]

But May 1 came and Ed was not in a harness. He was in a bed in the Hotel Westminster. He had a high fever and was diagnosed with grippe, a word used at the time to describe respiratory ailments, including influenza. On May 4 he was admitted to Angelus Hospital by Dr. C.W. Cook. Whatever he had didn't leave him until May 14 and he didn't get to Chicago until the 18th. He told Rowland he was ready to pitch up to his old form. Rowland said he would be given a trial in the near future. He worked out for a while with catcher Tommy Daley, who said Ed had better stuff than he did anytime in 1913. He was scheduled to pitch batting practice the next day, but didn't because of the cold weather.

On May 18 Ring Lardner wondered, in rhyme, if Big Ed wasn't being delusional in his insistence that he could pitch again.

> Welcome to you Eddie!
> We're glad you've not forgotten Chicago, Illinois.
> The fans rejoice to see you, And all the players, too.
> But are you certain Eddie,
> That there's a place for you?
>
> Conceding that your souper
> Will prove to be O.K.
> And that you'll zip 'em through there in your old-fashioned way;
> Conceding you're a come-back,
> Rebuilt as good as new;
> Conceding you're the old Ed Walsh
> Is there a place for you?
>
> You were the life preserver,
> The savior of your mates;
> You rescued fellow flingers
> Who found themselves in straits;
> You were the noble captain
> Of Commy's wrecking crew
> But now the boys have learned to swim,
> Is there a place for you?
>
> There's auburn Urban Faber,
> With smoking, scorching speed.

First aid is one commodity
He doesn't seem to need.
Opponents think they're lucky
When they get a hit or two.
Watch him perform; then tell me,
Is there a place for you?

There's Joseph Benz the Butcher,
With moistened, murderous hook,
And eke a Hoosier hop ball.
Just give this bird a look.
The tallies gathered off'n him
Are far between and few.
He's one swell pitcher, Edward —
Is there a place for you?

Then lamp the demon huntsman,
Death Valley Jimmy Scott.
Did you ever see a curve ball to beat the one he's got?
Why just the mention of his name
Turns all the Browns to Blue.
Observe Jim Scott and tell me,
Is there a place for you?

Then pipe the other Eddie,
Ed Cicotte, son of France.
A base hit off that knuckle ball?
Doable? Not a chance.
A knuckle ball and noodle,
An aim that's straight and true.
Just once him over Edward —
Is there a place for you?

And gaze on Rebel Russell.
Of southpaw breed and sex.
He's got the curve ball with him;
He brought it back from Tex.
He's better than two years ago,
So get a close up view
Of this young man then whisper
Is there a place for you?

And Wolfgang, too, and Jasper;
I ask if anywhere
You'll find two fill in pitchers
As classy as this pair.
Pull seven bearcats, Eddie;
Pull seven, tried and true.

Just count them, Ed, then tell me.
Is there a place for you?

No. no; I'm only fooling.
Don't answer me, I say.
For Eddie, we're not ready
To send you on your way.
For if you are the Walsh of old,
Some one, I don't know who,
Will have to yield his pitching turn
And MAKE a place for you.

And if that grand old souper
Has lost for good its zip;
If there's no crack remaining
In that once matchless whip;
If you are not a come-back;
If you, old boy, are through.
Pick out a soft spot on the bench —
There MUST be room for you.[45]

By June 3 Walsh had still not left that soft spot on the bench, except to help Rowland coach the bases. He'd gotten no closer to the slab. That night the Sox left for Boston to start a 20-game Eastern swing. The next day the train stopped in Springfield, Massachusetts, and Big Ed left the team to go home to Meriden after he received the news that his wife had been in an automobile accident. He left expecting to join the Sox in New York the next week, but the rumor was that he would not be seen again all season.

On June 8 the Giants said Christy Mathewson would be out for several weeks after being examined by a nerve specialist. "He is suffering from a nervous disorder of the left shoulder. Unable to sleep more than three hours a night because of the pain. Veteran baseball men who have discussed the case with Matty believe he has the same nerve affliction as Ed Walsh. Any violent exercise causes sharp pains to shoot through his shoulder and neck."[46]

On June 14 still another poem was published about Big Ed and his predicament by a noted writer, Grantland Rice.

As you stand coaching on the line
To help relay Doc Rowland's sign,
Forgotten on a Winning Nine,
I wonder if, amid the blur,
Dull memories begin to stir

> And speak again of Days that Were?
> I wonder if you seem to hear
> The echo of a roaring cheer
> That hailed you in a vanished year?
> Of flashing curve and blinding steam
> From days when you were All the Team?
> Or if, when rival batsmen clout
> With savage swing the pill about,
> And there is none to curb the rout,
> If, in your dream, you seem to see
> Stalking across the swarded lea
> The mighty Walsh that used to be?
> And as, in spectral-toned review,
> Amid acclaim that was your due,
> The golden vision comes to you,
> How does it strike your vaunted pride
> To feel the arm, once true and tried.
> Now dangling helpless at your side?[47]

Maybe it was because the Sox were winning without Big Ed, or maybe in private talks he told Rowland, as Rice's poem said, that his arm really was useless. In any case it wasn't until Friday, July 16, in Chicago, over halfway through the season in the team's 81st game, that Ed Walsh pitched for the first time. It was in the final game of an A's series. The Sox were in first place at 51–29, one game ahead of the Red Sox.

The announcement that Walsh would pitch came the day before, so the fans were ready. Rowland and Comiskey timed Big Ed's start with the day they raised the 1914 City Series pennant and the result was the largest weekday crowd of the season, over 28,000. Though the *Tribune* account of the day referred to Big Ed's appearance as a "comeback," it wasn't clear whether it was a comeback or a good-bye.

> With 28,000 friends of all ages, sexes, colors and previous conditions of homage rooting intensely for him, Edward Alright Walsh, veteran spitball monarch, came back yesterday, achieving a personal triumph unequaled in baseball. Backed by eight white-hosed athletes battling grimly, silently, determinedly for him, Big Ed licked the Athletics 6–2.
>
> No comeback could have been more complete or satisfying. If every last detail of the occasion had been made to order from the weather to the victory it could not have been more perfect. From the instant Walsh appeared to warm up until he was carried off the field on the shoulders of his admirers it was one continuous ovation for the greatest diamond hero the south side has known.
>
> For the flag ceremony a band led three squads of Uncle Sam's own soldiers

from Fort Sheridan carrying the stretched pennant. After raising the pennant they marched back to the front of the big stand and collected about home plate. With Walsh at the center of a big human horseshoe, a chest of silver and a loving cup were handed to the spitball king while several batteries of cameras worked overtime. Then the band broke up the party by playing The Wearing of the Green and the real comeback started.

The instant the last out was made a flock of rooters leaped from the stand to the field and carried him proudly to the Sox bench where Walsh was unable to escape the scores of admirers who pressed from every side to shake his hand.[48]

Walsh walked three, struck out five, and gave up six hits. He got out of trouble in the eighth. A walk and two singles scored a run and put runners on second and third with only one out with Schang and Lajoie due to bat. Walsh struck Schang out and induced Lajoie to pop out. The results on paper sounded like vintage Walsh, but the pitcher on the field did not pitch like him. He rarely if ever threw the spitter, but relied on a slow curve that was described as "dinky."

The *Los Angeles Times* said, "Control is all Walsh owns. Showed everything but his old speed." *The New York Times* said, "He seldom resorted to the moist ball but depended mostly on a slow curve and his expert knowledge of opposing batters."

However he pitched, Big Ed could still draw a crowd. On July 21 he pitched two scoreless innings in Henry, Illinois, in an exhibition against the Henry Grays. Over 5,000 paid $4,153, the largest crowd in Henry in six years. The Grays won 3–2. He could draw a crowd as an umpire, too. On August 2 he went to Des Moines to umpire a game there for his former teammate Frank Isbell, the team owner. The game drew the largest weekday crowd of the year in Des Moines.

Around that time the *Boston Globe* said Big Ed would coach the Yale pitchers in 1916. Walsh had coached the Yale pitchers in indoor winter practices before, but this time, said the *Globe*, "he will remain with the men as late in the spring as possible." On July 29 after a rainout in Boston, Walsh motored home to Meriden, intending to join the team in New York and pitch a game against the Yankees. But it wasn't until September 5 that Big Ed made his second comeback of the season. Again he pitched a complete game, throwing slow curves that looked easily hitable but weren't. He beat the Naps 4–2. In the third Eddie Collins knocked in a run with a double and then scored all the way from second on an infield out. In the outfield for the Sox that day was Shoeless Joe Jackson. He'd been acquired from the Cleveland Indians for Braggo Roth, Ed Klepfer, and $31,500 on August 21.

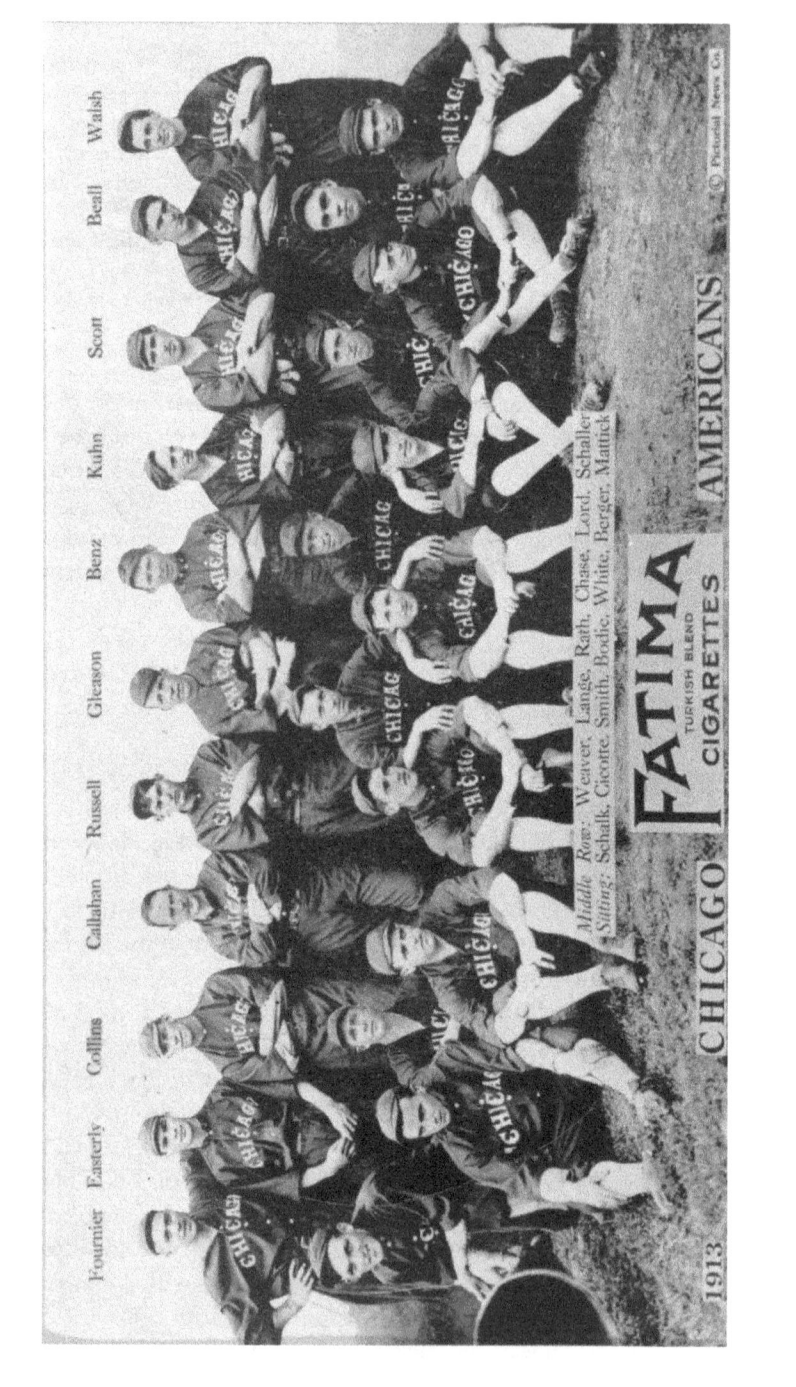

A month's rest was all Big Ed needed before his next and last start of the season on October 2 in Chicago against the Browns on Army Day. Ed pitched a shutout and the Sox won 8–0. He gave up six hits, four in the eighth and ninth, struck out three and walked two. Carried at full salary for the entire 1915 season, Big Ed pitched in three games. He finished 3–0 with three complete games. Appearing in that October 2 game made him eligible for the City Series, but he didn't play. He coached first base as the Sox won the series for the fifth consecutive time.

The winter of 1916 found everyone in denial. A new doctor known as "Bonesetter" Spencer made a house call to Meriden in January and declared that Ed Walsh was ready to take his regular turn in the box.[49] On February 11 Rowland denied a rumor that Big Ed would be released and said he expected Ed to be on hand in Mineral Wells, Texas, where the Sox were going to train that spring after five springs in California. Sure enough, Big Ed left Meriden for Texas on March 7, telling the *Chicago Tribune* "his old whip has regained all its wonderful strength and he is confident he will be in condition to take a regular turn."

March 15 was the first day of training. Players were allowed to warm up their own way. Some threw the medicine ball. Others took batting practice. All the pitchers, except Big Ed, took a turn throwing batting practice. Big Ed didn't play in any of the early spring games, but took on a coaching role. He worked with Horace "Hod" Eller, a rookie spitballer from Indiana, who threw four hitless innings against the regulars in his first outing.

On March 28 Big Ed volunteered to pitch for the Sox regulars against the second team who were dubbed the Mineral Wells Volunteers. The game was billed as the World's Championship of Texas. Warming up, Big Ed had good speed but no control. He had to let up to throw strikes in the game and gave up four runs in the first inning. After a five inning workout a few days later Big Ed admitted he was not ready to pitch and relegated himself to the second team as the right fielder. When the Sox broke camp and headed north to Chicago, Big Ed went home to Meriden. Comiskey was still carrying him on the roster and he was drawing full salary, probably around $5,000 or $6,000.

On May 13 the Sox played in Boston. On the 15th they went to New Haven, only 20 miles from Meriden, for an exhibition game. Walsh motored over and asked for a chance. He pitched three innings and declared "I never had more stuff in my life."

Opposite: **Walsh stands at far right in this photograph, used by Fatima Cigarettes, of the 1913 White Sox.**

On May 29 he pitched four scoreless inning in Toledo against a team of players from the street railway and light company. Finally on June 14 in Chicago against Washington, Rowland agreed to let Walsh try still another comeback. The game was billed as a match up between Big Ed and the Big Train and it drew 15,000. Big Ed Walsh lasted 2⅓ innings. He walked two and gave up four hits and four runs. The *Washington Post* predicted that Walsh was done once and for all. "The Nationals won a ball game at Comiskey Park this afternoon. They picked on a 'Cripple,' Ed Walsh. Probably sounding the death knell of this once famous slabbist."

The *Tribune* described the sad scene. "His exit in the third was one of the more pathetic episodes ever seen on a ballfield. Somehow one couldn't help the feeling that never again would we see the once famous pitcher on the mound. He had about 12,000 of Chicago's loyal fans pulling for him perhaps as they never pulled for an athletic favorite before."

In the first inning after walking the first man, he fanned the next two. When the inning ended Big Ed walked off to wild applause and had to tip his cap three times. In the third when Rowland pulled him, he walked off with his eyes down and never looked up to the fans who were applauding wildly again. He ran down the tunnel to the clubhouse, avoiding his teammates and manager. Johnson didn't pitch at all and the *Tribune* printed an apology. "Johnson was kept up the greater part of the night by the illness of his father-in-law, who was visiting in Chicago, and consequently did not feel fit to pitch a game of ball." Ban Johnson investigated and threatened to fine Washington $500.

Big Ed pitched two more exhibition games in June in Waukegan, Illinois, and Indianapolis, where 4,000 fans cheered loudly for the five innings he worked. On June 25 he refereed the feature wrestling match between Paul Martinson and Herman Koch at the annual field day at Comiskey to benefit the House of Good Shepherd.

The Sox left for an Eastern swing the evening of July 4, but Walsh stayed in Chicago. A week later he traveled on his own and met the team in Boston on July 12 where they were playing the third of three consecutive double headers against the Red Sox. Hardly anyone took notice when Big Ed pitched the last inning of the second game, the last inning he would ever pitch for the Chicago White Sox. Back in Chicago, Big Ed stopped going to the Sox games most days, which was fortuitous for two Chicago school girls on July 28. Big Ed saved them from drowning after they fell off a raft in Lake Michigan. Big Ed happened to be at the beach and jumped in and saved them.

"He swam ashore with one and then went after the other. She pulled him under. He tore himself loose, knocked her unconscious then carried her to safety."⁵⁰

The last news of Ed Walsh in 1916 came on the last day of the year. Former umpire Billy Evans, who was in a second career as a sportswriter was asked in his syndicated "Baseball Queries" column if Ed Walsh should attempt still another comeback in 1917. "As much as I would like to believe that Walsh has a chance to regain former effectiveness," Evans wrote, "I am unable to do so. I believe Walsh is through as a big leaguer. He's paying the penalty for overwork. When he was good he used to pitch two seasons in one."

The next day Big Ed was officially given his unconditional release. Immediately, speculation arouse over what he would do next. A story said he would manage the Des Moines club now owned by Frank Isbell. Another story said Comiskey offered to set him up in business in Meriden or anywhere he would select. On April 3 it was reported in the *Washington Post* that Walsh wanted a tryout with the Cubs. None of these things panned out.

On May 24 Big Ed was given permission to work out with the Giants. McGraw agreed to give him a shot if he saw the doctor who cured George Chalmers. Big Ed dressed in a Giants road uniform before a game and worked out, causing a commotion in the stands when he was recognized, but never signed with the Giants. On July 21 he was signed by the Boston Braves after manager George Stallings watched him work out on the recommendation of a mutual friend from Meriden, where Big Ed was staying in condition with outdoor workouts at his home. When he got to Boston the Cubs were in town. He stopped by their hotel to visit. On July 31 he appeared in a Braves uniform. He pitched batting practice and coached third base during the game. The Cubs beat the Braves 3–1. The *Tribune* intimated that maybe Ed's workouts weren't as strenuous as they might be. "It was a rather tame ballgame for the small crowd, most of whom took more interest in the presence of Ed Walsh on the coaching lines than in the players. Big Ed can coach just as handsomely for the Braves as he ever did for the White Sox. The only difference in his appearance was the uniform fitted him more tightly."

On August 2 Big Ed made still another comeback, starting a game for the Braves in Chicago against the Cubs. Comiskey was there on the field before the game when Walsh was presented with a bundle of roses. Big Ed pitched five scoreless innings and left with a 1–0 lead. The crowd of 9,000 yelled madly for a curtain call when a relief pitcher came out in the sixth, but Big Ed was in the locker room and didn't come out.

He pitched for a second time in Boston on August 22. Batting in the second inning he was hit behind the ear by a fastball by Doak "Mule" Watson. The ball bounded into the grandstand. Big Ed was carried from the field and was unconscious 20 minutes. He was thought to be seriously, even fatally injured, but it turned out he did not have a fractured skull and he was all right in a few days. On September 5 he finally pitched his last major league game. Likely realizing that was the case, Stallings, appropriately, let him finish what he started. Inappropriately he gave up 16 hits, struck out only three and was beaten by Brooklyn 8–1. He was 36 years old.

In Chicago the White Sox won the American League pennant, their first since Big Ed Walsh carried them there with his breakout season in 1906. Big Ed sent this telegram to Comiskey: "Congratulations on winning American League championship. Hope you will have further success by winning World Series. Although I am not with the Club, my heart is still with you."

14

Arm Trouble

With Big Ed washed up after the 1912 season at age 31, two questions presented themselves. One, what was wrong with Big Ed's arm? And two, was his injury caused simply by overwork or did throwing the spitball aggravate it? In 1914 nobody could tell him what was wrong with his arm.

> The doctors all had their theories. None of them agreed what was the matter with my arm, but they agreed on one thing. They were perfectly willing to take any loose change I might have lying around for their services. I was robbed systematically and almost invariably.
>
> What was most mystifying was I could never seem to find out what ailed the arm. Some days I could warm up and pitch for two or three innings without much trouble, but then the arm would go dead and begin to ache. I felt like my best friend had deserted me.
>
> Just what was the matter with my arm, I don't know and no one else does. It's one of the mysteries of baseball what affects pitchers' arms and I guess my own case is as big a mystery as any of them. Whether it was because I had worked too hard and got rundown, or had strained the arm that last game of the series against the Cubs in 1912, or pitched too early after less than my usual amount of spring training, or displaced a ligament as Bonesetter Reese claimed, or had plain rheumatism as I think, I don't know.[1]

In the spring of 1915 when he stayed in California seeking a remedy, he came to believe in Bonesetter's theory. "Walsh has a hunch that one of his shoulder ligaments has slipped around on the back of his neck, a position contrary to the laws of nature, or has become otherwise misplaced. And yet he has been unable to prove this to the satisfaction of himself or friends."[2]

During spring training with the White Sox in Los Angeles in 1914 Ed drove a Haynes automobile equipped with an electric shift loaned to him by E.W. Leslie, the manager of the local Haynes dealership. After driving the car he told W. B. Cochran, president and general manager of the Haynes Auto Company, that he intended to buy a new Haynes as soon as he returned to Chicago. This prompted a bizarre theory about Ed's arm trouble. "Ed Walsh frowns on the gear shifting act of automobiling although he is a regular motor-car fan. Many of his friends claim the trouble with his pitching arm was largely due to overwork caused by gear shifting. He admits the plausibility of the theory and has fallen for the electric gear shift. While ordinary pitchers could shift gears for a living without fear of injury, Walsh's arm is of a different mechanism. The soreness is located somewhere beneath the shoulder joint and the treatment is rest. The doctors orders are to leave gear-shifting alone."[3]

There were other theories about Ed's arm which had nothing to do with overwork. Writing in the *Atlanta Constitution,* Hugh Fullerton pinpointed Ed's trouble to a specific incident. "Many fans and players have the idea that he hurt his pitching arm through overwork. Such is not the case. One day he was playing catch and toss with Father Quill, the Chicago priest, and carelessly threw a ball sidearm in such a manner as to snap the shoulder muscles out of place and the arm was never as strong afterwards."[4]

Another story had it that Ed injured the arm during spring training in California throwing a medicine ball. Jack Quinn — a fellow Pennsylvania coal country product who pitched 22 years in the majors and retired in 1933, two days after his 50th birthday — said at a Boston Chamber of Commerce luncheon in 1923 that he knew when and why Big Ed's arm went bad.

> I have been pitching professional baseball since 1900 and never had a sore arm. I know just what my arm will stand and nurse it along accordingly. It is just as good now as it ever has been.
>
> One reason pitchers' arms go bad on them is because so many of them haven't sense enough to admit when their arms are sore. They try to go on pitching and the first thing they know their arms are gone forever.
>
> That's how Ed Walsh lost his arm. He had been scheduled to open a series against the Yankees in 1912 and, although his arm had been bothering him for quite a spell, he insisted on pitching the game. He managed to get away with it that day, but three days later the manager asked him to pitch and Ed was so intent on beating the Yankees that he consented. Pitching that game ruined him. He was never the same thereafter.[5]

Dr. William Charlton, a current orthopedic surgeon who specializes in arthroscopic treatment of shoulder disorders in Pennsylvania near Big

Ed's hometown, reviewed the available information on Big Ed's shoulder problem and offered a diagnosis. "Based on my experience with throwing athletes and Walsh's complaints, it is thought that Walsh suffered from internal impingement. This disorder occurs in overhead throwing athletes. The essential patho-physiology of internal impingement involves abnormal contact of the humeral head (ball) against the glenoid (socket) in extreme positions of shoulder movement.

"Internal impingement is a spectrum of disease from tendon irritation to tearing of the adjacent rotator cuff. It is certainly possible that Walsh developed internal impingement that progressed with the absence of a proper diagnosis and rehabilitation to result in a rotator cuff tear." Dr. Charlton does not believe the injury occurred from one incident, but was the result of overuse.

Big Ed's overwork is documented by the powerful statistics. Though his record shows he pitched in 14 seasons, in the first two seasons he pitched only 247 innings combined and in the last five he appeared in only 37 games combined. The core of his career was the seven seasons from 1906 to 1912. Ignoring 1906, when he became a regular halfway through the season, and 1909, when his holdout and his brother's death limited him to 230 innings, Big Ed averaged 57 games in the other five seasons and led the league in each. He averaged 403 innings and led the league in four of the five seasons. This does not count his post-season work in the City Series games, spring games, exhibition games or the pitches he threw warming up. In 1908 when he appeared in 66 games he warmed up in many games in which he did not appear. Ed probably threw thousands more pitches in the off season. His son Bob recalled how he used to work out at home in the winter. "I can remember many times he'd be up in our attic practicing. We had a mattress with a hole in it. He'd stand at the other end and throw. He hit the hole every time."[6]

While Ed was reeling off 300 and 400-inning seasons no one said he was being overworked. But once it became clear that his arm was ruined, baseball people chimed in with their opinions. Billy Evans posed a question. "Is it possible that every pitcher and catcher has just so many games in his system? Despite all kinds of treatment to which he has been subjected, I fear Walsh is through. With ordinary work he ought to have five or six more years ahead of him. Walsh did 15 years pitching in eight."[7]

That there are only so many pitches in an arm is accepted logic now, but it was something of a radical theory when Bill Evans suggested it in 1915, when many baseball people believed that pitchers got stronger with more work. Big Ed himself believed that. "All the years warming up for a call almost everyday and pitching in 60 or more games a season and more innings than any other pitchers my arm had never been sore. My shoulder developed muscular strength that I thought could stand the wear and tear of all the pitching."[8]

Hugh Jennings was one baseball man who believed the spitball ruined arms before their time. "No delivery ever so taxed a pitcher's arm. It was like throwing a tennis ball as hard as possible. No genuine spitball pitcher ever lasted long. Ed Walsh had a powerful physique and mixed the spitter with his fastball. As a starter and relief pitcher he was the best of his time, but he did not last long. The spitball killed his arm."[9]

Rube Waddell was ahead of the curve on this one. As early as 1905 he said the spitter was an arm killer. "The reason I don't pitch the 'spitball' is because it injures the arm. It has to be thrown with a jerk, and it won't take long for this to throw a man's arm out. Furthermore, if a man uses the 'spitball' all the time, he will find that it interferes with his ability to throw any other kind of curve."[10]

Christy Mathewson, who tinkered with the spitter in '05, dropped it quickly. He believed it was hard on the arm. But some pitchers and managers believed the spitball was easy on the arm. Chesbro once said, "The spitball is less trying to the arm than an ordinary curve ball. It does not involve such a twist as you deliver the ball."

That theory was bolstered by Chesbro's 1904 season when he pitched 454 innings and won 41 games seemingly without effect. But the facts show that Chesbro's effectiveness and workload dropped precipitously after 1904. His innings pitched dropped by hundreds each of the next three years. In 1907 he pitched only 207 innings. At age 35 in '09, his last season, he was 0–5 with an era of 6.14 in just 15 games.

Cy Sanborn, a writer for *Sporting Life* and the *Chicago Tribune*, believed it was clear the spitball injured arms. "That the spit ball is hard on the arm there is hardly a question. If the spit ball didn't injure Jack Chesbro's arm, why is he going into retirement? He says that he believes a year's rest will bring him back as good as ever. Chesbro is a big, strong, healthy-looking 200-pound athlete, and if his arm is good he would hardly pass up a $5,000 contract. If his arm is bad, then the spit ball put it on the bum. Bill Dineen once used the spit ball with success. Now Dineen is one of the strongest opponents of the spitter. Dineen says himself that it has taken him two years to recover from injuries his arm was subjected to by the use of the spit ball."[11]

Big Ed defended the spitter in 1913 in *Baseball Magazine*. "Many people consider that the spitball is hard on a pitcher's arm. If it is, it is news to me. I have pitched it for some time. I'm 31 years old and if the spitball is so hard on a pitcher's arm it seems to me that I ought to know about it. For a spitball, after all, is only a special type of fastball. It is pitched with great speed with the first two fingers wet."[12]

Later in that story Ed seemed to acknowledge the overwork hurt his effectiveness. "I was not able to do my best work under such circumstances. No pitcher can go into the box and work as I have and do his best work. It is impossible and I lay no claim to impossibilities." He also insisted that Callahan, his manager in 1908, was not to blame for the overwork. "If anyone makes the statement I was sore at Callahan for the extra work they don't know what they are talking about. He is one of the finest men I ever met and I would do anything in the world for him. If I was overworked it was my fault. He used to come to me and say, 'Ed I hate to ask you to pitch after all the work you have done, but I am trying to make good and don't know what to do.' I would tell him I was glad to do whatever I could. There were always the friendliest feelings between us."

There is evidence that the spitball resurrected careers and also ended careers early. Al Orth was 34 years old and in his 13th season in 1906 when he resorted to the spitball. He had his best season ever for the Highlanders, leading the A.L. in CG, 36; IP, 338; and wins, 27. His ERA dropped by a full run from 1904 to 1906. Glenn Liebhardt is an example of a spitball pitcher who flamed out early. In the Southern League in 1906 he pitched five double headers and was considered the best pitcher in the league. In 1907 as a rookie with Cleveland he won 18 with 2.05. In 1909 he got in only 12 games and was out of baseball at age 26. Jimmy Dygert had a similar career. He was 21–8 with the A's in 1907, among the leaders in walks and strikeouts, but was out of baseball after 1910 at 26.

There are pitchers who went on and on throwing the spitter. Urban "Red" Faber was one of the 17 spitballers grandfathered in when the pitched was outlawed in 1920. He went on throwing it until 1933 when he was 45 years old. Stan Coveleski, another of the grandfathered pitchers, pitched until 1928 when he was 39. Jack Quinn, who was one of the 17, was also from Pennsylvania coal country. He pitched until he was 50.

It doesn't seemed likely there was anything about the mechanics of the spitball that made it either hard or easy on pitchers' arms. But Walsh said he always threw it as hard as he could with fastball arm action. It was probably that, rather than the simple act of wetting the fingers, which hastened Ed's end. In the early part of the century, convinced by Chesbro's 1904 numbers, the White Sox managers, Fielder Jones and Nixey Callahan, believed that spitball pitchers could pitch more often than conventional pitchers. Given Big Ed's effectiveness, and the fact that he never complained, they also pitched him so often because they wanted to win.

Then there was the effect of Big Ed's physicality. As the nicknames like "Big Reel" and "Big Moose" imply, Ed, 6' 1" and 190, was a big man for the time. But many of Big Ed's contemporaries, especially pitchers, were as big or bigger. Jim "Hippo" Vaughn was 6' 4", 215. Walter Johnson was 6' 1", 200. Cy Young was 6'2", 210, Rube Waddell was 6' 1½" and 196. Jack Coombs was 6', 185. Jay Carl Cashion, a rookie for Washington in 1911, was 6', 200.

But Walsh had a tremendous physique developed as a youth in the mines. Ray Schalk used to say he had shoulders like a schoolhouse. Big Ed had a physical air about him that led Charlie Dressen to famously say, "He's the only man who can strut standing still." To managers he just looked like a player who could pitch all day, every day.

15

Big Ed: Manager

After the 1917 baseball season Big Ed went back to Meriden and managed an amateur football team. He had played football back in Plains and Wilkes-Barre, and liked it, but there isn't much record of him being involved in football in any way as an adult. Years later, in the 1950s when football was broadcast on television, Ed never missed a game. Though he followed baseball and stayed connected to it in different ways until he died, he said he much preferred watching football on TV.

In any case when the Meriden team he managed that fall played a team of soldiers from Camp Danvers in Massachusetts, Ed donated $300 for the camp's athletic fund after the game.[1] After football season Ed just hung around the house with his wife and boys, who were then 10 and 12, and waited for it to get cold enough to go ice fishing.

On January 2 his major league baseball career ended officially, once and for all, when the Braves gave him his unconditional release. In February there was a newspaper story about baseball players objecting to being "snapped," which was slang for getting photographed. Many of them considered it bad luck and Ed was among them. "We venture to say no man ever got a picture of him on the day he was supposed to pitch."[2]

In early March of 1918 Ed coached the Yale University pitchers at New Haven and, with the U.S. immersed in World War I, he took a job with the Marlin Arms Company in New Haven. The company had a defense contract to make machine guns for the Army. He worked there for the rest of 1918 and played with the plant's baseball team. He didn't pitch, but he batted .400 as an outfielder. In March of 1919 the *Bridgeport Telegram* broke the story that Ed would try a comeback with the American Association Milwaukee Brewers managed by "Pants" Rowland. "Will I coach?" Ed said when asked about the offer. "No I think not. I don't know what Rowland wants me to do, but I suppose it's a little bit of everything. I don't know if he still has faith in my arm, I hope so, for I think there is something in it yet. A little careful work when warm weather sets in may start me going again." Then he said something no one wanted to hear. "Who knows? Perhaps I'll get another try in the majors."[3]

The news caused a stir in Milwaukee where Rowland made the announcement at a dinner given by the Rowland Booster Club and said he "expects the Big Fellow to work regularly."

Big Ed arrived at the Brewers training camp in Evansville, Illinois, on April 6. Among his duties was working with Al Cooke, an infielder who was described as Walsh's protégé. Walsh worked with him for three weeks, but Cooke was sold to Memphis. The St. Louis Cardinals stopped in Evansville for an exhibition game and beat Milwaukee 9–7. Big Ed played a few innings in the outfield and hit a double. He won the first game he pitched in Milwaukee, beating St. Paul 6–1. He gave up five hits, struck out four and walked three. But on July 7 he resigned saying he just couldn't deal with the abolition of the spitball in the American Association. He let it be known that he was willing to accept a manager's job with a minor league team. On July 11 it was reported that Ed would join the Duluth White Sox in the outlaw Range-Lakes League the next Sunday when Duluth was scheduled to play Hibbing. Walsh sent a telegram to R.J. Carnes, owner, saying he accepted the terms, but there is no record that he ever did show up.[4]

It is known that on July 22 Walsh took in a Sox double header from a box seat. He chatted with a reporter and said he might get a coaching job at the University of Wisconsin. He also bragged about his latest game, golf, and said he hit a drive 371 feet one of his first times out.[5] Back home Ed took work as a deputy sheriff in New Haven County for a few months, but he still yearned to work in baseball. In December of 1919 he applied for the manager's job with the Bridgeport Americans in the Connecticut State League. But Bridgeport was negotiating with Gene McCann, a Cincinnati scout, who had managed Bridgeport a few years earlier. When McCann signed with Cincinnati, Walsh was expected to be hired. It was said that "baseball fans are all steamed up at the prospect."[6]

On January 21 in 1920 Clark P. Lane Jr., the owner of the Bridgeport club, announced he had signed Big Ed Walsh as player-manager. Bridgeport, 35 miles southeast of Meriden on the deep Black Rock Harbor on the Long Island Sound, was a shipbuilding and whaling center in

15. Big Ed: Manager

the mid–19th century. By the 1920s Bridgeport was a thriving industrial center with more than 500 factories and a booming immigrant population which made it the largest city in the state. Its most famous resident was P.T. Barnum who built four mansions there before his death in 1891.

A few days later Ed attended the league meeting with Lane, where he was kept busy shaking hands with magnates. Teams admitted for 1920 in addition to Bridgeport were Hartford, Waterbury, Pittsfield, New Haven, Providence, Worcester, Springfield and Albany. It was agreed to play a 140 game season from April 28 to September 11. The league was officially named the Connecticut State League, but because it had teams in other states it was sometimes called the Eastern Association. Signing Walsh, who still had star power, was considered a coup for Connecticut baseball. It was thought he immediately made Bridgeport a contender and was expected to develop young pitchers. "He knows how to bring out all the stuff in a twirler and has spent a lot of time with youngsters in the big show."

Big Ed had some history in Bridgeport. "So far as I personally am concerned I am greatly pleased at the prospect of being here this year as my first professional game of baseball was pitched here in 1902 when I was a member of the Meriden club. The club officials have promised to go the limit in matters of cooperation in every way to bring out a winning ball club here. That's my aim, too. I understand there is the nucleus of a good ball club already signed. As it gets warmer and folks begin to think about baseball we will be in position to inform the fans of some things that will show we've been quietly at work."[7]

It was hoped that Walsh's connection to the White Sox would help bring in players. Walsh even had designs on making Bridgeport an unofficial farm team for the White Sox. Walsh was friends with Sox manager Kid Gleason and expected Gleason to make a pitch to Comiskey about some kind of arrangement, but it never did develop.[8] In April the team secretary, Jimmy Kelly, tried to get the Braves to come to Bridgeport for a Sunday game on April 25, three days before the opener. The deal feel through. He then tried to get a Negro team from New York, but finally settled for a local all-star team. Of an expected crowd of 4,000 only 900 showed in wet, cold and windy weather to see Walsh's Fence Busters. The team was also called the Walshmen or the Walshzers or Moosers, after the Big Moose, one of Walsh's nicknames.

Big Ed's roster of 16, including himself, included position players Hank Bracket, a speedy outfielder; twin brothers Ray Grimes and Roy Grimes at first base and shortstop; Shorty Emerick at catcher; and a speedy

Chinese-Hawaiian outfielder named Bill "Buck" Lai, who joined the team after touring the United States with the University of Hawaii team. Among the pitchers were Ed Lennon, the number one from the previous season, and Ed's brother, Marty Walsh, who was at least 40 years old.

On May 5 the Americans went into first place by beating Albany 5–4 with a four-run rally in the bottom of the ninth, with Lai getting the winning hit. On May 18 Bridgeport stopped a New Haven seven-game winning streak 8–1. Ed Lennon was the winning pitcher. Team statistics through May 18 showed Big Ed was 3 of 6 as a pinch hitter. Big Ed wasn't the only well-known major leaguer managing in the league. Charles "Chief" Bender was a player-manager with New Haven. Bender's major league career paralleled Big Ed's. He had pitched with the A's from 1903 to 1912 and he and Big Ed had pitched against each other numerous times.

The day after the Americans stopped New Haven's win streak, Bender pitched and New Haven won 7–5. Bender's speed was described as blinding and he struck out nine, but he did give up 11 hits. Bender singled in the eighth and scored when George Nutter hit a home run described as one of the longest ever hit at the park. On May 28 injuries forced Big Ed to put himself in the lineup in Pittsfield, Massachusetts. He played the entire game at third base and he went 3 for 5 and scored the winning run with two outs in the top of the 10th, as Bridgeport beat Pittsfield 4–2. At that point Bridgeport was 17–6 with a one-half game lead over New Haven. By June 7 Bender's New Haven team had moved into first place with a 23–10 record. Bridgeport was second at 21–11. They started a series of four games against each other on the 8th, two at Newfield Park in Bridgeport and then two in New Haven. One headline read, "Ugh! Heap big Indian Chief Bender and his tribe of macing pastimers will pow-wow at Newfield Park tomorrow afternoon."

Bridgeport entered the series beset with injures. "Walsh himself is taped from knee to thigh and all over his back. Buck Lai is out with a fractured wrist. Shorty Emerick has water on the knee."

The teams split the four games. Chief Bender won the first and last games and Bridgeport won the two in between. In the fourth game Bender had a perfect game with two outs in the ninth. Big Ed pinched hit and broke up the no-hitter with a line single to left. He later scored on a walk and single by Orr. New Haven won 4–1. New Haven kept its one and one-half game lead. No other team in the league was over .500. After the game the teams were treated to a chicken dinner and a tour of the new jail by Meriden sheriff Tom Reilly and the custodian of the New Haven jail.

On June 22 Ed's brother Marty Walsh started and beat New Haven

10–4. Though he gave up 10 hits, he threw the spitball in the pinch and got key outs. He walked one and struck out three. Ed didn't play in that game but was batting .301, 21 for 69, as a part-time third baseman and pinch hitter. On July 9 the Americans had a chance to go into first place but lost to Hartford 5–1. Marty Walsh started and gave up four in the first inning, but settled down the rest of the way and struck out five. His record for the season couldn't be found, but it was said that his "losses are as common as dust on parlor furniture."

On July 24 Big Ed was thrown out of the game by the umpire at Pittsfield. He wouldn't leave and had to be escorted by the Pittsfield police. It was the second time he was tossed. On July 26 Roy Grimes played his last game with Bridgeport after being signed by the Giants. He went out with a big bang. He was 4 for 4 with a walk and a grand slam home run in a 12–1 win over Waterbury. Brother Ray was signed by the Cubs after the season. At that point Big Ed was 27 for 96, .281

By this time Bridgeport, though in fifth place, was in a wild pennant race where the top five teams were within two and one-half games. New Haven was 46–37. Bridgeport was 44–40. Two days later, after a 4–3 loss to Chief Bender and New Haven, Big Ed learned he had been suspended indefinitely by Eastern League president Dan O'Neill. Making matters worse, on July 29 during a 4–2 loss to New Haven, Emerick, the team's second leading hitter after Ray Grimes, was hit in the head by a pitch and was expected to be out five days.

Walsh came back on August 1 to a team that was five and one-half games out in fifth place and with the injuries mounting. Marty Walsh and Lennon both had sore arms. Big Ed started at third base batting second. He was 1 for 4 with two runs scored in an 8–3 loss to Hartford. The Americans' record dropped to 47–44. The team was left with two healthy pitchers, Shanty House and "Lehigh" Ed Stauffer. Despite the sore arm Marty agreed to pitch the next day and lost to Hartford 3–1. He struck out five. Ed played third again. He was 1 for 3. On August 11, after going 2 for 3 with a double off the fence leading off in a 3–2 win over Waterbury, Big Ed was fifth in team batting at .284, having played in 47 of the 100 games. He pitched just three times and went 1–1. In 22 innings he gave up 22 hits, walked six and struck out six. On August 25, Lai, who had been in Philadelphia lining up work in the off season with DuPont, was back. Big Ed put Lai at third and benched himself. He could hit, but increasingly was having a tough time running. Of his 33 hits, four were doubles and the rest singles. After a double header split with Albany that day, the Americans were 61–56 and still in the race. They were in third place two and one-half games behind Bender's New Haven Club, but went 9–14 the rest of the way to fade to sixth. They had to win the last game of the season to get back to .500 at 70–70.

A dark side of Big Ed emerged during the 1920 season. As a ballplayer he seemed to be well-liked. He was beloved by fans of all the A.L. teams and he had many friends among the players and managers, though he did clash with some of them, notably Hughie Jennings. As a manager and coach, though, Big Ed was unpopular with the umpires and players. In Bridgeport he rode players and expected them to play hurt. When Lai broke some small bones in his left hand he continued to play against his doctor's advice. When the pain became too much he asked to be taken out, but, as Lai was one of the team's best players and a pennant race was on, Big Ed didn't want to hear it. On August 8 the *Bridgeport Sun Herald* called for Ed to resign. "Ed Walsh must quit his job as manager of the Bridgeport club or the city will be without a ball club before many days." The newspaper story referred to the Lai incident, to Big Ed's suspension of center fielder and fan-favorite Gene Martin, and to the defection of pitcher Ed Lennon. Big Ed accused Martin of intentionally letting a single roll away for a home run. The player denied it and claimed Big Ed had been on him all season without cause. Martin made a report to the National Association of Minor Leagues demanding to be paid for the time he was on suspension. He vowed not to play for Big Ed again. Two weeks later he was sold to Pittsfield. According to the newspaper story Lai and Lennon made the same vow. "Lai has decided to quit the Bridgeport club at the end of the season and return to the Hawaiian islands and forget he ever saw Big Ed Walsh." Lennon didn't even wait for the season to end. He jumped the club the day before the story broke. "Lennon is now at his home in Philadelphia and will not return to Bridgeport under any consideration."[9]

This dark side of Big Ed was punctuated in the last game of the season when the backup catcher, a player named Skiff, refused to play and sat in the grandstand saying, "I would not catch for Ed Walsh. He's not worth it."[10]

Michael J. Bielawa, a historian with the Bridgeport Public Library and author of a book on Bridgeport baseball, said Big Ed was unpopular with the fans due to his strange in-game strategies and because had a hard time dealing with his players' shortcomings. "He thought players should play hurt," Bielawa said. "I guess because he was so great he took things for granted. He had a burning desire to win. There was a lot of dissension among the players. After the season he was pretty much run out of town."

Ed's own son Bob experienced Ed's impatience with players' mistakes. "He couldn't bear to lose. He saw me lose a ball game 1–0 once and bawled the hell out of me all the way home because I threw the wrong pitch."[11]

Even as early as 1909 there was evidence that Ed did not have the personality to be a coach or manager. That spring Ed was dismissed as pitching coach at Yale University "owing to a disagreement the famous twirler had with Head Coach Lush."[12]

December 30 it was announced Bridgeport had fired Big Ed and hired Gene McCann. Even so it was rumored that Big Ed would be hired to manage at Jersey City in 1921. Nothing ever came of that, though, and he wound up in Oneonta, New York, with a semipro team there, which sported three future major leaguers. Eddie Farrell, a 20-year-old infielder from nearby Johnson City who would go on to an 11-year major league career beginning in 1925 with the Giants, was the shortstop. Pitcher Owen Carroll also reached the majors in 1925 with Detroit. He pitched 10 seasons in the majors. Al Hermann, the second baseman, got in 32 games as a utility infielder for the Red Sox in 1923 and '24. Oneonta won the Southern Tier title under Big Ed, who turned 40 that season. He pitched one game and shut out Binghamton 3–0. "He was quite an attraction," said Dr. Francis Marx, president of the Oneonta Athletic Association. "We beat most of the major teams who came to play us including the A's."[13]

On August 11 the White Sox came to Oneonta to play Ed's team. It was declared Ed Walsh day and the ballpark was packed as Big Ed pitched three innings. "The Sox treated the old master kindly, but when a youngster named Scalon entered the game Eddie Mulligan and Yam Yaryan hit home runs over the distant center field fence."[14]

16

Big Ed Doesn't Like the Jeers

Publicly, at least, there were no complaints about Big Ed's coaching style after the season in Oneonta in 1921, but he was not offered that or any other coaching job in 1922. In December he went to the major league winter meeting in New York City where he was pictured in the New York papers throwing snowballs with Ty Cobb on a city street. He met Judge Landis in the hotel lobby on a Wednesday afternoon. That evening he met with Ban Johnson and was offered an umpiring job as the ninth man on the American League staff. Two or three umpires worked games in 1921.

"Baseball owes you such a position," Johnson said. "I think you are a man eminently qualified for the position. I am adding to my staff a man whose loyalty to his team was always a by-word. No player showed more conscientiousness in the performance of his duty."

Big Ed seemed happy to be back in major league baseball. "I have health and strength and ambition. I know the game and it will be no fault of mine if I do not justify Johnson's confidence in me."[1] It's not known what Ed's salary was, but a good estimate is about $3500–$4000 for the season. In the February issue of *Baseball Digest,* writer John J. Ward made a plea to fans to go easy on Big Ed, the umpire: "Next summer when Big Ed is wearing a blue suit and a windpad and calling them as he sees them, be easy on the comments and the pop bottles, for that tall athletic form behind the plate was once the greatest pitcher in the United States."

Big Ed began his umpiring career in March handling a Braves-Washington series with second-year umpire Bob Hart in St. Petersburg, Florida. He worked his first regular season game on April 13 in Boston with Tom Connolly, who was in his 25th season, and Frank Wilson. On June 11 President

Johnson released Wilson, reducing the staff. Big Ed was retained, but Big Ed was not a conventional umpire. Billy Evans, a future hall of famer who umpired and wrote a syndicated baseball column, once found Big Ed hitting fungos to outfielders before a game. When Evans confronted him about it Big Ed said, "He was hitting them lousy so I thought I'd show him how."[2]

In May a poem titled "I Wonder" about Big Ed the umpire and signed by Hoosier Pete appeared in the *Chicago Tribune*.

> I note Ed Walsh, ex-pitcher,
> Has donned the guesser's mask,
> And though I wish him all success
> In this most thankless task,
> I cannot help but wonder
> If the close ones look the same
> From behind the pan with another man
> Hurling an air tight game
> As they did when HE graced the rubber
> With the count at two and three
> And he slipped across a spitter
> That the ump couldn't see;
> If he signals "safe at second"
> And they jeer him to his face
> Will he think of the plays of ancient days
> He viewed from the coaching space?[3]

The poet was on to something. Ed was indeed thinking of his playing days when he umpired. The first time he umpired in Chicago he got a standing ovation when he was announced before the game. During the game he was booed because he made a close call that gave opponents runs and the Sox lost. Not long after that, he quit saying, "It's a helluva business. All jeers and no cheers. I'd rather remember the cheers." His umpiring career lasted 87 games.

In January of 1923 Big Ed attended a banquet dinner for "Wild Bill" Donovan, the manager of the New Haven club which won the Eastern League championship and a playoff with International League champion Baltimore. Guests included Hughie Jennings, Frank Frisch and Kid Gleason.[4] It was Donovan who had beaten the White Sox for Jennings and the Tigers to clinch the A.L. pennant on the last day of the 1908 season. In February Walsh was signed by the White Sox as an assistant to Manager Bill Gleason to replace Johnny Evers, who coached in 1922 but hadn't been heard from over the winter. Rumors were Evers would stay in the East as a coach for the Yankees or be named New York State boxing commissioner

Ed was a tremendous fungo hitter. He held the record for distance for a time, but he got in trouble for hitting fungos to players as an umpire in 1922 (George Grantham Bain Collection, Library of Congress).

by Governor Al Smith. Evers didn't respond to inquiries about whether he would return to the Sox, so Walsh was hired. Big Ed left for Marlin Springs, Texas, the Sox training site, on February 26 from Chicago with pitcher Frank Woodward, catcher Ray Schalk, outfielder Johnny Mostil, trainer Bill Buckner and Gleason. Three hundred fans saw them off at the LaSalle Street Station

"Walsh was kept busy greeting old friends and new. He looked to be in the best of condition. He towered above the crowd and had a word and greeting for all. He was eager to get into his togs and start his duties. He declared he was out to put the Sox hurling corps at the head of the league list."[5]

Among the pitchers in camp were Dixie Leverett, Charlie Robertson, brothers Homer and Ted Blankenship, Red Farber, Frank "Stubby" Mack, George Connolly and Ed's own personal project, Frank Woodward, who was 23–12 with New Haven in the Eastern League in 1922. Big Ed brought him to Chicago for the trip to Texas. Woodward led the Eastern League in games and strikeouts. This was his fourth trial with the big leagues. He played briefly with Philadelphia and St. Louis in the N.L. and tried out with Washington the previous spring. Woodward would get into two games in 1923, the last of his career.

Big Ed's job was to loosen the hurlers up. His method was to lead them on a 12-mile hike beginning at 9:30 A.M. the first day. The next day was the first day of a full workout and it was noted, "The practice wasn't as snappy as might have been, owing to the fact that several of the fellows showed up with stiffened underpinnings, the result of yesterday's 12-mile tramp."[6]

The 1923 season was uneventful on the field for Big Ed. The Sox finished in seventh place 69–85, 30 games behind the pennant-winning Yankees. The staff's ERA was 4.05, fifth in the league. Red Farber was the only pitcher with a winning record at 14–11. Something that happened off the field during the 1923 season made much bigger news than anything the White Sox did on it. On August 26 Big Ed escorted Mrs. Grace Comiskey, daughter-in-law of Charles Comiskey, the Sox' owner, to the hospital to visit her husband, Louis. On their way back, just as they were about to enter the Comiskey home, they were robbed by three men of $10,000 in jewelry and locked in the cellar of the house. They were released by Mrs. Comiskey's sister Alice Ready. On September 5 police arrested three men breaking into a basement apartment on Grand Boulevard. Grace Comiskey's stolen jewelry was found in their homes.[7]

After the season the Sox defeated the Cubs in the City Series. During a clubhouse celebration Kid Gleason told the players he was quitting. He pointed at the name Eddie Collins on an empty locker and said, "That fellow's misfortune was what broke us up. The club was never the same after that."

Collins injured his knee in July on the last game of a long road trip. At that point the Sox were 18–9 and one-half game out. Collins missed three weeks. By the time he came back, the Sox were out of the race and on their way down to seventh place.

With wrinkles around his eyes, Ed shows his age. This may have been about 1922 when he went back to the White Sox as a coach at age 41.

The day after the City Series, Gleason walked into Comiskey's office and placed his resignation on the desk. After three years of trying to rebuild the team wrecked by the 1919 World's Series scandal, he had given up. The shattering of his 1919 team was a blow from which he never recovered. Rumors of a successor included the names Eddie Collins, Harry Hooper, Frank Chance and Big Ed Walsh. Frank Chance was the Old Roman's choice, though Big Ed was retained as a coach. But Chance, who was sick at home in Los Angeles, resigned on February 17 just days after being hired. Comiskey refused the resignation and sent Chance a telegram saying he didn't care when he reported as long as it was before the season. "I will not accept Chance's resignation until I at least have a chance to talk with him. I think he is the best man we could have selected and I don't want to lose him. It will make little difference if Frank is on hand at Winter Haven. We can turn that part of the work over to his assistants."

The Sox were training in Winter Haven, Florida, that spring. With Chance home sick the bulk of the work that spring fell to Big Ed and Evers, who had come back as a coach.[8] Ed left Meriden on February 28 and was the first to arrive in Florida. He had a letter from Chance with some ideas about what he wanted him and Evers to do. They were to stay until April 1 when they had an exhibition game scheduled against the Giants in Orlando and then go northward and play some exhibitions at small towns on the way to Chicago for the April 15 opener. With 35 athletes invited to camp, Evers and Big Ed had their work cut out for them. They worked the players hard in the heat. Evers worked with the batters, spending a lot of time on bunting. Ed worked with the 16 pitchers in camp, including Roy Moore, who was bought from the Red Sox. "Two more days of this weather and we will be in better shape than when we left Marlin last spring to start north," Big Ed said. On March 7 Evers went to Orlando to "attend the last hours of Pat Moran" and Walsh ran the team. The Sox were investigating the possibility of buying property to establish a permanent spring training home. They were offered five acres on the shore of a lake, an orange grove and construction of dormitories for $10,000.[9]

On March 23, a Sunday, Schalk and Big Ed took a group of players golfing. Some managers, like Clark Griffith, Sisler, Cobb and McGraw, banned their teams from golfing, but the Sox had no such rule. The only rule was 11:30 P.M. bedtime and there was no trouble enforcing that one as there wasn't anywhere to go around Winter Haven in 1924.

Chance never made it to Florida and Eddie Collins, who was supposed to help Big Ed and Evers, didn't get there until two days before they left. It was said the team didn't appear to be much stronger than '23 except for pitching, which seemed improved. Red Farber was in tremendous shape and throwing hard, the *Trib* said: "He has everything that has made him noted as the 'iron man' to succeed Ed Walsh."

Chance arrived in Chicago on April 11, four days before opening day. He was greeted by 2,000 fans at the Northwest Station. Chance was bronze and chunky and didn't look like a sick man. A new policy established in 1924 was fine with Big Ed. Umpires were told to keep old balls in play as long as possible. "When they were shooting that new ball into the game every time it became the least bit soiled or some batter lodged a complaint, it was pretty tough on a fellow to strike his stride and many a rookie went back to the bushes before he got a fair start."

In mid–May Chance stayed in Chicago during an Eastern swing by the Sox. Evers took sick and Big Ed ran the team himself on May 16, 17, and 18 in Boston. In the last of those games, Big Ed, who was coaching first base, and the Sox were victimized by a hidden ball trick. With runners on first and third in the seventh, Clark, the Boston first baseman, tagged out Roy Elsh who had singled to right field. Boston won the game 5-4. Retrosheet lists Big Ed's managerial record as 1–2. That was about on par with the team's overall record as they finished last in the A.L. in 1924.

After the season the White Sox and Giants went on a tour of Europe. Big Ed went as the umpire. The New York team managed by McGraw included Meusel and Stengal and Hugh Jennings as coach. They played games in Montreal on October 13 and 14 and sailed for England on October 15 on the *Mount Royal*. They played games in London, Birmingham, Manchester, Glasgow, Edinburgh, Dublin, Belfast, and Paris. Big Ed was confounded when French youths yelled "death to the arbiter" at him during the game in Paris. Ed didn't know what was going on until it was explained it was the equivalent of the American bleacher cry, "Kill the umpire."[10]

After the tour broke up in November, Jennings and Evers and a couple of others went to Rome for an audience with the pope. Comiskey and his party went to Berlin. Big Ed, Lyons and Clancy went on a tour of World War I battlefields with guide Hank Gowdy. They reassembled in Paris on November 23 to sail home on the *Leviathan*.

Big Ed stayed with the White Sox as a coach in the 1925 season, but in 1926 he turned his attention to something more important — his sons were stepping onto the athletic stage.

17

Little Ed and Big Bob

In the 1927 edition of *The Dome*, a Notre Dame University yearbook, one of the Fighting Irish baseball pitchers was described this way: "Indications that he will be the equal of his dad, the former Chicago White Sox twirler, were evidenced by Ed Walsh, who handled half the pitching assignments last Spring."

Young Ed Walsh was born February 11, 1905, in Meriden, just a month before his father left for the spring training of his second major league season. Though often called "Ed Jr.," Big Ed's son was not strictly a junior. His name was Edward Arthur Walsh. Big Ed's name was Edward Augustin Walsh. Growing up the son of a famous major leaguer, Ed, and his brother, Bob, who was born in 1907, sometimes spent time during the baseball seasons in Chicago or in hotels in Boston, New York and Philadelphia when the Sox went on Eastern road trips. But after five-year-old Ed became ill at a hotel in Philadelphia in 1909, increasingly his mother, Rosemary, stayed in Meriden during the seasons where she had a supportive family.

By the time he was 15 young Ed was already 6' and 160 pounds. He played football in high school and in the summers pitched for South Meriden, a semipro team. In June of 1922 when he was 17 he struck out 14 against the Mohawks, considered one of the best semipro teams in the area. After high school Ed went to St. John's Prep in Danvers, Massachusetts. In 1923 and 1924 he played football, baseball, and hockey. He was the football team's kicker and received honorable mention as an All-Massachusetts halfback. In November of 1922 he kicked a field goal from a difficult angle from the 30-yard line with 10 seconds left as St. John's beat St. James 5–2. In 1923 he kicked 35- and 43-yard field goals and ran 38

17. Little Ed and Big Bob

yards for a touchdown in a 12–6 win over Newton. A story about the game in the *Boston Globe* portrayed young Ed as a one-man team: "Edward Walsh Jr., son of the famous old big league pitcher, and 10 other football players defeated Newton High. Walsh gave one of the greatest exhibitions of punting ever seen in a scholastic game."

Pitching for the St. John's baseball team he defeated the Harvard freshmen in front of major league scouts Fred Mitchell of the Braves and Hugh Duffy of the Red Sox. During the summers while he was at St. John's he went back to Meriden and pitched for South Meriden and Insilco, the International Silver Company team. His catcher was Frank Woodke, a professional from the Connecticut State League. He played against Howard Burkett of Los Angeles in the Pacific Coast League; Dick Tuckey, a veteran of the Connecticut State League; and Paul Hopkins, a Colgate star who got in 11 games with the Senators in 1927 and '29.

Young Ed was 20 in the fall of 1925 when he enrolled in Notre Dame. As a prep student he was considered a sophomore. He reported to football practice where Knute Rockne declared he was the only player on the team who could punt. But a knee injury kept him out that season and he never did play a down for the Notre Dame football team. On March 2, 1926, Rockne, who was also the athletic director, hired Big Ed as battery coach of the baseball team.[1] *The Dome* had this to say: "The acquisition of 'Big Ed' Walsh as a coach of the pitchers was a step toward the advancement of baseball at Notre Dame to a high plane."

What direct effect Big Ed had on the Notre Dame pitchers during his coaching tenure — which lasted only as long as his son's career from 1926 to 1928 — isn't known, but Notre Dame

Knute Rockne said Young Ed was the best punter on the team. Ed reported to practice, but after a knee injury stuck to baseball (Notre Dame Archives).

pitching did advance both in quality and quantity during those seasons. The Notre Dame head coach, who used young Ed in half the spring games in 1926, was Dr. George E. Keogan. Under him in 1926, Walsh and two other pitchers, Elmer Besten and Steve Ronay, pitched most of Notre Dame's 26 games. Walsh got off to an inauspicious start for the Irish, losing his first three. Walsh did not play on April 3 when Notre Dame played Georgia Tech in Atlanta before three big league scouts, Billy Doyle, Tigers; Jack Doyle, Cubs; and Charley Hickman, Indians.[2]

In the third of his early losses, on April 14, young Ed pitched four innings, gave up just one hit and struck out six, but lost 6–4 to Bradley Tech. The Irish made 14 errors. On April 30 he sprained his ankle sliding into third and missed three weeks. Later in the season he pitched effectively. Three of young Ed's games in 1926 stand out. He beat Western Reserve University 4–2 with a four-hitter and 15 strikeouts. He beat Georgia 4–2 on a four-hitter with 10 strikeouts and shut out Northwestern on a three-hitter with 16 strikeouts.

Tom Mills took over as head coach in '27 and Walsh didn't get as much work as he had the previous season. It wasn't that young Ed wasn't

Ed warms up for Notre Dame. He finished his collegiate career with an 18–6 record (Notre Dame Archives).

17. Little Ed and Big Bob

a top flight collegiate pitcher; he was. By the time he was a senior he was considered the team's ace and was known as "The Strikeout King." He didn't pitch more because Notre Dame — with Walsh, Besten, and Ronay back and three first-year pitchers — was loaded with pitching under Mills in 1927 and '28. The staff even had a nickname, "The Big Six."

In 1927 William Joseph Sullivan, Jr., the son of Bill "Sully" Sullivan, Big Ed's catcher during his heyday with the White Sox, joined the Notre Dame team, and Sully joined the coaching staff. Sully's son went by "Joe" at Notre Dame. He did have experience as a catcher and there was speculation that the Irish would have an Ed Walsh–Sullivan battery, just as the White Sox had when they won the World's Series in 1906. But Mills had a catcher and needed a second baseman, a job he gave to Joe, who was also selected team captain for 1926. That Rockne would hire two former major leaguers as coaches just when their sons enrolled in Notre Dame and joined the baseball program would be far too coincidental to be anything more that what it was — a package deal. Walsh and Sullivan, the elders, got to watch their sons play up close and do a little coaching for some small compensation, while the Irish got their sons for the baseball team.

With the Walshes and Sullivans, the Irish improved from 13–13 in 1926 to 15–6 in 1927 to 23–8 in 1927. Young Ed was 5–0 in 1927 and in 1928 closed his collegiate career with a flourish by winning his last nine, including a 20–1 win over Harvard in Cambridge, Massachusetts, when he scattered seven hits and hit a home run. After a 0–3 start young Ed finished his Notre Dame career 18–6.

Big Ed's younger son, Bob Walsh, joined the Notre Dame team in 1928, during his brother's senior season. Bob got in only one game, then switched to track and field the next spring and became one of the best shot put throwers in the country. Bob, bigger than both his brother and father at 6-foot-4 and 210, was undefeated in the shot put and discus, including the two big Midwest events, the Ohio Relays and Indiana State Meet. He set a Notre Dame and Indiana state record in the shot with a heave of 47' 6".

When young Ed's collegiate career ended on June 16 in 1928, his father went to Chicago to join the Sox as a coach. Young Ed followed in a few days and on July 4, less than three weeks after his last collegiate game, young Ed pitched in a major league game for the White Sox. He lasted only four innings in his debut, giving up four runs, five hits and five walks. The Browns won 11–8 and young Ed took the loss. The Browns' manager,

At 6' 4" Bob Walsh was even bigger than his father and brother. He was a record-setting shot put thrower at Notre Dame (Notre Dame Archives).

Dan Howley, was impressed with young Ed's speed. "His dad asked me what I thought of the kid after the game and I told him I liked him and I meant it," said Howley. "I believe he'll make a winning pitcher. His dad as a coach with the White Sox will be a big help to him. Naturally, being just out of Notre Dame, you can't expect him to burn up our league at the start. College boys can't do that."[3]

Young Ed's first major league win was in Boston in the second game of a double header on July 14 when he beat the Red Sox, 11–2. He yielded only six hits, all singles, struck out four and walked three. New Yorkers got their first glimpse of young Ed on July 21 and he pitched one of the best games of his otherwise unremarkable career. He pitched six innings of no-hit ball against the Yankees. In the seventh the no-hitter and shutout were broken up by Babe Ruth with his 39th home run of the year. Ed balked a runner in later in the seventh and wound up losing 2–0 to George Pipgras. Ed appeared in 14 games with the Sox in 1928, starting 10 and completing two. He was 4–7 with a 4.96 ERA and more walks than strikeouts. The next season Walsh was back with the White Sox as a fifth starter. He started 20 games and was 6–11 with a 5.65. He walked 64 with only 31 strikeouts in 129 innings. In 1930 he started only four games and relieved in 33, with similar results. He was 1–4 with a 5.38 ERA.

Browns manager Howley was likely right in his assessment that college pitch-

17. Little Ed and Big Bob

ers aren't ready for the big leagues. With that in mind, though three years too late, the Sox sent Walsh to the minor leagues at Louisville in the American Association in 1931. Though the deal was payment to the Colonels for outfielder Mel Simmons, strings were attached to the deal to allow the Sox to recall Walsh. The next season, 1932, the Sox gave him one more shot but he was released after just four games and 20 innings when he gave up 26 hits, 19 runs and 13 walks. In his last major league start, on September 11, 1932, the dream battery that had been suggested at Notre Dame was fielded by the White Sox. As a come on for the fans, Ed Walsh "Jr." pitched and Billy Sullivan, Jr., caught. After his release young Ed hung around the minors for a couple of seasons which were unremarkable except for one game. On July 26, 1933, pitching for Oakland in the PCL, Ed ended a 61-game hitting streak by an 18-year-old San Francisco rookie by the name of Joe DiMaggio.

Big Ed, right, and his son were at Notre Dame in the 1920s. Big Ed was a Notre Dame coach. The pair was together as player and coach with the White Sox in 1928 and '29 (Notre Dame Archives).

Four years later Edward Arthur Walsh was dead at 32. He died of rheumatic fever in a bed in an upstairs bedroom of his parents' house in Meriden. Ned Carney, a Walsh nephew who still lives in Meriden, recalled visiting Ed on his deathbed. "I gave him a horse chestnut. And he gave me a lollipop. That's all I remember."[4]

Big Ed's son Bob was signed by the Yankees after graduating from Notre Dame in 1930. In 1931 Bob pitched for the Cumberland Colts of the Mid Atlantic League. He stayed in the Yankees chain for six years, but never reached the majors. Injuries didn't help. On April 24, 1935, Bob was pitching for Indianapolis in the American Association against Columbus when he was spiked, badly lacerating his hand, and he missed two months. He was at Richmond in the Piedmont League in 1937 and was having his best year at 9–1 when he got hit in the head with a line drive that ended his career. "That pitch really conked me. Messed me up for six months. I couldn't walk."[5]

18

Big Ed: Old-Timer

During his sons' careers at Notre Dame, Big Ed continued to work for the Sox as a part-time coach and scout. His working relationship with the White Sox, which had begun when he was a rookie pitcher in 1904, ended once and for all in the spring of 1930, his son's last full year with the Sox. That March he was traveling home to Meriden after being in Florida to watch his son with the White Sox when he was stricken with appendicitis. On March 27 he was operated on in Meriden. He was described as a "very sick man" and wasn't declared out of danger for two weeks. That experience convinced Big Ed, by now approaching 50, that he should quit chasing baseball jobs and stay closer to home. The death of his son Ed in November of 1937 further solidified that choice. Taken by rheumatic fever, Young Ed was only 32. Just that summer he had been healthy enough to try out with Minneapolis in the American Association. He came back to Meriden from San Antonio, Texas, where he had been living, on Labor Day and died in his parents' home. His mother was devastated and Big Ed did not want to leave her home alone anymore. Being home gave Big Ed time to pursue his second love — hunting with his beloved dogs Spot, Diamond, Queen and Sox.

"My hunting days go back to when I was first old enough to handle a gun and that is about as far back as I can remember. I was working in the mines and it is a dingy, dusty trade, and an unhealthy life underground. No wonder I was glad to get out into the open, to tramp through the green fields and feel the cool shade of the woods. When I look back to that time it seems so far away it doesn't seem real to me. I used to hunt rabbits in the fields and on the edge of the woods when I was only a breaker boy. My hunting experiences meant much to me when I was in the mines. They were a great holiday. A few rabbits, a few squirrels and once in a while a quail. I never went far from home and for this simple game it wasn't necessary. The coal mines are in rugged country with ridges and valleys generally timbered. I seldom went out that I wasn't successful."[1]

Finding game around Meriden wasn't as easy for Big Ed as it had been in Pennsylvania as a youth. He liked to travel around central Connecticut in his automobile looking for game, but insisted he was always a true sportsman who followed game laws. "I am not criticizing game laws they are necessary no doubt, to prevent all the wildlife from being killed off, but it is exasperating to come on a good shot at a deer and have to pass it up as a law-abiding citizen."

On one trip Ed came across five fawns with a mother deer which had been killed by a train. He stayed with the young deer until game wardens came and captured them. Most of his adult life Ed dreamed of taking a true wilderness hunting trip, but never did. As close as he got was on trips with Comiskey to Wisconsin.

This was Big Ed's son Ed with Louisville in 1932. Five years later he was dead at age 37. Big Ed and his wife, Rosemary, were devastated.

"It doesn't pay a married man with a family to support to dream of long hunting trips off into the wilderness, where things are really as they used to be when Columbus came over, and meet bears and moose face to face; and I may never be able to take such a trip. But there is nothing outside of pitching in another world's series that I should like so well."[2]

In the early 1930s Big Ed took up golf and was soon amazing golfers with long distance drives on the original layout of the Old Meriden golf course, then nine holes. From the tee of the 264-yard ninth hole, using a brassie, he once drove a ball over the green and on top of the clubhouse 40 yards beyond. It was said he could tour the nine holes around par using only the brassie.[3]

Over the years Ed had invested money in a $14,000 showplace house on Hanover Road in Meriden and built two other houses. He lost two of the houses during the Depression and nearly went broke. In January of 1936, he took a job with the government's Works Progress Administration, or WPA, for $150 a month teaching and lecturing about sports and character around the state. He was fired in August because of his constant tirades over softball. It was said his insistence on teaching kids baseball had disrupted several softball leagues around the state.[4] From a newspaper story about his firing: "The bones of contention narrow down to two points: he lectured to boys that he considered softball a game for old men, especially those who had passed the age when they could attain maximum proficiency in baseball; and he stressed that playing professional baseball could bring rich monetary rewards."[5]

In the late 1930s Meriden mayor Francis Danaher, son of Cornelius Danaher, who brought Walsh to Meriden in 1902, gave Big Ed a job with the City of Meriden at the water filtration plant at Broad Brook Reservoir. Big Ed sometimes said he was employed as a chemical engineer, but he was more of a glorified night watchman. Ned Carney, the nephew who still lives in the Meriden area, said Big Ed used to let Ned and his friends fish in the reservoir where he worked, but rarely talked about his baseball career. From what Big Ed's nephew said, and because of a dearth of research materials on Big Ed after his son's death and into the mid–1940s, it seems that Ed didn't relish living the role of the old baseball star during that time.

But something happened in New York City on April 23, 1946, that brought Ed out of the closet. The Baseball Hall of Fame veterans' committee selected 11 inductees — Jesse Burkett, Frank Chance, Jack Chesbro, Johnny Evers, Clark Griffith, Tommy McCarthy, Joe McGinnity, Eddie Plank, Joe Tinker, Rube Waddell and Big Ed Walsh. He was one of only five — Burkett, Griffith, Tinker, and Evers being the other four — who were still living. By the time they were formally inducted on July 21, 1947, only four were still living. Johnny Evers died in the interim. Of the four, only Big Ed, who made the 200-mile drive with his wife, son Robert and Robert's wife, attended the ceremonies. National League president Ford Frick officially dedicated the plaques. He introduced Big Ed and Eddie Plank's son. Big Ed recited a poem in memory of deceased Hall of Famers about a hunter's cabin on which the door was always left open for the old-timers to come in and rest.[6]

Does Big Ed belong in the Hall of Fame? A case could be made that he does not as his window of greatness was only seven seasons and he doesn't have 200 wins. But there is that all-time low ERA of 1.82, the four 20-plus win seasons, which included one of 40. He led the A.L. in appearances four times, strikeouts twice, ERA twice, pitched a no-hitter and five one-hitters and was 2–0 in his only World's Series with a 0.60 ERA and 17 strikeouts in 15 innings.

His peers believed he was one of the greatest. In 1916 *Baseball Magazine* came up with a formula to rate pitchers based on innings, strikeouts and winning percentage and Big Ed was no. 1 over Mathewson and Johnson. In 1924 Honus Wagner named an all-time American League team for the *Los Angeles Times* and named Walsh his no. 1 pitcher. Cobb, though he had a lifetime average of .347 against Big Ed, said he and the other batters batted differently against Big Ed. "No man could go to the end of the bat and get a hit off that fella unless it was by sheer luck. In my day nearly all of us were choke hitters. Against Walsh we'd grip that bat even shorter and be satisfied to get a piece of the ball."[7]

In Meriden there was no doubt Ed belonged in the Hall. Two months after his induction, on September 20, 1947, the Meriden Kiwanis Club sponsored a "Big Ed Walsh Day." The day started with a downtown parade. A police escort led three drum corps and a string of convertibles containing Big Ed, Mickey Harris representing the Red Sox, Urban "Red" Faber representing the White Sox, and Sibby Sisti representing the Boston Braves. They paraded to the ball field for a game between the Meriden Insilcos and the Middletown Giants for the benefit of the Kiwanis Club's Underprivileged Children's Fund. Jimmy Piersall batted third and played left field for the Insilcos. Ed threw out the first ball and was presented with an inscribed silver bowl by Mayor Danaher. "Big Ed is still carrying his frame gracefully and appears capable of turning in a good performance on the mound."[8]

There was a reception that evening and a game the next night between the Insilcos and a comedy team called the New England Hoboes.

Big Ed's wife died in May 1949. A Daughter of Union Veterans of the Civil War, she was 69. That was right around the time that a new form of baseball came to Meriden — Little League. For its second year, 1950, the Meriden Little League formed two divisions, the Jack Barry Division and the Ed Walsh Division. Barry, who was born in Meriden in 1887 and lived most of his life there, was the shortstop for the A's famed "$100,000" infield from 1909 to 1914. On May 29, 1950, fit-looking with his hair still dark at age 69, Big Ed threw out the first ball at the Little League opening day in Meriden. He fell in love with Little League. "I wouldn't miss opening day for anything in the world," he said and declared his intention to attend as many games as possible.[9]

In 1951, 750 fans saw him throw out the first pitch and 600 came out in 1952. On Memorial Day weekend in 1953, 90-year-old Connie Mack, who got his start as a professional in Meriden in 1883, came for the opening of a new Little League park, arriving in a chauffeur-driven Cadillac. Big Ed was waiting on the sidewalk. Mack grabbed his hand and said, "If we had someone like you on the club this year, we'd win the pennant."[10] Rain washed out the program and Mack had to return to Philadelphia. The next day 1,500 fans came out to the formal dedication and to see Big Ed Walsh toss out the first pitch.

True to his word Ed didn't show up just for opening days. He hung around the Little League park a lot. The kids called him "Uncle Ed" and besieged him for autographs. "The kids would stand there all wide-eyed and all," said Joe Budwitz, a longtime league scorer and officer. "He'd tell the kids how lucky they were to be in a league and a league that had equipment and he'd tell the parents how lucky they were to have their kids involved in sports."[11]

In 1953 he was in the press box for the league championship game in September and gave a talk during the trophy presentation. That same summer he went to Williamsport for the Little League World Series. He picked the series winner just by watching kids warm up, and was right. Joe Sims from Birmingham, Alabama, beat Schenectady, New York, 2–1.[12]

In 1955 Ed's health started to deteriorate. He was hit hard by arthritis. He still managed to get out of bed and toss a pitch to open the Little League that May, but went home immediately following the opening ceremonies.[13] Two years earlier though, in March of 1953, Walsh, then 72 and looking like he was 55, was surprised to read in the local newspaper that he was retired from the Broad Brook Reservoir. "I would like to know who authorized my retirement as due to ill health and why I was not told in advance." He said he was not responsible for a rash of errors at the plant where a large amount of water was lost. The board listened but decided to fire him, saying the job was too arduous a task for the old ballplayer. "You can't just fire a man after 15 years of faithful service," he said. But they did, and voted him a pension of $75 a month.

As an old retired man Big Ed embraced the beloved old Hall of Famer role. On August 15 in 1954 Big Ed appeared at an Old Timers game in Yankee Stadium with Dazzy Vance, George "Hooks" Wiltse, Carl Hubbell, and Cy Young as one of five hall of fame pitchers with no-hit games. He went to Cooperstown for induction weekend every year and followed baseball closely and loved to talk about it. His favorite pitchers were Robin Roberts of the Phillies and Billy Pierce and Virgil Trucks of the White Sox. "All three are calm and cool out there. They have rhythm and the knack of keeping a batter off stride, something a pitcher must do to be a winner. Just as important they stay ahead of the hitters most of the time."[14]

He hated intentional walks and suggested batters be given two bases when intentionally walked. "The fans pay to see Mickey Mantle and Ted Williams hit, not walk. Why Mantle bunts I'll never know. If I could hit the way he does, I'd never bunt."[15]

He predicted that Williams would break Ruth's single season home run record of 60, but that Mantle had missed his best chance in 1956. But he hated home runs, the live ball, and called for the reinstatement of the spitball until he died. When Herb Score was struck in the face with a line drive Ed blamed what he called the "rabbit ball."

"Everything else in the game favors the hitters. Livelier baseballs, smaller ballparks. They've practically got the poor pitchers working in straight jackets. Those guys have a right to make a living, too. I admire the pitchers today who throw the pitch. Some people call them cheaters, they're not. They're just guys doing everything to win. If I were a manager I'd like to have a whole staff of spitballers."[16]

In an interview on his 76th birthday in 1957, which was syndicated by United Press International, he called modern baseball a joke. "We were a tougher breed then. There were fewer rules. And we didn't need coaches to tell us what to do. The trouble today is that there aren't enough good pitchers in the league. Too many .300 hitters. Too many home runs because ball parks are shorter and too many rules." When Reds manager Birdie Tebbets accused Lew Burdette of throwing the spitball, Big Ed said, "If Lew used it, I hope he continues to do so. As for Tebbetts, he ought to keep his mouth shut."

After Ed lost his job at the reservoir, he moved in with friends in Meriden, Mr. and Mrs. Henry MacAleer. When the MacAleers moved to Pompano Beach, Florida, in April of 1957, he went with them. His son Bob made arrangements for a flight on Eastern Airlines from Windsor Locks, Ontario. It was big Ed's first flight.

Just before and after he moved to Florida, stories began to circulate that Big Ed was broke. The AP ran a story which said he was living on only $50 a month from the Veteran Baseball Players Association. Big Ed, likely out of pride and embarrassment, denied the story. He said he had an annual $900 pension from Meriden and $100 monthly from Social

Security, in addition to the $50 a month from the old-timers association. Even if that were true it was still less than he made playing baseball some half century earlier.

The stories of his destitution wouldn't die. One writer visited him and noticed a pile of signed baseballs on his desk and wrote that Big Ed told him fans had sent him the balls to sign, but that he didn't have money for postage to send them back.[17] Big Ed was a prolific signer, but his own estimate that he signed 30,000 a year and 1,500,000 in his lifetime seems impossibly high.

In response to Big Ed's plight, the White Sox proclaimed June 22, 1958, as Ed Walsh Day. By this time he was 77 and in a wheelchair. He cried as he was wheeled to the pitcher's mound and given a long standing ovation by a crowd of 12,114. Someone yelled, "throw a spitball, Ed" and he wet his fingers and, laughing all the while, threw a ball a few feet to 66-year-old Ray Schalk who, as a rookie in 1912, had caught Ed a few times.

Chicago mayor Richard Daley was introduced to Ed near the dugout. Daley, who grew up a few blocks from the park said, "I used to see you pitch. You were a great one." Ed signed baseballs and posed with old teammates, catcher Jim Hart and pitcher Lou Fiene. Fiene had an old picture of himself, Doc White, Jim Scott and Big Ed seated around a piano. "That was our barbershop quartet," Ed said.

Also on the field to honor Ed were Hall of Famers Red Faber, Ted Lyons, Luke Appling, Al Lopez, and Mickey Cochran. Dizzy Dean was up in the radio booth. Charles Comiskey II, grandson of the Old Roman, who had died in 1931, also met with Walsh and followed the group out to the mound for the ceremony. Comiskey and his sister, Mrs. Dorothy Rigney, forgot differences for a day. They were in court over an estate dispute.

A group called Baseball Anonymous gave Ed a check for $1500 and said donations were still coming in. They expected to raise $5,000. Walsh watched the game and flew back to Florida two days later. On August 21 that year Ed was honored once more. He and Cy Young, then 87, were introduced at Bob Carpenter's Old Timers Game at Shibe Park in Philadelphia before a Phillies-Dodgers game.

Big Ed died on May 26, 1959, in Pompano Beach, Florida, 12 days after his 78th birthday. Fittingly, before his death to he got to spend time with one of the most important men in his life. A year earlier Billy "Sully" Sullivan, friend, mentor, teacher, teammate and manager, though 83 himself, came to Florida from Oregon for Ed's 77th birthday party.

Notes

Chapter 1

1. http://home.epix.net/~captclint/history.html.
2. Robert Wiebe, "The Anthracite Strike of 1902: A Record of Confusion," *Pennsylvania Historical Review* 48, 229–251.
3. *Sporting News*, January 9, 1957, 14.
4. Ibid.
5. F.C. Lane, "The Spit-ball King," *Baseball Magazine*, March 1913, 41.
6. *Washington Post*, "Walsh Credits Dame Fortune," November 24, 1912, S2.
7. Lane, 41.
8. Martin Corcoran, letter to Sid Keener, November 27, 1957.
9. Ernest P. Lanigan, director of Baseball Hall of Fame, from a series called *Firsts of the Famous*; and from an unattributed story in Walsh's Hall of Fame file.
10. *Washington Post*, November 24, 1912, S2.
11. *Baseball Magazine*, September 1913, 98.
12. *Sporting News*, January 9, 1957.
13. *Bridgeport Telegram*, July 9 and 13, 1902.
14. *Wilkes-Barre Record*, March 11, 1904.

Chapter 2

1. *Wilkes-Barre Record*, "A Tribute to Walsh," March 11, 1904.
2. *Chicago Daily Tribune*, "White Sox at Fort Worth," March 6, 1904, 8.
3. *Chicago Daily Tribune*, "White Sox at Marlin Springs," March 8, 1904, 8.
4. Ibid.
5. Ibid.
6. *Chicago Daily Tribune*, "White Sox Gain 12-Inning Victory," March 15, 1905, 8.
7. *Chicago Daily Tribune*, "Comiskey Arrives at Dallas," March 12, 1904, 8.
8. *Chicago Daily Tribune*, "White Sox Break Camp," March 20, 1904, 11.
9. Dave Larson. This SABR biography was the source of information about Jones and Davis.
10. *Chicago Daily Tribune*, "White Sox Win an Easy Contest," March 29, 1904, 9.
11. *Chicago Daily Tribune*, "White Sox Romp in Snow," April 10, 1904, 9.
12. F.C. Lane, "The Spit-ball King," *Baseball Magazine*, March 1913, 41.
13. Ibid.
14. *Chicago Daily Tribune*, "White Sox Make Thrilling Finish," May 8, 1904, 9.
15. *Chicago Daily Tribune*, "Great Pitching Beats White Sox," August 18, 1904, 6.

Chapter 3

1. *Iowa City Citizen*, "Spitball Honor Given to Chic Fraser," August 5, 1919, 5.

2. Al Spink, *Atlanta Constitution*, "Spit-Ball Pitching Will Be Considered," Dec 10, 1919, 6.
3. *Chicago Daily Tribune*, December 18, 1904.
4. *Chicago Daily Tribune*, "Nines Are Hard at Work," March 12, 1905, 1.
5. *Chicago Daily Tribune*, "Sox and Pelicans Game Is Blocked," March 12, 1905, A1.
6. *Baseball Magazine*, March 1913, 41–59.
7. L.H. Gregory, *Baseball Digest*, "True Spitter Didn't Spin," September 1950, 71.
8. Harry A. Williams, *Los Angeles Times*, "Walsh Is Confident," April 25, 1915, I7.
9. Howard Peck, *Courant Magazine*, "How Big Ed Got the Spitball," December 16, 1956.
10. *Baseball Magazine*, March 1913, 41.
11. *Washington Post*, "Walsh Credits Stricklett with Discovery of Spitter," March 15, 1914, SP2.
12. *Chicago Daily Tribune*, "Sox Rooters Ask: How About Walsh," January 25, 1914, B1.
13. *Washington Post*, March 15, 1914, SP2.
14. *Indianapolis Star*, "Spitter Requires Strength," May 29, 1910, 3.
15. *Baseball Magazine*, March 1913, 41–59.
16. *Baseball Magazine*, "As He Told," July 1917.
17. *Baseball Magazine*, "Manager Declares That This Delivery Injures," March 1913, 51.
18. *Chicago Daily Tribune*, January 22, 1905.
19. *New York Evening Telegram*, September 22, 1916.
20. *Washington Post*, "No Spitball for M'Guire," April 17, 1910, MS8.
21. I.E. Sanborn, *Chicago Tribune*, "Majors Scheme to Circumvent Freak Pitches," December 5, 1915, B4.
22. *Sporting News*, January 9, 1957.
23. *Sporting Life*, August 3, 1907.
24. *Baseball Magazine*, "As He Told," July 1917.
25. *Baseball Magazine*, "Ed Walsh Has a Word to Say in Its Defense," February 1912.
26. *Sporting Life*, September 27, 1913.
27. *Sporting Life*, "Deadly Spitball," May 18, 1907.
28. *Chicago Daily Tribune*, "His Latest and Best Joke," April 13, 1905, 6.
29. *Washington Post*, March 20, 1910.
30. *Chicago Daily Tribune* (1872–1963); Dec 19, 1920, A1.
31. Sanborn, *Chicago Tribune*, December 5, 1915, B4.
32. James Crusinberry, *Chicago Daily Tribune*, "Kick Spitball Out of Pastime," December 18, 1917, 15.
33. *New York World*, February 26, 1918.
34. *Chicago Daily Tribune*, "Walsh's Arm Is Gone," December 19, 1920, A1.
35. Story in Hall of Fame file, not attributed.
36. *Sporting News*, January 9, 1957.

Chapter 4

1. *Chicago Daily Tribune*, "Pennant Races to Begin Today," April 14, 1905, 6.
2. *Chicago Daily Tribune*, July 15, 1905.
3. *Chicago Daily Tribune*, "No World Series if Sox Win Out," October 5, 1905, 6.
4. *Meriden Daily Journal*, "Told by Player and His Wife," October 16, 1906.
5. *Baseball Magazine*, September 1913, 98.
6. Gregory, *Baseball Digest*, September 1950, 71.
7. *Baseball Magazine*, March 1913.

Chapter 5

1. *Washington Post*, "Comiskey Was Baseball Star," January 12, 1913, S2.
2. *Baseball Magazine* 12, No. 4 (February 1914): 21–28.
3. *Ibid*.
4. *Washington Post*, Baseball Notes, January 4, 1906, 8.
5. *Chicago Daily Tribune*, "Playing Dates for Americans," February 15, 1906, 8.
6. *Los Angeles Times*, "Nig Smith's Self-Reserve," March 12, 1906, II; and *Washington Post*, "Threat to Join Outlaws," March 26, 1906, 8.
7. *Washington Post*, "Stone Goes to White Sox," January 28, 1906, S1.

8. *Chicago Daily Tribune*, "White Sox Land in Crescent City," March 15, 1906, 10.
9. Ibid.
10. *Chicago Daily Tribune*, "White Sox Easily Win," March 25, 1906, A2.
11. *Washington Post*, March 25, 1906, S1.
12. *Chicago Daily Tribune*, "Walsh Figures in Pitching Feat," May 7, 1906, 10.
13. From a story in his Hall of Fame file, dated June 24, 1933.
14. *Chicago Daily Tribune*, June 24, 1906, 10.
15. *Chicago Daily Tribune*, August 24, 1906, 10.
16. *Boston Daily Globe*, August 4, 1906, 7.
17. *Chicago Daily Tribune*, August 4, 1906, 10.
18. H.S. Fullerton, *Chicago Tribune*, "New Foe for Sox but Same Result," August 11, 1906, 10.
19. Fullerton, *Chicago Daily Tribune*, "Sox Reach Top of Pennant Ladder," August 13, 1906, 6.
20. *Chicago Daily Tribune*, August 19, 1906, A1.
21. *Chicago Daily Tribune*, September 11, 1906, A1.
22. *Chicago Daily Tribune*, September 15, 1906, 11.
23. *Los Angeles Times*, "Eddie Collins Tells How He Started," January 3, 1927, 10.
24. *Chicago Daily Tribune*, "Get the News Standing in the Rain," October 4, 1906, 2.

Chapter 6

1. *Chicago Daily Tribune*, "Four Umpires in Series," October 7, 1906, A1.
2. Ibid.
3. *Chicago Daily Tribune*, October 8, 1906, A1.
4. *Chicago Daily Tribune*, October 10, 1906, A1.
5. *Meriden Daily Journal*, October 16, 1906.
6. Ibid.
7. Ibid.
8. *Chicago Daily Tribune*, October 12, 1906, A1.
9. *Chicago Daily Tribune*, "Notes on the Game," October 14, 1906, 2.
10. Ibid.
11. *Meriden Daily Journal*, October 16, 1906.
12. *Washington Post*, "Commy Popular Man," October 19, 1906, 8.
13. *Chicago Daily Tribune*, "White Sox's Flag; Beat Cubs 8 to 3," October 15, 1906, 1.
14. *Wilkes-Barre Record*, "Duck Walsh Honored," October 25, 1906.
15. *Wilkes-Barre Record*, "Duck Walsh the Spitball Wizard," October 29, 1906.
16. *Washington Post*, September 25, 1913.

Chapter 7

1. *Chicago Daily Tribune*, March 5, 1907, 10.
2. *Chicago Daily Tribune*, "Sox Marooned in Southern Texas," March 8, 1907, 10.
3. *(Elyria, Ohio) Evening Telegram*, Wednesday, July 24, 1907, 4.
4. *Chicago Daily Tribune*, "News Surprises Comiskey," March 29, 1907, 12.
5. *Chicago Daily Tribune*, "Sox Speedy Plays Beat Colonels," A1.
6. *Chicago Daily Tribune*, "Fast Fielding Brings Victory," 14.
7. *Boston Daily Globe*, "Expects to Repeat," April 7, 1907, 9.
8. *Chicago Daily Tribune*, April 7, 1907, 14.

Chapter 8

1. *(Elyria, Ohio) Reporter*, April 1, 1907, Page 8.
2. *Chicago Daily Tribune*, April 14, 1907, "Sox Win Like Champs of Old," A1.
3. *Chicago Daily Tribune*, April 20, 1907.
4. *Chicago Daily Tribune*, April 27, 1907, 10.
5. J. Ed Grillo, *Washington Post*, December 9, 1908, 8.
6. *Chicago Daily Tribune*, May 5, 1907, 10.
7. *Chicago Daily Tribune*, June 20, 1907, 8.
8. *Chicago Daily Tribune*, June 30, 1907, 8.

9. Hek, *Chicago Tribune*, "In the Wake of the News," August 6, 1907, 7.
10. *Washington Post*, September 1, 1907.
11. *Chicago Daily Tribune*, September 9, 1907.
12. *Chicago Daily Tribune*, October 2, 1916, 15.
13. *Chicago Daily Tribune*, October 14, 1907.
14. *Oakland Tribune*, "Funny Incidents of the Major Leagues," January 19, 1908.

Chapter 9

1. *Chicago Tribune*, May 14, 1908.
2. *Wilkes-Barre Record*, May 13, 1908.
3. *Boston Globe*, June 21, 1908.
4. *Washington Post*, July 5, 1908, S3.
5. *Boston Globe*, July 14, 1908.
6. *Boston Globe*, August 18, 1908.
7. *Washington Post*, September 19, 1908.
8. *Chicago Tribune*, September 29, 1908.
9. *Chicago Tribune*, October 3, 1908.
10. *Baseball Digest*, "The Day I Fanned Lajoie," March 1945, 10.
11. *Chicago Tribune*, October 5, 1908.
12. *Baseball Digest*, March 1945.
13. *Boston Daily Globe*, January 1, 1922, 51.
14. *Chicago Tribune*, March 9, 1909.

Chapter 10

1. Red Smith, from his column in the *New York Herald Tribune*, May 31, 1959.
2. *Washington Post*, August 6, 1916, S2.
3. *Boston Daily Globe*, January 5, 1923, 11.
4. *Los Angeles Times*, March 1, 1925, A3.
5. *Washington Post*, December 4, 1908, 8.
6. *Washington Post*, "Ed Walsh Is Iron Man," January 10, 1909, S4.
7. *Washington Post*, "Johnson Won't Sign," January 14, 1909, 8.
8. *Washington Post*, "Ed Walsh Wants $7,500," February 4, 1909, 8.
9. *Washington Post*, February 7, 1909, S4.
10. *Chicago Daily Tribune*, February 27, 1909, 7.
11. *Washington Post*, March 28, 1909, S4.
12. *Baseball Magazine* 12, no. 4 (February 1914), 21–28.
13. *Chicago Daily Tribune*, April 2, 1909, 6.
14. *Chicago Daily Tribune*, April 16, 1909, 13.
15. *Chicago Daily Tribune*, April 22, 1909, 8.
16. *Chicago Daily Tribune*, April 25, 1909, 8.
17. R.W. Lardner, *Chicago Daily Tribune*, April 30, 1909, 10.
18. *Chicago Daily Tribune*, May 2, 1909, B1.
19. *Wilkes-Barre Record*, "Plains Man Meets with Serious Injury," May 5, 1909, 1.
20. *Chicago Daily Tribune*, May 17, 1909, 12.
21. *Chicago Daily Tribune*, August 14, 1909, 10.
22. *Chicago Daily Tribune*, September 15, 1909, 10.

Chapter 11

1. *Chicago Daily Tribune*, February 25, 1910, 12.
2. *Los Angeles Times*, March 19, 1910, I6.
3. *Chicago Daily Tribune*, April 29, 1910, 9.
4. *Chicago Daily Tribune*, May 3, 1910, 13.
5. *Chicago Daily Tribune*, July 1, 1910, 12.
6. *Chicago Daily Tribune*, July 15, 1910, 8.
7. *Chicago Daily Tribune*, August 6, 1910, 9.
8. Lardner, *Chicago Daily Tribune*, August 18, 1910, 10.
9. *Chicago Daily Tribune*, August 25, 1910, 10.
10. *Boston Daily Globe*, September 1, 1910, 7.
11. *Chicago Daily Tribune*, September 10, 1910, 10.
12. *Chicago Daily Tribune*, September 27, 1910, 1.

Chapter 12

1. Ralph Berger, SABR biography.
2. *Chicago Tribune*, April 21, 1911.
3. *Chicago Tribune*, May 4, 1911.
4. *Chicago Tribune*, May 23, 1911.
5. *Chicago Tribune*, June 2, 1911.
6. *Chicago Tribune*, June 14, 1911.
7. *Chicago Tribune*, June 22, 1911.
8. *www.baseballlibrary.com/baseballlibrary/ballplayers/C/Cobb_Ty.stm*.
9. *Washington Post*, July 7, 1911, 8.
10. *Washington Post*, August 5, 1911.
11. *Chicago Tribune*, August 28, 1911.
12. *Washington Post*, October 15, 1911.
13. *Chicago Tribune*, October 19, 1911.
14. *Chicago Tribune*, June 14, 1912.
15. *Chicago Daily Tribune*, October 9, 1912, 24.
16. Chicago Tribune, October 18, 1912, 21.
17. Details of the City Series were taken from the *Chicago Tribune*, October 8–18.

Chapter 13

1. *Atlanta Constitution*, October 22, 1912, 8.
2. *Chicago Tribune*, October 22, 1912, 15.
3. Ibid.
4. *Chicago Tribune*, January 15, 1913, 6.
5. *Los Angeles Times*, February 5, 1913, II2.
6. *Chicago Tribune*, February 18, 1913, 11.
7. *Chicago Tribune*, February 19, 1913, 11.
8. *Chicago Tribune*, February 21, 1913, 11.
9. *Los Angeles Times*, March 6, 1913, III2.
10. *Chicago Tribune*, February 26, 1913, 11.
11. *Chicago Tribune*, March 10, 1913, 10.
12. *Chicago Tribune*, March 18, 1913, 13.
13. *Chicago Tribune*, April 1, 1913, 5.
14. Ibid.
15. *Chicago Tribune*, April 6, 1913, 15.
16. *Chicago Tribune*, April 8, 1913, 13.
17. *Chicago Tribune*, April 10, 1913, 13.
18. *Chicago Tribune*, April 16, 1913.
19. *Chicago Tribune*, April 21, 1913.
20. *Chicago Tribune*, May 12, 1913.
21. *Washington Post*, May 24, 1913, 8.
22. *Chicago Tribune*, May 19, 1913, 17.
23. *Chicago Tribune*, May 25, 1913, 15.
24. *Chicago Tribune*, May 29, 1913, 17.
25. *Chicago Tribune*, June 3, 1913, 15.
26. *Chicago Tribune*, June 14, 1913, 15.
27. *Newark Daily Advocate*, "Remarkable Cure of Newark Boy," April 22, 1914, 5.
28. *Washington Post*, "Reese Aids Players," January 7, 1912, S2.
29. *Los Angeles Times*, "Reese Fixes Walsh," August 20, 1913, V1.
30. *Baseball Magazine*, "Mystery of the $100,000 Arm," September 1914, 31.
31. *Baseball Magazine*, "The Mystery of the $100,000 Arm," September 1914.
32. *Los Angeles Times*, February 28, 1914, II3.
33. Harry A. Williams, *Los Angeles Times*, March 7, 1914, III3.
34. *Chicago Tribune*, March 24, 1914, 11.
35. *Chicago Tribune*, March 29, 1914, B1.
36. I.E. Sanborn, *Chicago Tribune*, April 13, 1914, 8.
37. Sam Weller, *Chicago Tribune*, July 19, 1914, B1.
38. *Washington Post*, August 30, 1914, 42.
39. *Chicago Tribune*, August 27, 1914, 8.
40. *Baseball Magazine*, September 1914.
41. Ibid.
42. Chicago Tribune, "Sox Arrive," February 21, 1914, B1.
43. *Chicago Tribune*, March 2, 1915, 9.
44. *Los Angeles Times*, April 25, 1915, VII7.
45. *Chicago Daily Tribune*, May 18, 1915.
46. *Los Angeles Times*, "Matty's Arm Like Walsh's," June 8, 1915, III1.
47. *Boston Globe*, June 14, 1915, 6.
48. I.E. Sanborn, *Chicago Tribune*, "28,000 Cheer Walsh," July 17, 1915, 11.
49. *Los Angeles Times*, "Baseball Talk," January 29, 1916, 16.
50. *Chicago Tribune*, July 29, 1916.

Chapter 14

1. *Baseball Magazine*, September 1914, 27.
2. *Los Angeles Times*, "Strange Case Puzzles Baseball," March 3, 1915, III3.
3. *Los Angeles Times*, "Electric Gear Shift Saves Pitcher's Arm," March 22, 1914, VII4.
4. *Atlanta Constitution*, July 19, 1919, 10.
5. *Boston Daily Globe*, March 1, 1923, 10.

6. *Meriden Record and Journal*, August 29, 1980.
7. Billy Evans, *Atlanta Constitution*, January 17, 1915, A3.
8. *Baseball Magazine*, September 1914, 27.
9. From Jennings' syndicated column in the *Atlanta Constitution*, December 22, 1925, 11.
10. *Washington Post*, June 4, 1905.
11. *Sporting Life*, "The 'Spit' Ball," April 20, 1907.
12. *Baseball Magazine*, March 1913, 51.

Chapter 15

1. *Washington Post*, November 16, 1917, 8.
2. *Atlanta Constitution*, February 17, 1918, A3.
3. *Bridgeport Telegram*, March 29, 1919.
4. *Chicago Tribune*, July 11, 1919, 19.
5. *Chicago Daily Tribune*, July 22, 1919, 15.
6. *Bridgeport Telegram*, January 20, 1920, 10.
7. Ibid.
8. *Washington Post*, January 26, 1920, 8.
9. *Bridgeport Sun Herald*, "Walsh Is Thorn in Side," August 8, 1920.
10. *Bridgeport Evening Post*, "Skiff Refuses to Play," September 13, 1920.
11. *Meriden Journal and Record*, August 29, 1980.
12. *Baseball Magazine*, May 1909, 52.
13. *Oneonta Star*, May 27, 1959, 12.
14. *Chicago Tribune*, August 12, 1921, 9.

Chapter 16

1. *Washington Post*, December 15, 1921, 17.
2. Steve Scarpa, *Meriden Record-Journal*, "Spitball Wizard," April 30, 2005, A4.
3. *Chicago Daily Tribune*, May 31, 1922, 24.
4. *New York Times*, January 26, 1923, 14.
5. *Chicago Tribune*, February 23, 1923, 15.
6. *Chicago Daily Tribune*, March 4, 1923, A4.
7. *Chicago Daily Tribune*, August 27 and September 6, 1923, 5.
8. *Chicago Daily Tribune*, February 18, 1924.
9. *Chicago Daily Tribune*, March 5, 1924, 25.
10. *New York Times*, November 14, 1924, 1.

Chapter 17

1. *Chicago Daily Tribune*, February 27, 1926, 14.
2. *Atlanta Constitution*, April 4, 1926.
3. *Galveston Daily News*, September 27, 1928.
4. Ned Carney, telephone interview, January 2007.
5. Ken Robinson, *Meriden Record and Journal*, August 29, 1980.

Chapter 18

1. *Baseball Magazine*, September 1913, 98.
2. Ibid.
3. *Courant Magazine*, December 16, 1956.
4. *Bridgeport Sunday Herald*, "Walsh Handed Pink Slip," August 16, 1936.
5. Steve Scarpa, *Meriden Record-Journal*, "Spitball Wizard," April 10, 2005, A4.
6. Dan Parker, *Daily Mirror*, January 30, 1946.
7. Prescott Sullivan, *San Francisco Examiner*, May 27, 1959.
8. *Meriden Record*, September 20 and 21, 1947.
9. *Meriden Record*, May 31, 1954.
10. Frank Corkin, *Meriden Record*, June 1, 1953.
11. *Meriden Record-Journal*, August 29, 1980.
12. *Baseball Magazine*, "The Inside Story," November–December 1954.
13. *Meriden Record*, May 29, 1955.
14. Jerry Holtzman, *Sporting News*, July 2, 1958, 7.
15. Joe Williams, syndicated column, August 25, 1956.
16. Scarpa, *Meriden Record-Journal*, "Spitball Wizard," April 10, 2005, A4.
17. Lou Black, *Meridan Journal*, "Ed Walsh Pained," February 18, 1957.

Bibliography

Magazines

Baseball Digest, 1902–1917
Baseball Magazine, 1902–1926
Courant Magazine, 1956
Sporting Life, 1907
Sporting News, 1902–1917

Newspapers

Atlanta Constitution, 1912
Boston Daily Globe, 1904–1917
Bridgeport Evening Post, 1921–23
Bridgeport Sun Herald, 1921–23
Bridgeport Telegram, 1921–23
Chicago Daily Tribune, 1904–1917, 1925–1958
Daily Mirror, 1946
(Elyria, Ohio) Evening Telegram, 1907
(Elyria, Ohio) Reporter, 1907
Galveston Daily News, 1928
Indianapolis Star, 1910
Iowa City Citizen, 1919
Los Angeles Times, 1904–1917
Meriden Daily Journal, 1902–1906, 1939–1958
Meriden Record and Journal, 1980
New York Evening Telegram, 1916
New York Herald Tribune, 1959
New York Times, 1924–1958, 1982
New York World, 1918
Newark Daily Advocate, 1914
Oakland Tribune, 1908
Oneonta Star, 1959
San Francisco Examiner, 1959
Washington Post, 1904–1909, 1917
Wilkes-Barre Record, 1902–1906

Books

Campbell Bartoletti, Susan. *Growing Up in Coal Country*. Boston: Houghton Mifflin, 1996.
James, Bill. *Historical Baseball Abstract*. New York: Villard Books, 1988.
Kashatus, William. *Diamonds in the Coal Fields*. Jefferson, NC: McFarland, 2002.
Smiles, Jack. *"Ee-Yah": The Life and Times of Hughie Jennings*. Jefferson, NC: McFarland, 2005.
Smith, Ken. *Baseball's Hall of Fame*. New York: Grosset & Dunlap, 1974.
Thorn, John. *Total Baseball*. 7th ed. Kingston, NY: Total Sports, 2001.
Wolff, Rick. *The Baseball Encyclopedia*. 4th ed. New York: Macmillan, 1990.

Web sites

www.baseballlibrary.com
www.cityofmeriden.org
http://pages.cthome.net/jbll/history.htm
www.retrosheet.org

www.sabr.org
www.wesleyan.edu/ctgeology

Other

Rhone, Rosalind D. "Anthracite Coal Mines and Mining." *The American Monthly Review of Reviews*, November 1902.

Baseball Hall of Fame: Clippings from Ed Walsh's File, letter to Sid Keener.

Society of American Baseball Research biographies of Fielder Jones and Charles Comiskey.

Index

The Alamo 82
Altrock, Nick 19, 20, 21, 28, 33, 43, 45, 46, 48, 57, 59, 65, 66, 70, 71, 72, 81, 87, 92, 94, 103
American Association 18, 40, 54, 187, 205, 207
American Revolution 4
Anson, Cap 30, 72, 119, 130
Appling, Luke 213
Atkins, J.C. 4
Atlanta Constitution 164, 182
Atz, Jakey 106
Auerbach, August 56

Barry, Jack 210
Baseball Digest 31, 194
Baseball Hall of Fame 209–210
Baseball Magazine 8, 29, 34, 51, 52, 161, 163, 168, 184, 210
Bender, Chief 25, 138, 140, 190, 191
Berger, Henie 119
Bernhard, Bill 62
Berry, Claude 132
Bevan, Floyd 74
Bielawa, Michael J. 192
Birmingham, Joe 101, 108
Blackburne, Russell 128, 130, 135
Blair, Dr. James 159
Blankenship, Homer 196
Blankenship, Ted 196
Bodie, Ping 137, 138, 139, 141, 158
Boston Globe 60, 115, 175, 201
Bracket, Hank 189
Bradley, Bill 105

Bridgeport Americans 188–193
Bridgeport Sun-Herald 192
Bridgeport Telegram 187
British Parliament 4
Brouthers, Dan 50
Brown, Mordecai 68, 71, 145, 146, 149
Brush, John T. 53
Buckner, Bill 196
Burdette, Lew 212
Burkett, Howard 210
Burkett, Jesse 209
Burnham, Walter 13, 16

Callahan, Jim "Nixey" 15, 16, 17, 20, 22, 54, 137, 146, 147, 151, 153, 154, 155, 156, 157, 158, 161, 169, 185
Camp, Walter 71
Cantillion, Joe 114, 115
Carnes, R.J. 188
Carney, Ned 205, 209
Carney, Rosemary 12
Carpenter, Bob 213
Carroll, Owen 193
Carroll, Raman 82
Cashion, Jay 142, 186
Cates, Eli 106
Chadbourne, Chet 65
Chalmers Automobile Company 144, 145, 169
Chance, Frank 67, 75, 148, 198, 199, 209
Charlton, Dr. William 182–183
Chase, Hal 50, 60
Cheney, Larry 35, 81, 149

223

INDEX

Chesbro, Jack 24, 26, 28, 30, 33, 36, 49, 60, 116, 184, 185, 209
Chicago Examiner 15
Chicago Tribune 16, 22, 24, 43, 44, 46, 58, 65, 70, 72, 86, 87, 101, 104, 114, 120, 129, 130, 133, 134, 140, 144, 147, 148, 152, 154, 157, 159, 163, 170, 174, 177, 178, 179, 184
Chouinard, Felix 144
Cicotte, Ed 158
Cincinnati Commercial-Tribune 52
Clancy, Bud 199
Clarke, Nig 101, 139, 141
Cobb, Ty 8, 88, 92, 94, 99, 116, 129, 132, 136, 138, 140, 141,143, 144, 194, 198, 210
Cochran, Mickey 213
Cohan, George M. 75
Cohen, Will 115
Cole, Leonard 167
Collins, Eddie 60, 122, 135, 143, 169, 175, 197, 198
Comiskey, Charles 14, 16, 20, 22, 26, 31, 38, 43, 46, 48, 49, 50, 51, 52, 53, 53, 56, 58, 69, 77, 79, 82, 87, 103; Walsh holdout 113–120; 128, 137, 138, 151, 152, 157, 158, 163, 168, 169, 174, 177, 180, 197, 199
Comiskey, Charles, II 213
Comiskey, Grace 197
Comiskey, J.L. 84, 152
Comiskey Park 118; opening130–131, 145, 154
Connecticut State League 11, 12, 188, 189, 201
Connolly, Tomy 62, 104, 143, 194
Connor, Roger 50
Conroy, William "Wid" 62
Cook, Dr. C.W. 171
Coombs, Jack 122, 133, 135, 138
Corcoran, Martin 8, 9, 79
Cornell University 83
Corridon, Frank 29
Coughlin, Bill 87, 88, 89
Coveleski, Stan 42, 185
Cravath, Gabby 104
Crawford, Sam 57, 88, 94, 99, 111, 138, 141, 166
Cross, Lave 63

Daley, Richard 213
Daley, Tommy 171
Dallas State League 17
Danaher, Cornelius 11, 13, 209
Danaher, Francis 209
Davis, George 18, 23, 54, 57, 65, 66, 70, 77, 86, 124
Davis, Henry 123
Dean, Dizzy 213
Demmitt, Ray 164
Desmond, Harry 159
DiMaggio, Joe 205
Dinneen, Bill 184
Dolin, Mike 116
Donahue, Jiggs 19, 25, 43, 54, 57, 61, 66, 72, 99, 124
Donovan, Bill 94, 99, 109, 110, 111, 195
Dougherty, Patsy 57, 43, 44, 71, 106, 125, 132
Dougherty, Tom 19
Downs, Red 94
Doyle, Bill 202
Doyle, Jack 202
Dressen, Charlie 186
Dryden, Charles 75, 88, 90, 91, 96
Drysdale, Don 60
Duffy, Hugh 138, 140, 142, 201
Duluth White Sox 188
Dundon, Gus 54, 57, 65, 66, 86
Dygert, Jimmy 185

Eastern League/Association 14, 189, 191, 196
Eberly, Rob 56
Egan, H. Chandler 71
Ehmke, Howard 74
Elberfield, Kid 63, 65, 96, 142
Eller, Horace 177
Elsh, Roy 199
Emerick, Shorty 189, 190
Engle, Art 143
Evans, Billy 63, 179, 183, 195
Evers, Johnny 67, 75, 77, 116, 195, 199, 209

Faber, Urban "Red" 42, 185, 197, 199, 210, 213
Falkenberg, Cy 119
Farrell, Eddie 193
Farrell, Frank 131, 132
Fell, Jesse 4
Felsch, Oscar 169
Fiene, Louis 31, 43, 57, 66, 67, 213
Flaherty, Patsy 20
Flick, Elmer 92
Ford, Russell 40, 139

Index

Fordham University 7
Fox River 168
Fraser, Chic 30
Fredricks, Charley 58, 117
Freeman, Buck 65, 80, 83
Frick, Ford 209
Frisch, Frank 195
Fullerton, Hugh 152, 182

Gandil, Chick 128, 132, 135
Ganley, Bob 106
Gessler, Doc 73, 142
Gleason, Bill "Kid" 165, 189, 195, 197, 198
Good, Wilbur 105
Graney, Jack 128
Great Fire of 1871, 71
Green, Danny 54
Gregg, Dave 138
Gregg, Vean 160
Griffith, Clark 23, 35, 38, 52, 87, 91, 103, 198, 209
Grillo, Ed 114
Grimes, Ray 189, 191
Grimes, Roy 189, 191

Haan, Ed 75
Hahn, Ed 57, 73, 76, 84, 124
Harkness, Fred 130
Harris, Mickey 210
Hart, Bob 194
Hart, General Fredrick 130
Hart, Jim "Hub" 44, 57, 213
Hartsel, Topsy 14
Hayden, Jack 60
Haynes Auto Company 182
Heitmuller, Henie 125
Hemphill, Frank 57
Henry Grays 175
Hermann, Al 193
Hermann, Gerry 86, 130
Hickman, Charles 202
Hildebrand, George 29
Hinchmen, Bill 109
"Hitless Wonders" 57
Hoffman, Larry 15
Hogg, Bill 65
Holmes, Ducky 53, 54, 56
Holway, John 30
Hopkins, Paul 201
Hopper, Harry 198
Hornsby, Rogers 114
House, Shanty 191
Howell, Harry 33, 44, 87

Howley, Dan 204
Hubbell, Carl 211
Huggins, Miller 83
Hurst, Tim 96, 94

International League 195
Isbell, Frank 57, 72, 103, 124, 179

Jackson, Joe 139, 140, 175
Jacobs, Benjamin 77
Jennings, Hughie 7, 8, 80, 88, 89, 92, 94, 108, 143, 162, 163, 184, 192, 195, 199
Johnson, Ban 52, 70, 79, 94, 120, 131, 152, 178, 194–195
Johnson, Walter 60, 113, 114, 115, 125, 127, 136, 138, 139, 146, 178, 186
Johnstone, Jim 69, 74
Jones, Benjamin Franklin 23
Jones, Davy 59, 89
Jones, Fielder 19, 22, 23, 24, 28, 31, 37, 43, 48, 49, 57, 65, 72, 75, 76, 77, 86, 110, 111, 141, 142, 185
Jones, Laura Ellen Parmenter 23
Jones, Richard 4
Jones, Tad 116
Jones, Tom 22
Joss, Addie 39, 66, 92; perfect game 107–108

Keeler, Wee Willie 8, 44, 61, 63
Kelly, "King" 51
Kentucky Colonels 85
Keogan, Dr. George 202
Kerr, Dick 114
Killian, Ed 99, 103
Kilpatrick, C. 85
Kirby, Dr. 90
Kirby, Fred 4
Kleinow, Red 65
Klepfer, Ed 17, 175
Kling, Johnny 71, 75
Koch, Herman 178
Kreitz, Ralph 145
Kruger, Art 128
Kruger, Earl 54

Lackawanna Railroad 4
LaFitte, Ed 139
Lai, Bill "Buck" 190, 191
Lajoie, Napoleon 85, 101, 109, 116, 139, 144, 145, 175
Landis, Judge Kenesaw Mountain 194

Lane, Clarke P. 188
Lane, F.C. 168
Lanigan, Ernest 114
Lanigan, H.W. 120
Lardner, Ring 113, 132, 134, 171
Lavender, Jim 40, 152
Lee, Robert E. 135
Lennon, Ed 190, 191
Leverett, Dixie 196
Leviathan 199
Liebhardt, Glenn 106, 119, 185
Little League World Series 211
Lopez, Al 213
Lord, Harry 137, 142, 144, 155
Los Angeles Times 153, 163, 170, 175, 210
Lush, Billy 118
Lyons, Ted 199, 213

MacAleer, Henry 212
MacGilligan, T.P. 100
Mack, Connie 12, 64, 136, 211
Mack, Frank 196
Mantle, Mickey 212
Manuel, Moxie 102
Martin, Charles 75
Martin, Gene 192
Martinson, Paul 178
Marx, Dr. Francis 193
Mathewson, Christy 145, 173, 184
Matthews, Bobby 30
Mattick, Wally 149
Mayflower 23
McAleer, Jimmy 54, 114, 152
McAndrew, Tom 80
McCann, Gene 188, 193
McCarthy, Tommy 209
McConnell, Amby 134, 137, 142, 145
McFarland, Eddie 54, 57, 66
McGee, Bruin 14
McGinnty, Joe "Ironman" 14, 209
McGraw, John 8, 18, 30; against spitball 40–41; 67, 198, 199
McGuire, Deacon 36, 91
McIntyre, Matty 88, 137, 139
McRoy, Robert 63, 69
Meany, P.A. 29
Memphis 19
Meriden, Connecticut 11, 12, 13, 14, 58, 79, 91, 98, 119, 120, 128, 131, 153
Merkel, Fred 110
Meusel, Bob 199
Mexican League 82
Mid Atlantic League 205

Milan, Clyde 143
Mills, Tom 202
Milwaukee Brewers 18, 188
Mitchell, Fred 30, 201
Mitchell, John 5, 79
Mitchell, Mike 97, 144
Moore, Ray 198
Moran, Pat 198
Mount Royal 199
Mulligan, Eddie 193
Mullin, George 99
Murphy, Charles 69, 77, 114
Murphy, Danny 95
Murphy, Dr. J.B. 63

National Commission 16, 46, 69, 77, 119
National League 18, 23, 35
New Orleans Pelicans 18, 19, 55, 84
New York Times 134, 170, 175
Northwestern League 50
Notre Dame 200–205
Nutter, George 190

Oakland Tribune 100
O'Brien, Buck 161
O'Connor, Jack 134
O'Day, Hank 62
O'Laughlin, Silk 46, 63, 69, 108, 109
Oldring, Rube 64, 93, 159
O'Neill, Bill 54, 57, 75
O'Neill, Dan 191
O'Neill, John 80
O'Neill, Mike 80
O'Neill, Tip 18, 86
Orr, Dave 50
Orth, Al 90, 185
Ortman, Lulu 85
Overall, Orval 125
Owen, Frank 18, 19, 25, 26, 57, 58 59, 62, 65, 66, 82

Pacific Coast League 16, 29, 155, 201, 205
Panama-Pacific Exposition 169
Parent, Freddy 108, 135
Parker, Doc 142
Patten, Casey 90
Patterson, Roy 19, 20, 43, 57, 58, 60, 62, 93, 98
Payne, Fred 143
Peabody College 56
Pennsylvania State League 9
Perrine, Bull 125
Perring, George 108

Index

Pfeffer, Fred 72
Pfiester, Jack 68, 75, 76
Piedmont League 206
Pierce, Billy 212
Piersall, Jimmy 210
Pipgras, George 204
Plains, Pennsylvania 6, 7, 8, 11, 79, 101
Plank, Eddie 25, 26, 95, 98, 105, 127, 135, 138, 164, 167, 209
Players League 52
Powell, Jack 98
Pulliam, Harry 69, 124
Purtell, Billy 128, 132

Quillen, Lee 86, 90
Quinn, Jack 182, 185

Radbourn, Charley "Old Hoss" 50
Rainey, Ed 9
Range-Lakes League 188
Ready, Alice 197
Reese, John "Bonesetter" 161
Reilly, Thomas 79
Reulbach, Ed 68, 72, 76, 125, 149
Rice, Grantland 114, 173
Rickey, Branch 91
Rigney, Dorothy 213
Roberts, Robin 212
Robertson, Charlie 196
Rockne, Knute 201, 203
Roe, Preacher 42
Rohe, George 44, 54, 57, 70, 71, 74, 75, 81, 103
Roosevelt, Theodore 5
Rossman, Claude 88, 89
Roth, Braggo 175
Rowland, Clarence "Pants" 169, 170, 174, 178, 188
Rowlus, Charles 56
Ruppert, Colonel 160
Russell, Reb 165, 166
Ruth, Babe 137, 204
Ryan, Jimmy 72
Ryan, Patrick 77

Saier, Vic 149
St. John's Prep 200–201
St. Louis Times 120
Sanborn, Cy 147, 164, 184
San Francisco Seals 137, 154
Schaefer, Germany 89, 90, 142
Schalk, Ray 159, 186, 196, 213
Schang, Wally 175

Schlei, Admiral 70
Schneider, Pete 94, 143, 144
Schreckengost, Ossie 64, 108
Schulte, Frank 67, 73, 74, 77, 145, 149
Score, Herb 212
Scott, Jack 135, 213
Seattle Mariners 141
Seybold, Socks 14
Shea, Daniel 75
Sheckard, Jimmy 67, 74, 152
Shibe Park 167, 213
Siever, Ed 57
Simmons, Mel 205
Sims, Joe 211
Sisler, Dick 198
Slagle, Jimmy 67, 70, 71
Smith, Al 196
Smith, Frank "Nig" 19, 20, 43, 53, 57, 58 59, 95, 99, 111, 124, 134
Somers, Charles 14
South Side Grounds 25, 63, 72, 75, 110, 130, 158
Southern League 185
Spalding and Brothers 9
Speaker, Tris 130, 136, 147
Spencer, "Bonesetter" 177
Sporting Life 39, 184
Sporting News 7
Springfield, Ohio 54
Steinfeldt, Harry 67, 72
Stengal, Casey 199
Stricklett, Elmer 16, 17, 20, 29, 30, 32
Stahl, "Chick" 60, 85
Stahl, Jake 125
Stallings, George 14
Stauffer, Ed 191
Stone, George 53, 54
Stovall, George 108
Stroup, Charles 56
Sullivan, Billy 19, 31, 32, 49, 57, 74, 89, 90, 103, 119, 120, 142, 169, 213
Sullivan, Billy, Jr. 203, 205
Sullivan, Ted 81, 154
Sullivan, Tom 50
Summers, Ed 99, 108, 132
Susquehanna River 3
Sweeney, Ed 139

Taft, William Howard 127
Tannehill, Lee 18, 25, 26, 46, 54, 57 59, 61, 70, 74, 103, 124, 131, 146
Tebbets, Birdie 212
Tenet, John K. 72

Texas Christian University 18
Thomas, Ira 123
Thorn, John 30
Tinker, Joe 67, 75, 117, 209
Towne, Jay 63, 86
Townsend, Jack 23
Tri-State League 54
Trucks, Virgil 212
Tuckey, Dick 201
Tuthil, Harry 110

Unglaub, Bob 94, 106
United Mine Workers 5, 6
University of Nebraska 44, 83
University of Wisconsin 188

Vance, Dazzy 211
Vaughn, Jim "Hippo" 142, 186
Veteran Baseball Players Association 212
Vickers, Harry 103
Vinson, Rube 57
Virginia League 123
Von der Ahe, Chris 52

Waddell, Rube 26, 64, 93, 96, 98, 100, 105, 133, 184, 186, 209
Wagner, Henie 94
Wagner, Honus 18, 85, 161, 210
Walker, Dixie 142
Wallace, Bobby 38
Walsh, David 5, 123
Walsh, Edward Arthur 81; at Notre Dame 200–205
Walsh, Martin 116, 119, 123, 161, 190, 191
Walsh, Robert 81, 183, 203–206, 209
Walsh, Tom 101
Ward, John 34

Warner, Jack 106
Washington Post 8, 10, 45, 53, 88, 113, 114, 115, 116, 134, 178, 179
Washington Monument 134
Watson, Doak 180
Weaver, Buck 146
Welch, Curt 52
Welday, Mike 86
Weller, Sam 139, 154
West Side Grounds 69, 110, 125, 149
Western League 52, 119
White, Guy "Doc" 19, 45, 46, 55, 58 59, 66, 70, 72, 76, 77, 89, 92, 99, 100, 110, 111, 136, 149, 213
White River 55
Wilkes, John 3
Wilkes-Barre, Pennsylvania history 3–4; 6, 9, 10, 19, 24, 65, 77, 79, 83, 98, 101, 134, 187
Wilkes-Barre Record 16
Willett, Ed 99
Williams, Ted 212
Wilson, Frank 194
Wiltse, George "Hooks" 211
Winter, George 93
Wood, Smoky Joe 138
Woodward, Frank 196
Work Progress Administration 209

Yale University 115, 116, 175, 187
Yaryan, Yam 193
Young, Cy 94, 102, 137, 162, 186, 211, 213
Young, Dr. George 39

Zeider, Rollie 130, 135
Zwilling, Alec 135

www.ingramcontent.com/pod-product-compliance
Ingram Content Group UK Ltd.
Pitfield, Milton Keynes, MK11 3LW, UK
UKHW041945140426
5217IPUK00014B/656